iPad® for Kids

Using the iPad to Play and Learn

Brian Proffitt

Course Technology PTR

A part of Cengage Learning

COURSE TECHNOLOGY
CENGAGE Learning™

Australia • Brazil • Japan • Korea • Mexico • Singapore • Spain • United Kingdom • United States

COURSE TECHNOLOGY
CENGAGE Learning™

iPad® for Kids
Brian Proffitt

**Publisher and General Manager,
Course Technology PTR:**
Stacy L. Hiquet

Associate Director of Marketing:
Sarah Panella

Manager of Editorial Services:
Heather Talbot

Marketing Manager:
Mark Hughes

Senior Acquisitions Editor:
Mitzi Koontz

Project and Copy Editor:
Marta Justak

Technical Reviewers:
Brown Partington and Carol Proffitt

Interior Layout:
Jill Flores

Cover Designer:
Luke Fletcher

Indexer:
Sharon Shock

Proofreader:
Chuck Hutchinson

For product information and technology assistance, contact us at
Cengage Learning Customer & Sales Support, 1-800-354-9706
For permission to use material from this text or product,
submit all requests online at **cengage.com/permissions**
Further permissions questions can be emailed to
permissionrequest@cengage.com

iPad, iPhone, iPod, iPod Touch, iOS, and OS X are registered trademarks or trademarks of Apple Inc. BlackBerry is a registered trademark of Research In Motion Limited. Droid is a registered trademark of LucasFilm Ltd. Android is a trademark of Google Inc. Linux is a trademark of Linus Torvalds. Microsoft, Windows, and Internet Explorer are either registered trademarks or trademarks of Microsoft Corporation in the United States and/or other countries. PalmPilot, Palm, and webOS are either registered trademarks or trademarks of Palm, Inc., a subsidiary of Hewlett-Packard Company. HP EliteBook is a trademark of the Hewlett-Packard Company. Dell Latitude is a trademark of Dell Inc. GTD and Getting Things Done are registered trademarks of David Allen and Co. Kindle is a trademark of Amazon Technologies, Inc. Wii is a trademark of Nintendo.

All other trademarks are the property of their respective owners.

All images © Cengage Learning unless otherwise noted.

Library of Congress Control Number: 2011930897

ISBN-13: 978-1-4354-6053-9

ISBN-10: 1-4354-6053-7

Course Technology, a part of Cengage Learning
20 Channel Center Street
Boston, MA 02210
USA

Cengage Learning is a leading provider of customized learning solutions with office locations around the globe, including Singapore, the United Kingdom, Australia, Mexico, Brazil, and Japan. Locate your local office at: **international.cengage.com/region**

Cengage Learning products are represented in Canada by Nelson Education, Ltd. For your lifelong learning solutions, visit **courseptr.com**
Visit our corporate Web site at **cengage.com**

Printed by RR Donnelley. Crawfordsville, IN. 1st Ptg. 07/2011
Printed in the United States of America
1 2 3 4 5 6 7 12 11

Acknowledgments

Oftentimes, people I know picture my life as an author as a solitary, lonely existence, where I randomly wander the moors in a tweed jacket smoking a pipe, punctuated by the occasional session of typing.

Um, no.

In truth, putting together any written work is a collaborative effort, because no author knows everything, and often needs someone to put him in his place. Such is the job of my long-suffering editors on this book Mitzi Koontz, Marta Justak, Brown Partington, and Sharon Shock, who get thanks for taking my content and crafting it into something better.

This book, though, was even more personal than having good editors. This book, it turned out, would have family.

My mother, whose name graces the masthead under the technical reviewer heading, is a retired elementary school teacher with 36 years of experience. When the idea of this book was first formed, I knew I would need her help with figuring out the nuances of education that would be ingrained in a teacher like her. She delivered stunningly, and her influence is felt in many pages of this book.

There was some generational help going the other way, too. My daughter, Aberash, and Brown's daughter, Alexa, came through with a coast-to-coast FaceTime session that was used in Chapter 8. Alexa is also the granddaughter of Marta, so three generations from two families have impacted the creation of this work.

This book also covered many different types of software applications. Several companies and developers generously donated copies of their apps to this book so they could be reviewed and discussed. For all of the people who graciously responded to my requests for help, thank you.

About the Author

Brian Proffitt is a technology expert who blogs on ITworld.com on Open Source technology and AllBusiness.com on matters concerning small business. He Twitters as @TheTechScribe on these and a whole wide range of technology sectors. Currently, he is an adjunct instructor at the Mendoza College of Business at the University of Notre Dame. Formerly the community manager of the Linux Foundation, he has also been managing editor of Linux Today (linuxtoday.com), a news and information site about all things Linux and Open Source. He is the author of numerous books on computer technology, including *Take Your iPad to Work*. His other works focus mostly on Linux, with a Mac and Windows book thrown in just for variety. He is also the author of a student guide on Plato. He makes his home in northern Indiana.

Contents

Introduction

With the right applications, the iPad can become more than just a device for watching videos, music, and electronic books. It can be a device that's used for teaching and imparting knowledge to children in nearly any environment.

This ability to teach anywhere opens up a wider range of knowledge for children than the obvious one of just having a mobile Internet-connected device. The iPad has apps that are specifically designed to build skills in reading, math, and writing. How many apps? Thousands. Some are good, some are not so good, and having tried a lot of them, I think this book has a collection of some very good apps that are available.

The apps offer parents and teachers flexibility, because they are small. Small in terms of size, so they're easy to download and install, and small in terms of price. Many of the apps featured in this book are free, some cost no more than $10, and many are somewhere in between. This way of doing things means that parents can pick and choose exactly what works for their kids and what's fun for them to use.

While a computer could handle just about all of these tasks, software is usually more expensive, and laptops can be inconvenient to carry around, but the iPad's flat form greatly simplifies mobility. Its longer battery life is a bonus, too.

Is the iPad right for every educational situation? Yes, it can be. Naturally, this is something this book will try to promote. But it won't be a fawning description: if there's a problem to avoid, this book will let you know.

Is This Book for You?

iPad for Kids is for all of you who want to get started using the iPad as a teaching tool for your kids. Think of this book as a personal tutorial, a one-on-one class with an expert user of the iPad. You get to stay in the comfort of your own home or school and learn how to do the following things:

* Familiarize yourself with the iPad controls and interfaces.
* Connect to the Internet with the iPad using WiFi or a cellular connection.
* Learn how to add apps and multimedia content to your iPad.
* Print documents from the iPad.
* Communicate with others via email.

* Teach kids from toddler-age to fourth grade how to read—and then read better.
* Explore and practice mathematic concepts.
* Discover the world of art and music.
* Have your kids see the world around them in new ways.
* Create documents, spreadsheets, and presentations for advanced school work.

Companion Web Site Downloads of Bonus Chapters

As this book was put together, it soon became apparent that there was a lot more information we wanted to impart to parents and teachers that wouldn't fit in these pages, so we've provided the information in the form of bonus electronic chapters on the Cengage Web site. You may download the additional chapters at *www.courseptr.com/downloads* and read them on your iPad. Here is a list of the online chapters:

* Chapter 18: "Homework: Documenting with Pages"
* Chapter 19: "Homework: Analyzing with Numbers"
* Chapter 20: "Homework: Presenting with Keynote"
* Chapter 21: "Homework: Printing"
* Chapter 22: "Homework: Mail"

Chapter 1
First Step:
Introducing
the iPad

It is not the first device of its kind, but there is little doubt that the Apple iPad family has revolutionized the consumer electronics market of the second decade of the 21st century. Okay, that's a pretty hoity-toity thing to say, full of all the market-y things that people hear about electronics all the time. But let's face it, there have already been millions of iPad devices sold, so there must be *something* to these shiny new devices, beyond the hype generated by Apple and its marketers that's making this device such a hot property.

With the iPad, like many successful products, there's a combination of things involved. Certainly all that marketing and sales timing helped. The iPad was introduced at a time when smartphones were just hitting their stride in the market: early adopters (which is code for "gadget-freaks") had pretty much found smartphone religion, and now normal people were getting converted, too. After 2007, more and more "regular" folks were buying smartphones, discovering the advantages of instant-on, highly mobile Internet and processing access. So, what changed in 2007? That was the year of the introduction of iPad's ancestor: the original iPhone.

With its sleek form factor, broad range of applications, processing speed, and superior coolness factor, the iPhone became a huge sales hit among consumers and business personnel alike. In that same year, Apple released what's considered to be the real predecessor to the iPad: the iPod Touch, an iPhone-like device without an onboard phone that connected to the Internet via wireless access points (WiFi).

Tech Term: WiFi

Throughout this book, I'll try to avoid heavy-duty tech terms, but sometimes they can't be avoided. So here's the first one: WiFi. WiFi is a way to get to the Internet through radio signals that transmit from a nearby, centralized station. Like 30–40 feet nearby. The plus side of WiFi is that the signal is usually very strong and rather fast. But the downside is that you have to be close to a WiFi device to use it. Cell phones use different radio signals that can have a range of miles away—but at the cost of slower speeds.

Today, the smartphone market is dominated by the iPhone, although other excellent smartphones exist, such as RIM's stalwart BlackBerry product line and the various Droid phone models running multiple versions of Google's Linux-based Android software. Even Microsoft has offerings in the smartphone market with its Windows Mobile 7 software, although sales of such devices are rather low.

Faced with some stiff competition, Apple has continued to improve its iPhone product line, most recently with the release of the iPhone 4 model. But in 2010, Apple decided to raise the bar again, this time announcing a long-rumored tablet device scheduled for release in April 2010: the iPad. In March 2011, success was repeated with the even bigger launch of the iPad 2.

What Is the iPad?

When Steve Jobs announced the iPad in January 2010, the initial reaction was rather mixed. After the initial excitement died down, critics pointed out that this "new" device was hardly more than a giant iPod Touch. Sure, the screen was bigger, and the apps looked better, but other than that, what could such a device offer to consumers? Tech pundits didn't know if they were coming or going with their opinions of this thing.

It turns out, they should have had some faith.

Perhaps the biggest draw to the iPad was the tablet form itself.

Tech Term: Tablet

In geek speak, a tablet is any device that has a flat interface and a size that approximates a notebook sheet of paper. The size of the device is key: personal digital assistants (PDAs) like the old PalmPilots certainly had flat interfaces, but their handheld sizes placed them in a different category than tablets.

Other examples of tablet devices include the Dell Latitude XT2 or the HP EliteBook 2740p—both devices that have a touchscreen interface, though with a swiveled screen that enables users to quickly convert these computers to traditional laptop devices, the kind with the hinge.

iPads don't have physical keyboards, and most applications don't even require a pen-like stylus to function. All you do is use your fingers to enter text and manipulate objects onscreen. With such a simple interface, and because the device itself is much lighter than laptops, notebooks, and even those itty-bitty, ultra-light netbooks, it is a large-screen device that is much more portable for users of all types.

Besides being large enough to read comfortably and watch the occasional movie, the screen is also a multitouch interface, which can be a unique experience for many electronic device users. In the past, touchscreens on PDAs, smartphones, or even the occasional kiosk were primarily single-touch interfaces, meaning that one and only one touch at a time was registered by the application running on the screen.

Beginning with the iPhone, and continuing with the iPad and iPad 2, there is multitouch, which enables users to touch and manipulate objects on the screen with more than one finger (or device) at a time. This interface enables users to shrink objects by "pinching" them or expand objects by fanning out their fingers. Or they can type capital letters onscreen by virtually "holding down" the Shift key on the keyboard on the screen.

But it's not just the hardware. Applications are the biggest key to the iPad family's success, if only by sheer numbers alone. Thousands of applications are available in the Apple App Store, free or otherwise, with a high percentage of them reviewed by other users. This social review system lets you find out quickly what's really going to work, and what may not. More than that, the stunning variety of apps available makes the iPad highly suitable for any number of uses.

Especially apps for your child.

The Educational Case for the iPad

With the right apps, the iPad can become more than just a content consumption device for videos, music, and electronic books. It can be an educational and content *production* device for kids as well, generating documents, spreadsheets, presentations, music, and video, while also giving children a window into a vast array of knowledge.

This ability to make content, given the right apps, immediately increases the iPad's value as a useful educational device. Students, parents, and teachers can have the tools to learn about new concepts and then turn around and create information based on that learning.

The potential education uses for the iPad are limited only by your ingenuity:

* Parents can let their younger children play with qualified apps that will provide hours of entertainment, while also practicing the basic skills of reading and mathematics.
* Teachers can use the iPad to create lesson plans and present engaging multimedia presentations at home or in the classroom.
* Older students can research new material and put that material together in traditional reports or cutting-edge multimedia presentations of their own.

These, of course, are just a few possible scenarios of iPad use for education. A computer could handle just about all of these tasks, of course, but even laptops can be a hassle to carry around and can require a good chunk of personal space to use. Not to mention the short life of a laptop battery, which often has you looking for a plug. The iPad's flat form greatly eases transport, and the 10-hour battery life means you won't be married to an outlet.

Is an iPad device right for every situation? It would be easy to get all excited and say "why yes, yes it is." But this isn't always the case. The design of the device itself should make you think about using it in certain instances. For example, an iPad has a large amount of glass, so using it in an environment where that glass can be damaged is obviously not a good idea. Care especially should be taken when younger children are using the device for just this reason. Still, with the right accessory—namely, a good carrying case—and some common sense, even that problem can be solved.

If you see possibilities for using the iPad with your child or students, the first thing you need to do is get yourself an iPad, which sometimes can be easier said than done.

Choosing the Right iPad

Before you buy an iPad, you need to figure out first which iPad you're going to get, particularly with the recent release of the iPad 2. A lot of people liked the looks of the iPad and held off buying one until the iPad 2 came out and shoppers mobbed the stores and Web sites looking for them. I am not proud to admit that I was one of those shoppers, and I paid my teenage daughter $50 to go stand in line at another store at the same time, coordinating with text messages. I blame my publisher.

Shopping rushes aside, while all iPads may look alike, there are two key differences found within all iPads that mean you get to choose between a total of six different iPad models.

 When choosing an iPad device, you may find yourself gravitating toward an iPad 2, the latest in the iPad family of devices. The good news is that from a retail standpoint, iPad 2s are no more expensive than the first iPad, and each model in the respective device families are similarly priced and with the same basic features.

However, there are key differences between the iPad and iPad 2 that should be taken into consideration.

First, the form factor of the iPad 2 is thinner and lighter than the original iPad. This is not a huge difference, but nonetheless it should be noted. Most of the time, you won't even notice it, unless you spend your time holding the device in one hand. Then the weight difference can be felt.

The two biggest differences between the devices are the faster processor in the iPad 2 and the onboard cameras in the iPad 2.

Tech Term: Processor

The processor in any computing device (iPad, computer, phone, microwave) is the part of the device that actually does all the computing work after you push some buttons to tell the device what you need (a movie, a document, a phone call, some popcorn). The faster the processor, the faster the device responds.

The faster processor does not change the apps that run on either version of the iPad, but it does increase the speed at which apps will run on the iPad 2. And it is noticeable. iPad apps were never pokey, but when compared with performance on the iPad 2, they are less responsive. Some apps, like Garage Band, can be used on the iPad, but they are recommended for the iPad 2 precisely because of its faster processor.

The cameras on the iPad 2, while not the greatest in the world, do give you the capability to run apps like FaceTime, a two-way videoconferencing app, and Photo Booth, a fun photo-morphing app. Many of the apps you will see in this book also use the cameras to take pictures of children to use as icons within the apps, should you choose. But even without the camera, you can upload an image and use it for the same purpose in the apps on an iPad.

The one big advantage of the iPad versus the iPad 2? Price. While only a year old, first-model iPads are being sold on the secondary market for big discounts from their original prices. Of course, this usually means buying a used iPad, with all the pros and cons of such a transaction. But, if you are on a budget, picking up an iPad on eBay or some other reputable vendor is a great way to get started.

The first choice point for any iPad or iPad 2 model is whether to get a WiFi or a WiFi+3G model. All iPads have the capability to connect to the Internet using WiFi access—the kind found in your home or most public businesses, like the coffee shop on the corner. This is usually pretty adequate, particularly within your own house, which should have its own wireless network.

If you don't have WiFi, ask your Internet provider. Most home systems include a WiFi network device, so you may have WiFi and not even know it.

iPad WiFi+3G models, on the other hand, can tap into the AT&T cellular network and connect to the Internet anywhere the iPad can receive the AT&T network signal. iPad 2s can use either AT&T or Verizon as a cellular carrier. WiFi+3G models uniformly cost $130 more than their WiFi-only counterparts retail, so using a WiFi-only device is obviously a real cost saver.

The other difference between iPad products is the amount of solid-state storage each device has. The iPad and iPad 2 are currently available with 16, 32, or 64 gigabytes of storage. The price of each model is directly proportional to the amount of memory. Table 1.1 displays the retail pricing of the iPad 2.

Table 1.1 iPad 2 Model Pricing (April 2011)

	16GB	32GB	64GB
iPad (WiFi)	$499	$599	$699
iPad (WiFi+3G)	$629	$729	$829

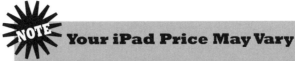

Your iPad Price May Vary

Because iPads are now only available on the secondary market, pricing on the models can vary significantly, depending on the seller.

Tech Term: Memory

The question of how much memory you need is one that plagues most iPad device users. While you may understand in the abstract that 16 gigabytes equates to 16,000 megabytes, which in turn represents 16,000,000 kilobytes, you may not know how that equates to real-world terms. (Not to mention, you may need a hobby.)

Check out Table 1.2, which puts together some numbers from Apple that do a better job of relating how big this storage is.

Table 1.2 iPad and iPad 2 Storage Comparison			
File (Average Size)	16GB	32GB	64GB
Images (1.5MB)	10,922	21,844	43,688
Songs (5MB)	3,276	6,552	13,104
Movies (700MB)	23	46	92
TV Shows (325MB)	50	100	200
eBooks (1.2MB)	13,653	27,306	54,612
Documents (50KB)	335,544	671,088	1,342,176
Presentations (100KB)	167,722	335,544	671,088

Looking at Table 1.2, you might wonder why in the world you would ever need to store 1.3 million documents, and that certainly seems unlikely. But these size comparisons can give you a more practical idea of what kind of storage capacity we're talking about.

From an education standpoint, you need to factor in how you will use the device. If you are going to be based in one central location, and plan to sync the device with a PC or Mac computer on a regular basis, then you will not need a lot of storage space. You can simply use your computer (and any storage device to which the computer has access) to handle storing files. In such a case, you should stick with one of the 16GB models.

If, however, you plan to be more mobile or otherwise be unable to sync on a regular basis, and will be handling a significant number of files, then consider purchasing one of the larger memory devices. It's likely that 32GB's worth of capacity is enough for most mobile use cases, unless you have a huge amount of multimedia files to lug around.

One good way for you to pin down the answer to the memory question is to look at all the files you must have to educate and entertain kids away from home, calculate the amount of memory those files need, and then triple that number. This calculation should account for the original files' storage and the potential of creating twice as many files while away from your base PC.

As for the decision on WiFi-only versus WiFi+3G, here the recommendation is not really going to be along financial lines. It would be easy to say, for instance, that all stationary iPad users should be fine without plunking down an extra $130 for 3G cellular connectivity. You've got WiFi set up in your home or school, so why bother with 3G?

This is where you should ask a key question: What happens when your Internet connection goes down? If losing Internet connectivity would harm your experience on the device, then it may be worth it to spend the extra money and get the WiFi+3G model. Most of the apps in this book, however, do not require always-on Internet connectivity, so you may want to consider that, too.

When 3G May Not Be a Good Idea

If you work in a region where AT&T or Verizon coverage is troublesome or nonexistent, you may need to reconsider the 3G options. One possible work-around, for instance, would be to use a mobile WiFi device from another cellular carrier and connect to the Internet via that device's WiFi network.

 The final decision in buying an iPad 2 is color: you have a choice between a white or black benzel (screen border) on the new iPad 2. This is strictly a preference issue, but the choice will need to be made, nonetheless.

With these choices in mind, you should be able to make an informed choice on getting the iPad or iPad 2 you need.

Getting an iPad Device

If you are fortunate enough to live near one of the hundreds of Apple retail stores, purchasing that needed iPad 2 should be a relatively painless process. Just walk in, pick out the one you want, and then take it home. To date, most U.S. Apple stores have caught up with the huge demand for these devices, and usually have them in stock, although it is still sporadic. Some of the WiFi+3G models are still lagging behind a bit. You may want to call ahead and see if the model you want is in stock before driving in to purchase it.

If you don't reside near an Apple store, you have two basic options: purchase the iPad 2 online or through an Apple retail partner, such as Target, Wal-Mart, or Best Buy. Be careful about expecting to actually see an iPad 2 at a retail partner, though; these stores often only get a handful of devices at a time, and they are usually snatched up very quickly.

The other route you might go is to check an AT&T or Verizon retail store, but here iPad 2s are even more scarce: only the largest stores in a given region will actually have the device in stock, while a big majority of such stores will have to order them from Apple directly.

The good news about any of these options is that the cost of the iPad, either online or at another retail store, is always the same. There's no markup when you purchase the iPad 2 somewhere other than an Apple store, and the online store will ship iPad 2s free of charge, so there's no additional cost there.

The bad news is, since most iPad 2 buyers use the online option to get their device, the delivery channel is exceedingly slow. As of this writing, Apple indicated one to two weeks to receive an iPad 2, and while this has been mostly true, anecdotal evidence has suggested otherwise; in some cases, shipping times of three weeks have been reported.

The option to go to a partner retailer, if there's one near you, may not be any better. You should definitely call ahead and see if there's an iPad 2 in stock. Be sure to specify which model you want. You don't want to get there and find out the retailer has models that don't meet your technical or budgetary requirements.

If you are not in a hurry to receive the iPad 2, you should definitely order it online. That way, you're working directly with Apple, and you won't have to dodge and weave past other shoppers to get the exact device you want.

Of course, getting an iPad is a little easier. If you find one at a reputable online vendor, you could have the device in your hands in a matter of days, at a lower cost.

Throwing in the Extras

When you purchase an iPad device, you may be tempted by all of the nifty-looking accessories you see around you in the actual or virtual store. You might be tempted to try one over the other, but here are some recommendations based on business-use cases.

* **Cases.** Available from Apple and a number of third-party vendors, a case is essential for anyone planning to transport the iPad device from one location to another. With a glass screen and a burnished metal exterior, the iPad device could easily be damaged without some sort of protective covering—not to mention that carrying the iPad device in full view in some public locations is an invitation to theft.

* **Smart Cover.** While not a full cover, the Smart Cover is very useful for protecting the iPad 2's screen, and when folded correctly, it serves as a portable stand. Magnets hold the cover in place and also serve to turn the device off and on when the cover is used. Plus, they're kind of cool.

* **Apple iPad Camera Connection Kit.** If you plan to connect any USB camera or SD flash drive to your iPad, then this accessory is essential. The ability to transfer photos, videos, or other files to your iPad without using an iTunes-equipped computer is a real time-saver.

* **Apple iPad Dock.** This is a great stand to park your iPad in an upright position while you sync or charge the battery.

* **A Bluetooth-capable wireless keyboard.** Available from Apple and third-party vendors, a wireless keyboard is a very essential tool for iPad. You might be tempted to purchase the Apple iPad Keyboard Dock and just get all-in-one functionality. I don't recommend this, because the Keyboard Dock means that your screen and keyboard are mated and any change in position between the two will be impossible. Also, if you prefer a more ergonomic keyboard, the Keyboard Dock will be ill-suited for you. It's better to get the Dock and a wireless keyboard separately.

Setting Up the iPad

When the big day comes and you bring that white box home, you will be very tempted to turn the iPad on and start playing with it right away. As with all good things, you will need to put a little effort into your iPad or iPad 2 before you can play with—er, *use* it wisely.

At the beginning of their operational lives, iPads must be connected to a PC or Mac computer that has iTunes 9.1 or higher installed at least once. iPad 2s need iTunes 10.2 or later. Linux machines, unfortunately, are not fully compatible with any iPad because of this iTunes requirement. You need iTunes at least once in the life of your iPad, in order to set up the iPad to talk to the Apple systems on the Internet.

PCs with Windows should have Windows XP Home or Professional (Service Pack 3), Windows Vista, or Windows 7 installed. Macs should have OS X 10.5.8 or later. Both kinds of machines should have available USB 2.0 ports.

If you don't have one already, you need an iTunes Store account. The iTunes Store is where the iPad will get apps even if you never sync to a computer again. While many iPad applications are free, you may want to purchase some applications later, so it's a good idea to get your account set up first.

To set up iTunes and an iTunes Store account, follow these steps:

1. Visit the iTunes Web page at *www.apple.com/itunes/* (see Figure 1.1).

Figure 1.1

The iTunes home page.

2. Click the Download iTunes link. The Download page will appear.
3. Confirm the operating system you are currently running and click Download Now. The installation file will be downloaded and saved to your system.
4. Follow the normal installation procedures you use to install software on your operating system to install iTunes.
5. After iTunes is installed and running, click the iTunes Store link in the left column of the application. The iTunes Store page will open, as shown in Figure 1.2.

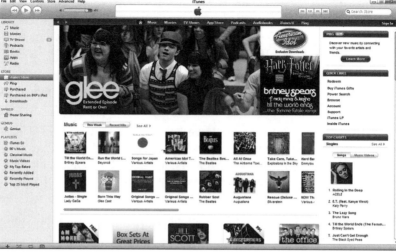

6. Click the Sign In link located in the upper-right corner. The account dialog box will open (see Figure 1.3).

7. Click the Create New Account button. The Welcome page will appear.

8. Click Continue. The Terms & Conditions page will appear.

9. Click the I have read… checkbox and then Continue. The Store Account page, shown in Figure 1.4, will appear.

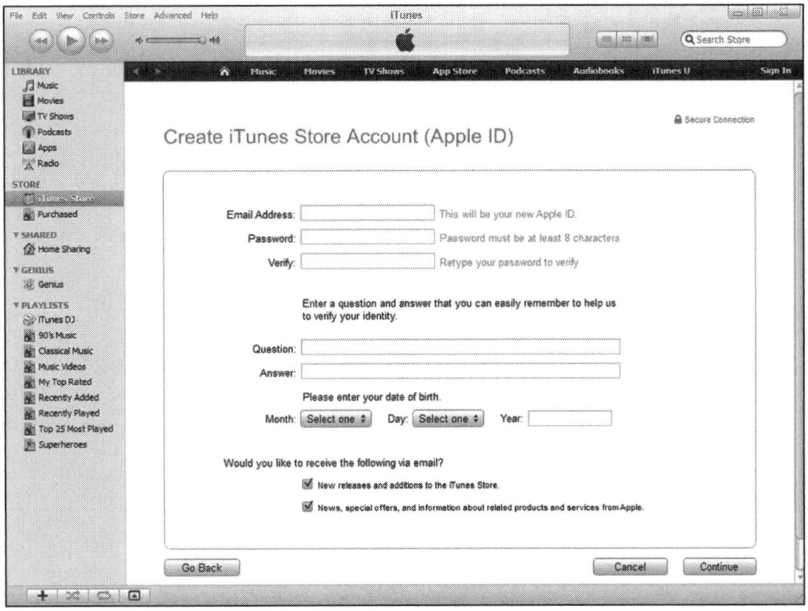

Figure 1.4

*The iTunes Store
Account page.*

10. Enter the pertinent information and click Continue. The Payment Method page will appear.

11. Enter your credit card or iTunes gift card information, your billing address, and click Continue. Your account will be created.

Once the iTunes account is created, you will now be able to set up your iPad device. When you first press the Sleep/Wake button along the top edge of the device, you will see a graphic depicting a USB cord being "plugged into" an icon representing iTunes. This means exactly what it signifies: you need to plug the iPad into your computer using the 10W USB Power Adapter that came in the box with the device. Simply pull off the power adapter from the USB end of the cord and plug it into an open USB port on your computer. Then plug the other end into the Dock Connector at the bottom of the iPad.

That's all you need to do. Your computer will automatically detect the iPad, start iTunes, and begin the Setup Assistant (see Figure 1.5).

Figure 1.5
The iPad Setup Assistant.

1. Click the Set up as a new iPad option and then click Continue. The second page of the Setup Assistant will appear (see Figure 1.6).

Figure 1.6
Define your iPad settings.

2. Type a name for your iPad.

3. Confirm that the two Automatically sync options are checked. This will enable your iPad's contents to be backed up on your PC or Mac.

4. Click Done. The iPad will be configured to your specifications and synced with your computer.

It is important to note that this first synchronization between your iPad and computer could take quite some time, particularly if you have any music or video files already in your iTunes library.

Conclusion

In this chapter, you learned about the not-so-secret origins of the iPad and iPad 2, and why this device has become so successful. You also were presented with the pros and cons of purchasing a particular iPad model. Finally, you learned how to set up iTunes, an iTunes Store Account, and the iPad itself.

While you're waiting for the iPad to finish its initial setup, grab a cup of tea while you wait, and come back for Chapter 2, "Second Step: Interfacing with the iPad." There, you'll learn about all of the iPad and iPad 2 controls and even some undocumented control features that may come in handy later.

Chapter 2

Second Step:
Interfacing with the iPad

Like most iPad customers, you were probably already aware of quite a few of the iPad's capabilities. Apple's massive marketing plan did a good job of highlighting the device so that by now most people know that the iPad is a touchscreen device, capable of connecting to the Internet and viewing a large variety of really cool stuff.

When you first get to use the iPad, you will find a sleek, simple device that doesn't seem to change that first impression. A few buttons, a single switch—seriously, how hard could this be?

The simplicity is certainly there, but there's also a lot more going on with the iPad than you'd think. In this chapter, you will learn how to use

* The controls of the iPad.
* The right way to use the touchscreen.
* The virtual iPad keyboard.
* The tools to configure the iPad.

Touring the iPad Device

Take a look at the iPad. You hold in your hands a 9½ by 7½-inch, half-inch thick tablet with a grand total of four controls (not counting the screen itself, which is the iPad's biggest control). As you can see in Figure 2.1, three of the controls are located near the "upper-right" corner of the iPad or iPad 2.

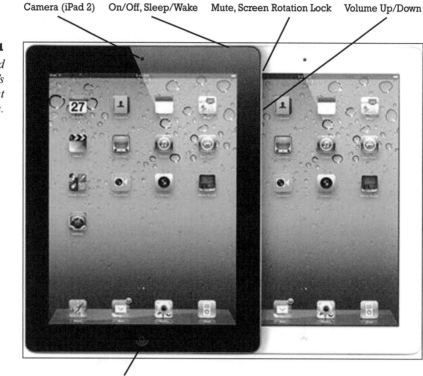

Camera (iPad 2)   On/Off, Sleep/Wake   Mute, Screen Rotation Lock   Volume Up/Down

Figure 2.1

The iPad's and iPad 2's minimalist controls.

Home

What Is Up? What Is Down?

The use of quotes in "upper-right" is deliberate. Since the iPad can be oriented in any direction, there really isn't a "top" or "bottom" for the device. For the purposes of this section, when I actually point out the position of controls, I'll assume that the iPad is oriented as shown in Figure 2.1, with the Home button positioned at the bottom of the device. If you want to be a rebel and hold the iPad differently, that's all you.

The control you will use the most is the Home button, located on the front of the iPad, centered below the screen. Click the Home button, and you will be taken immediately back to the last Home screen you were in. Since the iPad can use more than one application at a time, double-clicking the Home button will open the App toolbar and let you switch to any other open app. I'll get to that later in the chapter.

The On/Off or Sleep/Wake button is something you'll also use often. Its dual name hints at its multifunction capabilities. If you simply press the button quickly, it will put the iPad to sleep. "Sleep," in this case, is a very low-power state that will turn the screen off and prevent any other inputs until the Sleep/Wake button or the Home button is pressed again.

The thing to remember about the iPad being asleep is that while the iPad appears to be completely powered down, it's actually not. The device will be waiting quietly for you to pick it up and start working again, ready to pop on the instant you wake it up. To come back so quickly, the iPad has to be in a state of readiness that uses a teensy bit of power as time goes by. Very little, to be sure, but the drain on the batteries is real. Leave the iPad asleep for too long (over a couple of days or so), and it's possible you will find the batteries very weak or even drained when you come back to wake it up.

To prevent this unfortunate surprise, you can use the same button as an On/Off control. To turn the iPad completely off, press and hold the On/Off button for a few seconds. A red confirmation slide control will appear at the top of the window.

If you really want to power down the device, tap and drag the slide control to the right, and the iPad will shut down. If you hold the Sleep/Wake button down too long by mistake, you can tap the Cancel button on the bottom of the screen.

Once the device is really and truly all the way off, pressing and holding the On/Off button is the only way to start the power-on sequence. (This is to prevent any accidental bumps from turning the iPad back on and thus draining the batteries.) It takes a few moments to cycle all the way back on, so don't worry if it seems to take awhile.

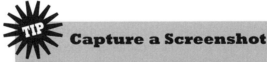

Capture a Screenshot

There's a cool little undocumented feature you can use with the Home and Sleep/Wake buttons. Hold the Home key down and then press the Sleep/Wake button at the same time. The screen will flash, and you'll hear the sound of a camera shutter. You've just taken a picture of your iPad's screen, which you will be able to view using the Photo app. In fact, all of the iPad pictures in this book were acquired using this method.

The Volume up/down control, located on the right side of the iPad, is pretty straightforward. Press the top of the control to turn the volume of the iPad's speaker up and press the bottom of the control to bring the volume down. This control is the master volume control for the iPad. Some applications, such as the iPod and video apps, have their own onscreen volume controls that handle volume just for those apps. This is something you should be aware of, because you might hear volume differences as you use different apps.

The mute or screen rotation lock switch is just above the Volume up/down control. The two names may seem confusing, but actually it's not. When the initial iPad was released, this switch only controlled the screen rotation, the effect that pivots the screen around so you can always read it. But Steve Jobs is rumored to have insisted on making the switch a mute control, just like a similar switch on the iPhone. A software upgrade on the iPad changed the function of the switch to just mute.

That decision, however, was met with user outcry, because many iPad users liked the screen rotation switch just fine, thank you. So, when the iPad 2 was released, Apple gave users the capability to decide for themselves. The switch can be used for one or the other function, based on a setting that users can change. (More on that later in this chapter.)

As a rotation lock, when the switch is in the up, or off, position, the screen will rotate freely based on the orientation of the device. Flip the switch to the on position, and the orientation of the screen will stay right where it is, no matter how you hold the device. This is useful, should you be reading something and don't want the contents of the screen to shift every time you move in your chair or set the iPad down.

As a mute switch, the up position enables sound, and the down position mutes the device.

There are other neat features on the iPad about which you should know. Figure 2.2 displays the top and bottom of the iPad device, where these important features lie. The location of these hardware features is identical on the iPad 2.

Figure 2.2

Other iPad hardware features.

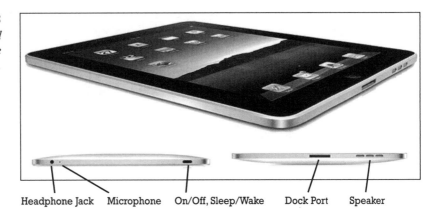

Headphone Jack   Microphone   On/Off, Sleep/Wake   Dock Port   Speaker

We've already reviewed the Sleep/Wake or On/Off button, so here are more details about the other features:

* **Headphone Jack.** This is a standard 3.5mm stereo headphone jack, to which you can plug in your favorite headphones.

* **Microphone.** This tiny hole is actually the microphone for the iPad. It does work well for everyday applications, but for higher-quality work, you may want to get a better microphone.

* **Dock Port.** This port is the primary way to connect the iPad to a PC or Mac, a power adapter, or an iPad Dock or Keyboard Dock.

* **Speaker.** This is where the sound comes from if the headphones are not in use. Try not to cover this up, so you will get better sound.

Now that we've looked at the other controls of the iPad, let's examine the most important control: the iPad screen itself. Most of the work you will do and the content you will view will be done on the screen, so it's a good idea to get the lay of the land.

When you press the Sleep/Wake or On/Off button for the first time, you will initially see the Lock screen (shown in Figure 2.3). This screen will stay visible until you slide the Slide to Unlock control or about seven seconds have passed—in which case the iPad will go back to sleep.

Figure 2.3

The iPad Lock screen.

To slide the control, place your finger on the gray arrow button and drag your finger to the right. This will open the Home screen, as shown in Figure 2.4.

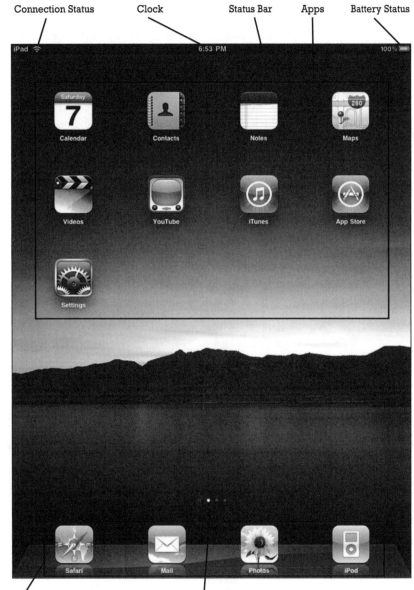

Figure 2.4

The iPad Home screen.

Connection Status   Clock   Status Bar   Apps   Battery Status

Favorite Apps   Home Screen Status

Here's a rundown of the different components of the Home screen:

✳ **Status Bar.** This area on the top of the screen is home to various status messages the iPad or its apps may display.

✳ **Connection Status.** This area displays the status of the WiFi connection the iPad is currently using. In 3G models, the connectivity to AT&T is also displayed.

✳ **Clock.** Here it shows the current time.

✳ **Battery Status.** This area displays the strength of the current battery charge. It also displays when the battery is being charged.

✳ **Apps.** Here are the icons that, when tapped, start the various applications that run on the iPad.

✳ **Home Screen Status.** This area displays which Home screen the iPad is currently showing and the number of available Home screens. The iPad can accommodate up to 11 Home screens.

✳ **Favorite Apps.** Here is an area that houses your favorite apps. This area is displayed on all the Home screens.

The look and feel of any of the Home screens will remain the same, regardless of how many or how few apps are displayed. Each Home screen can display 20 apps or folders, and the Favorites section can hold up to six applications or folders. As you can see in Figure 2.5, the same components are visible when the iPad is in landscape mode.

Figure 2.5

The iPad Home screen in landscape.

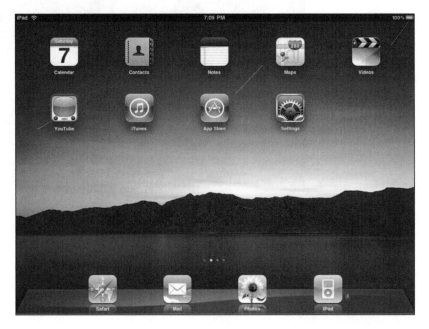

Another available screen on the iPad is the Search screen (see Figure 2.6), which is always located to the left of the Home screen. The Search screen enables you to find files and applications quickly on the iPad.

Figure 2.6

The iPad Search screen.

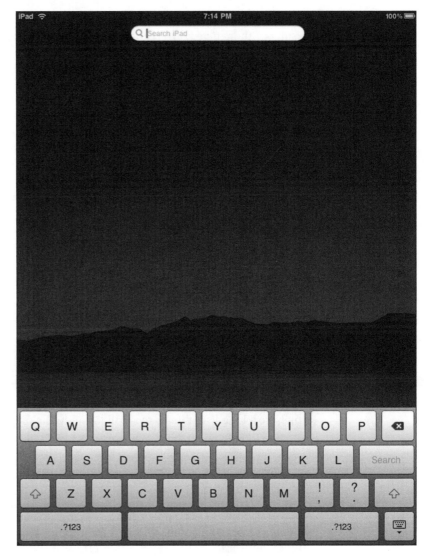

Having the Right Touch

Using an iPad is not like using a "typical" PC or Mac, where a mouse is used to move a cursor around a screen and clicking the mouse once or twice brings up menus, windows, and dialog boxes. No, the iPad has a different interface, one that differs from the now-familiar actions many people are used to on their computers, but definitely mirrors the way smartphones are used.

The most useful gesture is the tap. Tapping once on the screen will start an app, "press" a button, type a letter, or select an option on a list. The results of the tap vary from application to application, but it is directly analogous to a single click of a mouse.

A related gesture is the double-tap, which can also perform useful actions. In Maps, for instance, a double-tap will zoom in on that area of the map.

Pinching the screen on a given spot can zoom out from that spot. This may not be intuitive when you read it, but try it (Maps is a good app for this example), and it will make sense. Pinching serves to bring the edges of the area "in," thus creating the zoom-out effect. The farther away your two fingers (or finger and thumb) are when starting the gesture, the more dramatic the "zoom." To get the opposite effect, you can pinch out, which is how Apple refers to the motion of starting with two fingers together on the screen and moving them apart to zoom in. This is also referred to as "fanning," since you can fan your fingers out to achieve the zoom.

Panning, also known as dragging, is done by placing your finger on the screen and moving it around to display the area you want, or move an object or text around the screen. A related move is two-fingered dragging, which will scroll any window within a window.

Swiping, as you've seen in the previous section, is done by quickly pressing and dragging a control across the screen. Swiping is also how you can move from one Home screen to another. Flicking is a similar gesture: if you have a long list of items to scroll through, flicking a finger across the screen will simulate a quick scroll with some inertia behind it.

Some objects, particularly in iWorks apps, will contain objects that can be rotated. A special two-fingered move known as *rotating* will handle this. The best way to describe it is like grabbing an imaginary radio knob and twisting your fingers in opposite directions to rotate the object.

Finally, some applications will call for a long-press, also known as the "touch-and-hold." This gesture is pretty self-explanatory, and can be done by pressing any part of the screen for over one second.

Keep in mind, not every application will use every gesture. It varies from application to application, but these are the basic moves that will help you navigate the iPad when needed.

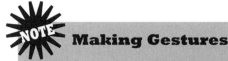

Making Gestures

All of the gestures that are unique to the iPad give the applications a common trait: many functions are done with an economical use of gestures and touches, with the least amount of input. You will see these traits recurring in many of the applications in this book.

Keying in the Keyboard

The most noticeable piece of hardware missing on the iPad is, naturally, the keyboard. Well, it's not really missing. Like the iPhones and smartphones being sold out there, the iPad relies on what's known as a virtual keyboard for users to enter text. That means the keyboard is driven only by software and appears directly on the screen, as displayed in Figure 2.7.

Figure 2.7
The iPad keyboard.

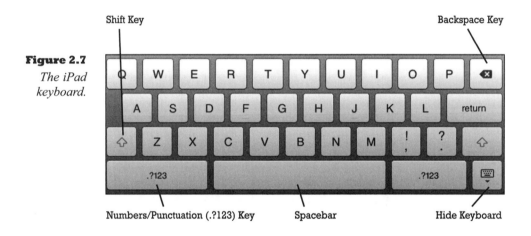

Keyboards appear whenever the user taps an area of the screen where text needs to be entered or changed (known as a field). Yes, it's "keyboards," plural, because as software, the keyboard can change itself to meet the needs of the environment in which you are typing.

Tech Term: Fields

A field is a place in a Web page or computer application where you, the user, enter information.

The keyboard in Figure 2.7, for instance, is the keyboard that displays when using the Pages app. But tapping on the URL field (the spot where Web addresses are entered) in the Safari Web browser shows some big differences (shown in Figure 2.8).

Figure 2.8

The iPad keyboard in Safari.

Check out the .com key, which is a nice shortcut for typing what falls at the end of most Web addresses. The Return key has been changed to Go, and common Web address punctuation has been added to the bottom row of keys.

Because each application developer may require a different set of common keystrokes, the variations of keyboards are potentially limitless. And that's just in English (more on that in a bit).

Referring back to Figure 2.7, note the .?123 key. Tapping this key will display the numbers and punctuation keyboard, shown in Figure 2.9.

Figure 2.9

The numbers and punctuation keyboard.

Symbols (#+=) Key   Main Keyboard (ABC) Key

If you tap the Symbols key, denoted as #+=, the symbols keyboard will appear (see Figure 2.10).

Figure 2.10

*The symbols
keyboard.*

To return to the main keyboard, tap the ABC key at any time. If you want to remove any keyboard from the screen, tap the hide keyboard key. The keyboard will be hidden until the next time you tap in a text-entry area.

Typing with the iPad keyboard is just like typing with a regular keyboard, but with some slick differences. For instance, if you find yourself typing a word that needs accented characters (such as résumé), then press and hold the "e" key and a popover menu containing several variations of the vowel will appear, with different accents and umlauts. Slide your finger to the correct variant (in this case, "é"), release the key, and the letter will appear in your text.

Not every key in a keyboard has these special keys available, so you will need to explore. Two very useful variant keys include

* Hold and slide the comma key to access an apostrophe without tapping the .?123 key.
* In the Internet keyboard in Safari, hold and slide the .com key to view the .org and .net variations.

Another hold-and-slide trick, which will take a little practice, is to type a letter, then slide your finger over to the .?123 key, and—without lifting your finger—slide to the number or punctuation mark you need and then let go. This will insert the character and return you right back to the ABC keyboard without having to tap the ABC key.

Moving Text Around

Most of us who have used computers are familiar with the writing capabilities of our machines when it comes to creating documents. We even take these features for granted, especially the cut, copy, and paste text functions.

But in the iPad, the question immediately becomes, how to cut, copy, or paste text without a mouse? Or a Ctrl key?

The answer is actually quite simple, and it's just a few taps away.

To cut or copy text, double-tap the word you want to edit. The word will be selected and an Edit menu will appear immediately above it (see Figure 2.11).

Figure 2.11

The Edit menu.

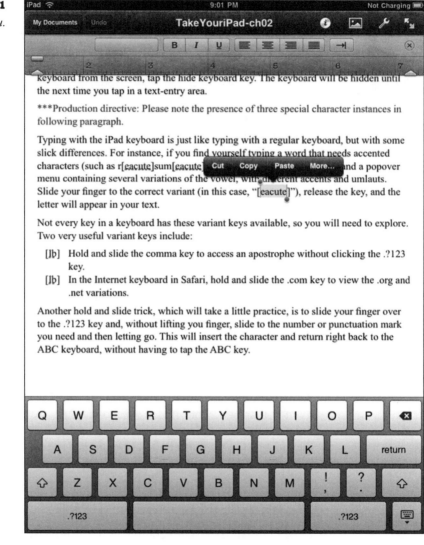

Tap Cut, and the word will immediately be removed from the document, but held in storage on the iPad's "clipboard," which is a temporary storage area for text and objects that have been cut or copied. If you tap Copy, the word will be stored on the clipboard, but not removed from the document.

Long-press the location in the document you want the cut or copied word to appear. The Edit menu will appear again. Tap Paste, and the cut or copied term will appear where you want it.

Clipboard Functionality

Text or objects in the clipboard can be pasted indefinitely until another passage of text or another object is cut or copied.

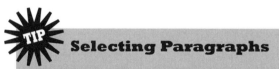

Selecting Paragraphs

To cut, copy, and paste an entire paragraph, triple-tap the paragraph to select all of it.

Configuring the iPad

Now that you have a good idea of the layout of the iPad, it's time to start customizing it to meet your personal needs. You can customize many things about the iPad, but for now we will focus on some of the more popular settings.

One of the first things users want to do is change the wallpaper on their iPad. While this seems trivial, let's face it, we all want to give things our own identifier.

To change the wallpaper:

1. Tap the Settings icon on the Home screen. The Settings app will open, as seen in Figure 2.12.

Figure 2.12

The Settings app.

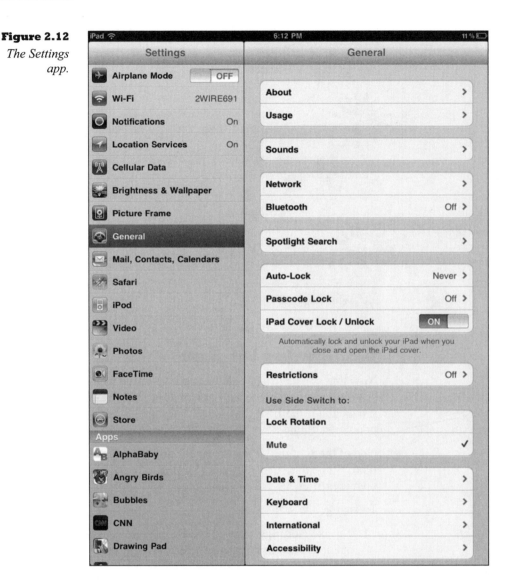

2. Tap the Brightness & Wallpaper setting. The Brightness & Wallpaper pane will open.

3. Tap the Wallpaper control. The Wallpaper pane will open (see Figure 2.13).

Figure 2.13

The Wallpaper pane.

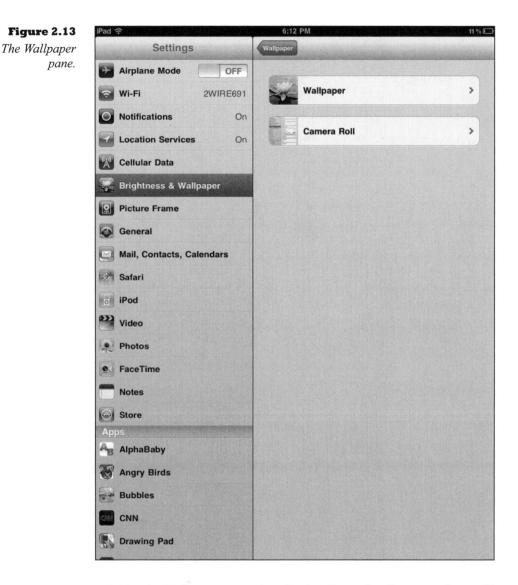

4. Tap the Wallpaper control again. A gallery of wallpaper options will appear.

5. Tap an option you like. The wallpaper will appear full-size, with an Options bar on top. You can use this wallpaper for the Lock Screen, the Home Screen, or Set Both (see Figure 2.14).

Figure 2.14

Choosing how to use the wallpaper.

6. Tap the option you prefer. The sample wallpaper will close, and the Settings app will appear.

7. Press the Home button. The new wallpaper will be visible (see Figure 2.15).

Figure 2.15

*The new
wallpaper.*

Users for whom English is not their native language will very likely want
to make a more significant change—the addition of a keyboard more
suited to their own language.

1. Tap the Settings icon on the Home screen. The Settings app will
   open.
2. Tap the General settings. The General pane will open.
3. Tap the Keyboard option. The Keyboard pane will open.
4. Tap the International Keyboards option. The International Keyboard
   pane will open.

5. Tap Add New Keyboard. The Add New Keyboard pane will open.

6. Tap an option. The option will be added to the International Keyboard pane.

To use an added keyboard, enter an app that uses a keyboard. Immediately, you will see a globe key in the keyboard (see Figure 2.16). This is the International Keyboard key.

Figure 2.16

The International Keyboard key is shown where the globe is.

To start the new keyboard, tap the globe icon to cycle through the available options. The name of the keyboard will appear in the spacebar as you type. Or long-press the globe icon to see an action menu of the available options (see Figure 2.17). Slide your finger to the desired International option and release. The keyboard will be set.

Figure 2.17

The International Keyboard options.

To remove an International Keyboard:

1. Tap the Settings icon on the Home screen. The Settings app will open.

2. Tap the General settings. The General pane will open.

3. Tap the Keyboard option. The Keyboard pane will open.

4. Tap the International Keyboards option. The International Keyboard pane will open.

5. Tap the Edit key. The pane will appear in Edit mode.

6. Tap the red delete icon for the keyboard you want to remove. The Delete button will appear (see Figure 2.18).

Figure 2.18

Removing a keyboard.

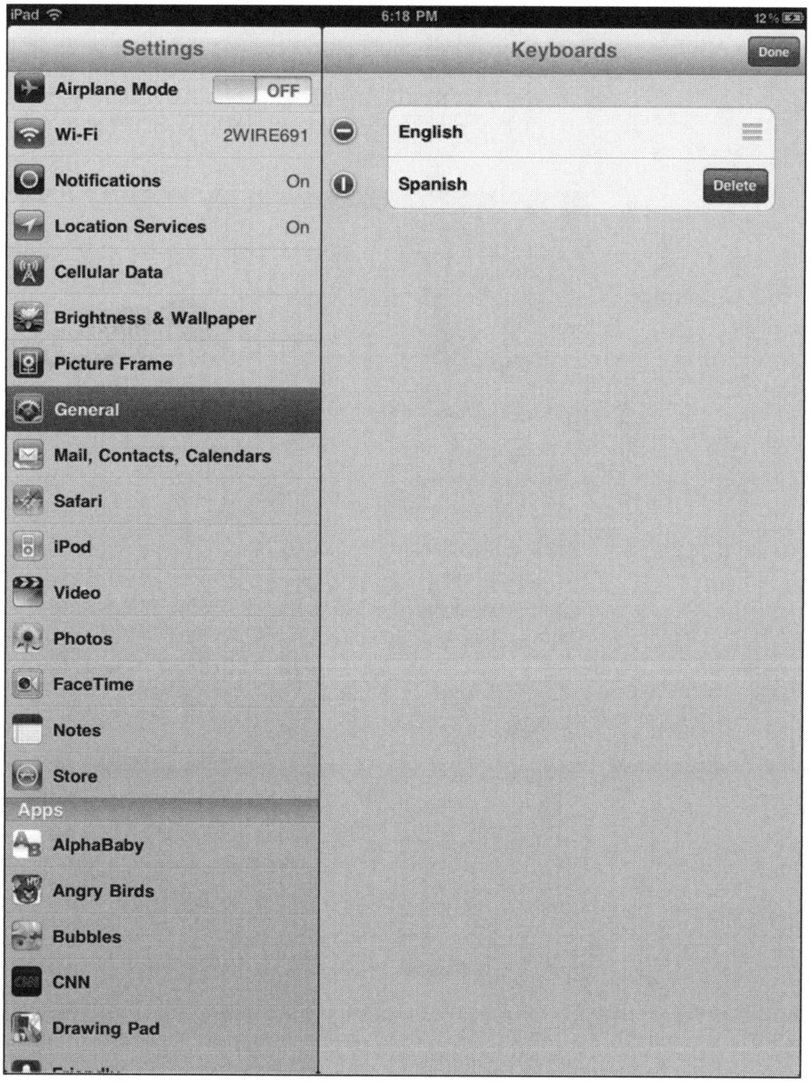

7. Tap the Delete button. The option will be removed.

8. Tap Done. The International Keyboard pane will return to Display mode.

For English users, there are additional keyboard enhancements that you may want to check out.

1. Tap the Settings icon on the Home screen. The Settings app will open.
2. Tap the General settings. The General pane will open.
3. Tap the Keyboard option. The Keyboard pane will open (see Figure 2.19), and the following options will be displayed.

Figure 2.19

General keyboard settings.

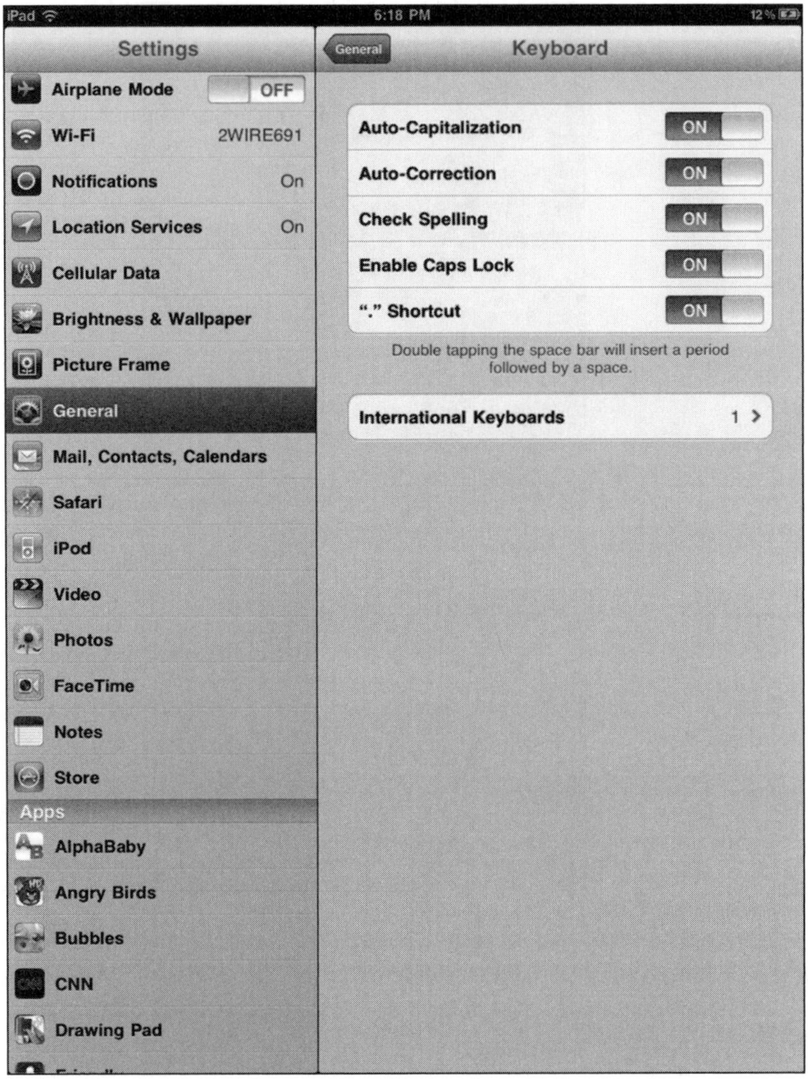

* **Auto-Capitalization.** Capitalizes the first letter after the end of a sentence.
* **Auto-Correction.** Displays suggested words from the iPad dictionary when iPad thinks you have made a spelling error.
* **Check Spelling.** Checks spelling within an opened document.
* **Enable Caps Lock.** Lets you start Caps Lock typing by double-tapping the Shift key.
* **"." Shortcut.** Inserts a period followed by a space when you double-tap the spacebar.

4. Select the options you want to activate or deactivate by sliding the appropriate control.
5. Press the Home button. The changes will be made.

Finally, as mentioned earlier in this chapter, you can specify whether you want the iPad's side switch to control muting sound or locking screen rotation.

To change the side switch action:

1. Tap the Settings icon on the Home screen. The Settings app will open.
2. Tap the General settings. The General pane will open.
3. In the Use Side Switch to: section, tap the option you prefer.
4. Press the Home button. The changes will be made.

Conclusion

In this chapter, you learned about the various hardware and software controls available on the iPad. You discovered the basic gestures needed to navigate the iPad interface and learned some handy shortcuts along the way.

In Chapter 3, "Third Step: Connecting with the iPad," you'll learn how to really, er, tap into the iPad's power by getting connected to the Internet, and you'll be that much closer to your family using the iPad. Provided you share.

Chapter 3
Third Step:
Connecting
with the iPad

On its own as a stand-alone device, the iPad is a great platform to view videos, listen to music, or play educational games. All you need to perform these and other tasks is the iPad itself and a connection to a local computer that lets you share files with the iPad.

That's all well and good, of course, but let's face it—we like devices like the iPad and iPad 2 because of their ability to visit and view content on the Internet.

Now, let's talk about the Internet a bit. It's important to remember that the Internet is no magical environment for work and play. It's just a big collection of computers that are connected to each other. What we get out of the Internet depends on how we look at it.

Apple's vision of the Internet is different than that of other computer or mobile device companies. Since the opening of the Internet to the public in the early 1990s, the original idea that software developers used when they built Internet software like browsers and email applications was this: show users everything, and let them figure out what is good. Like giving some people a tent, dropping them off in the middle of the forest, and saying "have at it."

In the last decade of the 20th century, the forest was not so scary, since content on the Internet was scarce, and because that content was such a novelty, it could not help but be interesting. That novelty didn't last long. As PCs and Macs got better, and networks got faster, content changed from static text and images to dynamic applications and multimedia experiences. The nature of the content grew much more diverse, ranging from the very good to the very ugly.

"Ugly" is not just a judgment on the taste or attractiveness of the content; it also means the content can be very unsafe for your computer and its data. Viruses, Trojans, and other forms of computer malware can lie hidden on even the most reputable of Web sites, if they've been hacked.

Tech Term: Malware

Malware is short for *malicious software*, and it describes any software that tries to get at your system and the information contained within. Some people classify spam messages as malware, but spam is just annoying, not a true threat.

Apple, particularly with its iPhone and iPad devices, has decided to leave the one-window-to-the-Internet approach behind and change to a more managed content approach. Safari, a traditional browser, is still available, of course, but other apps on the iPad family (and iPhone) present Internet content to you in very managed, "clean" environments. The analogy used today is the "walled garden": nature is still seen and enjoyed, but in a controlled fashion, not all wild and messy.

As adults, you and I may or may not agree with the walled garden approach, since some would see this as strangling freedom, but the good news is that you can either use this approach or abandon it and surf the Internet normally with the Safari browser. As parents and teachers, let's face it: there is a compelling argument for using individual apps to visit the Internet. The level of content control is much greater and can give parents a better sense of what their kids are seeing.

This is a tricky area, of course. Privacy, freedom of exploration, protection—these are all areas parents struggle with, especially when it comes to the Internet. What works for me and my family, for instance, may not sit well with your value system. We have a managed, age-appropriate system in the Proffitt household. My youngest in elementary school had regimented access to the Internet—only allowed to visit certain sites—until recently, when we started letting her explore a bit on her own. Our soon-to-be-in-high-school middle daughter has pretty much unlimited access, though her mother and I have discussions with her about what's happening with the social media sites like Facebook. We don't pry too much, but we do look for signs of trouble. Our oldest, about to go to college, has had free rein for quite a while.

However you want to approach the Internet, you will need to apply your values to the way the iPad gives you the Internet: processing content that is also segmented into defined channels. Instead of one-size-fits-all applications that manage different types of content, iPad apps work by piecing out content based on the app used. For example, this app does music, that app does video, while this one over here takes care of news.

Before we get to the Internet, it's important to connect to a more local computer, your iTunes-based PC or Mac. This was already done in Chapter 1, "First Step: Introducing the iPad," when you first configured your iPad, but now it's time to learn more about what iTunes can do for you.

In this chapter, you will learn how to

✳ Connect to and sync with iTunes.

✳ Connect to the Internet with WiFi.

✳ Connect to the Internet via 3G service.

✳ Troubleshoot Internet connectivity.

Connecting to iTunes

Because of the connectivity the iPad has to the Internet, it is possible to use iTunes with the iPad or iPad 2 just once in its operational life—at the very first configuration described in Chapter 1. Many people will do this, since music, videos, and applications you get with iTunes on a computer can also be purchased and downloaded "over the air" with iTunes on the iPad.

For casual use only, this approach is fine. But there is another good reason to use iTunes: even if you don't download a lot of content, syncing with iTunes will give you the very important benefit of backing up all of your iPad device's data.

As nice as the iPad and iPad 2 are, the truth is that things can—and will—go wrong. Your device could be dropped. Or damaged. Or lost. Even less drastic problems might happen—a poorly put-together app could freeze the iPad, and the only way to stop the problem might be to restore the device back to its original factory state (though thankfully such problems are very rare now). When that happens, having a backup of your iPad's data and settings is a great thing because you can direct iTunes to restore your data and put you right back where you were, with no loss of data.

For this reason alone, it is strongly recommended that users regularly sync the iPad with iTunes.

Auto and Manual Syncing

Synchronizing the iPad with iTunes is very simple, as demonstrated in Chapter 1: just plug one end of the USB/docking cable into the Dock port and the other end into the PC or Mac with iTunes installed. This will immediately start iTunes and begin the syncing process, as shown in Figure 3.1.

Figure 3.1

Syncing the iPad.

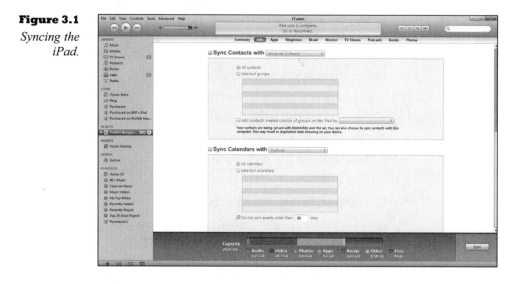

Depending on how long it's been since you last synced your iPad, this operation could take anywhere from one to several minutes. As it is syncing, your iPad will show a sync variation of the Lock screen, preventing you from working with the iPad until the sync process is completed. You can use the slide control to stop the synchronization, and most of the time this can be done with no ill effect. However, if you have a lot of data to back up, or you're adding or removing a lot of data from the iPad, stopping in mid-sync is not recommended.

After the sync operation is complete, you can disconnect the iPad from the computer. If you leave it connected, you can use iTunes to configure the iPad and the synchronization process.

With the iPad still connected to your iTunes-equipped computer, click the name of the iPad in the Devices section. The iPad's configuration pages will appear, as shown in Figure 3.2.

Figure 3.2

iTunes' iPad pages.

In Figure 3.2, the Summary page is displayed. This page reveals a lot of information about the status of your iPad, particularly the capacity of the device. If you are wondering if your iPad is running low on memory, this is the page to check.

The tabs along the top of the iPad window will navigate to other pages that will let you configure various aspects of the iPad directly from within iTunes. Click the Info tab, for instance, and you will find a page that will enable you to configure MobileMe, Apple's online storage service, as well as where the contacts, calendar, and email apps will collect their data (see Figure 3.3).

Figure 3.3

The iPad Info page.

If you make any changes to your iPad configuration anywhere in iTunes, then the Sync button in the iPad window will change to two buttons: Apply and Revert (see Figure 3.4).

Figure 3.4

Apply changes to your iPad.

Revert Button   Apply Button

To manually sync the iPad with the new changes, click Apply. To manually sync the iPad at any time, regardless of changes that may or may not have been made, simply click the Sync button in iTunes.

Choosing What to Sync

The iPad window in iTunes not only lets you configure iPad and its apps (which will be more thoroughly reviewed in Chapter 4, "Fourth Step: Using the iPad Apps"), but it also synchronizes file types from the iTunes computer to the iPad. This is important, especially if you have a very large collection of music or video files. Even at a maximum of 64GB, the iPad may not have the capacity to hold your entire multimedia collection. Or, if it does, it may not leave you enough room for apps or other data.

To demonstrate, let's specify which music files will be moved to the iPad.

1. With the iPad still connected to your iTunes-equipped computer, click the name of the iPad in the Devices section. The iPad's Configuration window will appear.

2. Click the Music tab. The iPad Music page will appear (see Figure 3.5).

Figure 3.5

The iPad Music page.

3. Click the Selected playlists, artists, albums, and genres option. The Options windows will appear, as shown in Figure 3.6.

Figure 3.6

Choose the music you want to sync.

4. In the Genres window, select the Classical option.
5. Click Apply. The music on your iPad will now include only the songs in this genre (see Figure 3.7).

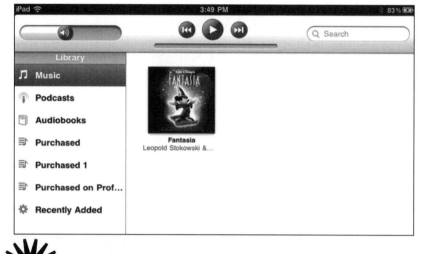

Mixing Your iPad Music

You can select music to sync to the iPad based on individual artists or any playlists you've created in the iPad or iTunes.

Restoring the iPad

As I mentioned earlier in this chapter, you can use iTunes to restore your iPad to either completely new factory settings (which is useful if you're going to sell the iPad and want none of your personal data on the device) or to the last backup you made.

Care must be taken that you only perform a restore operation when absolutely needed. This is a last-ditch solution for resolving issues with the iPad, mainly because it can take a very long time to restore the iPad.

Still, if all other options are exhausted, restoration can be a big help putting your iPad to rights.

1. With the iPad still connected to your iTunes-equipped computer, click the name of the iPad in the Devices section. The iPad's Configuration window will appear.

2. In the Summary tab, click Restore. A confirmation dialog box will appear (see Figure 3.8).

Figure 3.8

Confirm that you want to restore the iPad.

3. Click Restore. The confirmation dialog box will close, and the restoration process will begin.

CAUTION   **Do Not Disconnect**

Do not disconnect the iPad from the iTunes computer during restoration. Ever. No matter how long it takes. An incomplete restoration could create more problems on your iPad.

4. Once the restoration process reaches the halfway point, you will be asked to restore the device to factory new settings or from your last backup. Click the From backup option and then click Restore.

At the end of the lengthy restoration process, your iPad should be restored to its last backed-up state.

Using the WiFi Connection

After you have gotten the hang of connecting to iTunes, you should complete the connection circuit and get your iPad out on the Internet.

For iPad WiFi users, there is only one way to connect to the Internet—joining a wireless network. Luckily, such networks are rather common.

In many countries, high-speed Internet access is provided by Internet Service Providers (ISPs), such as telephone, cable, or satellite companies. These large ISPs provide fast Internet connectivity to home customers at relatively affordable rates, usually based on usage. Most broadband consumers have wireless access already, as their Internet connection devices (known as "routers") provided by the ISPs usually have connections for network cables ("wired") to your computer(s) and WiFi.

If your router supports wireless, it will broadcast a radio signal at a range of about 50 yards in the clear or throughout a typical two-story home, depending on the composition of walls, layout, etc. The signal is identified by a unique label, known as the SSID. The SSID is the name of the router's wireless network; think of it as the call letters of your favorite radio station. Knowing the SSID of your wireless network is important, although most of the time it will be pretty obvious what the SSID is.

That's because when devices like laptops and the iPad detect a wireless network, the device's software will also see the strength of the network and whether it's an open or protected network. If you are using your iPad in your local coffee shop, for example, you may detect a few nearby wireless networks, but the strongest one has the SSID "Cup_O_Joe," so it isn't hard to tell in this case.

CAUTION Make Sure That You Know the Network

If you are at all unsure what the right network is, do not connect to it—even if it looks right. I was once in a major bookstore chain and noted the correct SSID was accompanied by one that had a similar name, but not as strong and not as protected. A little walking around found a teenager sitting in the stacks with his own router, trying to catch unsuspecting customers to log on to his network and thus have their data intercepted. If you're not sure, ask the manager. If you are the manager, periodically check for the presence of SSIDs that look like your own establishment's network.name, but not as strong and not as protected. A little walking around found a teenager sitting in the stacks with his own router, trying to catch unsuspecting customers to log on to his network and thus have their data intercepted. If you're not sure, ask the manager. If you *are* the manager, periodically check for the presence of SSIDs that look like your own establishment's network.

For some networks, you may also need the key to the network. Public networks or some business networks will provide a completely open network for citizen or customer convenience. You might find the network to which you want to connect is protected (or locked) by a password, also known as a key. Before you can connect to the Internet through such a network, make sure that you have the key.

CAUTION Safety First

Unless you are on your own home wireless network, do not conduct any business or financial transactions on a wireless network—even if it's protected. Radio signals can still be received by malicious individuals and potentially decrypted. *Under no circumstances should you conduct any private business over an open network.* Ever.

Once you have the SSID and key in hand, you can connect the iPad to the Internet quickly.

1. Tap the Settings app. The Settings screen will open.
2. Tap the WiFi setting. The WiFi Networks pane will appear (see Figure 3.9).

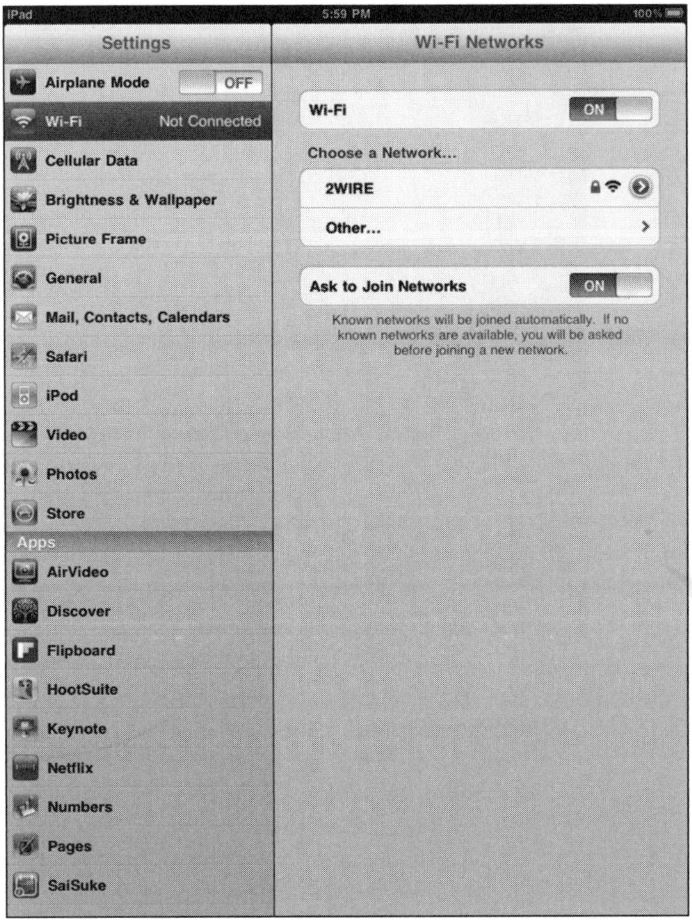

Figure 3.9

The detected nearby wireless networks.

3. Tap the network you want to join. If the network is protected, the Enter Password form will appear, as shown in Figure 3.10.

Figure 3.10

*Protected
networks will
need a
password.*

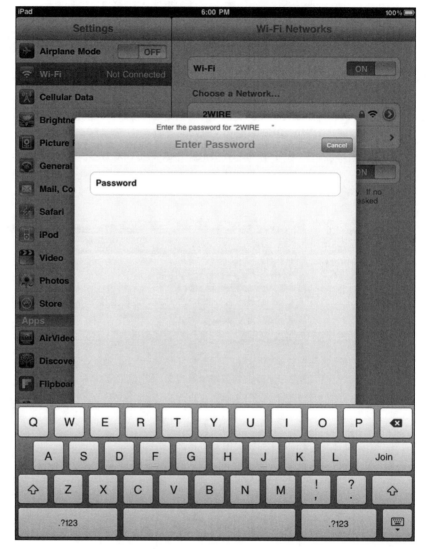

4. Type the password and tap the Join key. If the password is entered correctly, the network will be joined, as indicated by the check mark next to the network name.

One great feature of the iPad is that it will remember networks as you join them. So once you join networks in various businesses and locations, the iPad will keep track of them and auto-join them when you return.

Now that you're connected to the wireless network, you can start to use any iPad application that uses Internet connectivity.

CAUTION PassW0rds R ImportAnT!

Most WiFi systems have a password from the manufacturer built in, which is generally strong enough to be unguessable. If you change your system's password to something that you can remember better, be sure the password is strong. Don't use family names, pet names, birthdates, or anything easily guessed. Use upper- and lowercase and throw in a number or two to make it harder to figure out.

Using the 3G Connection

iPad WiFi+3G owners will have the added advantage of being able to connect to the Internet via a 3G cellular network, just like the one used by your mobile phone.

There are some important things to keep in mind when deciding to use the 3G connection. First, cellular connections will never let you work as fast as a solid WiFi connection. If you never work away from WiFi, then don't just activate the 3G for the sake of turning it on.

That said, the cool thing about using the iPad's 3G connection is that it's strictly pay as you go—no contracts needed. You sign up for the service, and you're set for the next 30 days. At the end of the 30 days, the plan will automatically renew, but you can cancel the plan at any time.

In the U.S., 3G service is provided by two carriers, AT&T and Verizon. Verizon is only available on the iPad 2, and you have to choose between the two carriers when you first buy the iPad 2. The pricing plans get a little tricky to compare, because AT&T has two payment options: up front (pre-paid) or at the end of the month (post-paid), while Verizon is paid after the month is over (post-paid). So how do they compare?

AT&T is available for both the iPad and iPad 2 and comes in one of two plans:

* 250MB for 30 days: U.S. $14.99
* 2GB for 30 days: U.S. $25.00

If you sign up for the 250MB plan and end up transmitting more data over the network than you planned, you will be asked to pay for the 2GB option. If you use 2GB up before the end of 30 days, you will have the opportunity to purchase one of the plans again for another 30-day period.

Under the pre-paid option, if you used 251MB in 30 days, it would cost $29.98 and 2.1GB would cost $50.00. But if you use post-paid, AT&T tacks on a $10.00/GB overage charge per gigabyte. This means that 251MB would still run you about $30.00, but 2.1GB would only be $35.00.

When you just look at AT&T alone, which iPad users will have to do, the post-paid option is definitely better if you run over your monthly traffic limit. AT&T 3G plans include unlimited WiFi at all AT&T hotspots, too.

 How does this compare to Verizon? All Verizon plans, as mentioned, are post-paid at

* 1GB for 30 days: U.S. $20
* 3GB for 30 days: U.S. $35
* 5GB for 30 days: U.S. $50
* 10GB for 30 days: U.S. $80

You can see that for just $5 more than the base AT&T plan, you can get four times the traffic allotment. Add $5 a month to the next level of AT&T, and you can get 50 percent more than the upper-level AT&T plan. If you plan on doing a lot of 3G network surfing, Verizon may be a better deal for U.S. citizens.

Canadian residents have similar plans in place through Rogers:

* 250MB for 30 days: C $15
* 5GB for 30 days: C $35

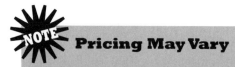

Pricing May Vary

iPad 3G options tend to be affordable in every country where they are implemented. Note that these are plans for residents of these nations: these are not roaming charges for, say, U.S. residents traveling abroad, which are far more expensive.

These prices were valid when this book went to press in the spring of 2011.

To sign up for 3G in the U.S., follow these steps:

1. Tap the Settings app. The Settings screen will open.
2. Tap the Cellular Data setting. The Cellular Data pane will appear (see Figure 3.11).

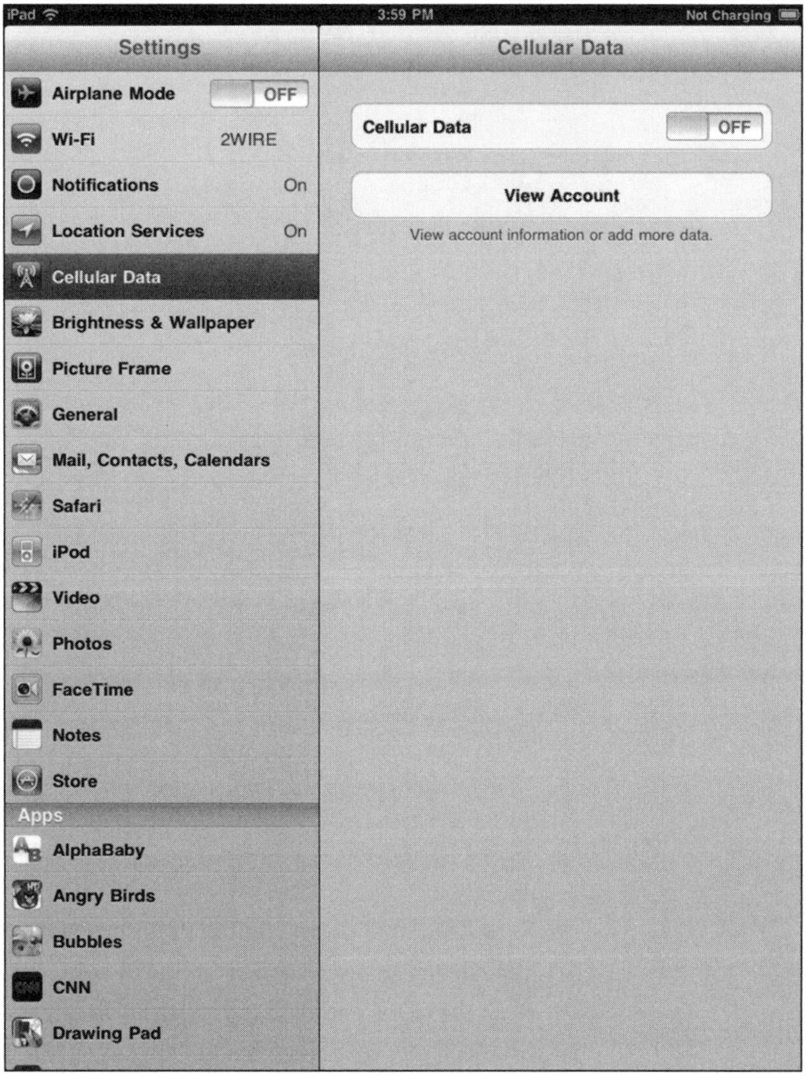

Figure 3.11

Configuring cellular access.

3. Slide the Cellular Data setting to On.
4. Tap the View Account button. The Cellular Data Account form will open (see Figure 3.12).

Figure 3.12

Sign up for a data plan.

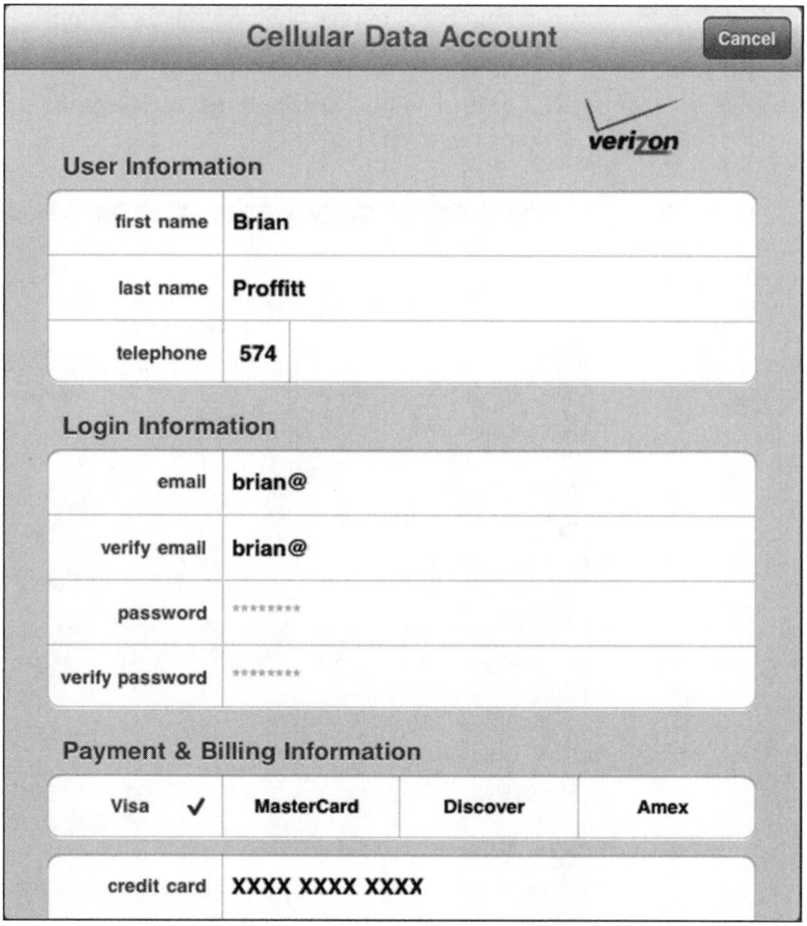

Cellular Data Account   Cancel

verizon

User Information

first name	Brian
last name	Proffitt
telephone	574

Login Information

email	brian@
verify email	brian@
password	********
verify password	********

Payment & Billing Information

Visa ✓	MasterCard	Discover	Amex

credit card	**XXXX XXXX XXXX**

5. Type in the appropriate information, providing an email address and a password that you will use to log in to the cellular network.

6. Tap the desired data plan. The selection will be denoted by a check mark.

7. Enter your credit card and billing information.

8. Tap Next. The Terms of Service page will appear.

9. Read the terms and then tap Agree. A Summary page will appear.

10. Confirm your information and then tap Submit. A notification message that your account will be updated will appear. Tap OK.

In a few moments, you will receive an Alert message indicating that your data plan has been activated. Tap OK to close the Alert box.

If you want to cancel or change your plan, return to the Settings app, tap Cellular Data, and then View Account to see the options available to you (see Figure 3.13).

Figure 3.13

You can always return to the Cellular Data Account form to change or cancel your plan.

Figure 3.13

You can always return to the Cellular Data Account form to change or cancel your plan.

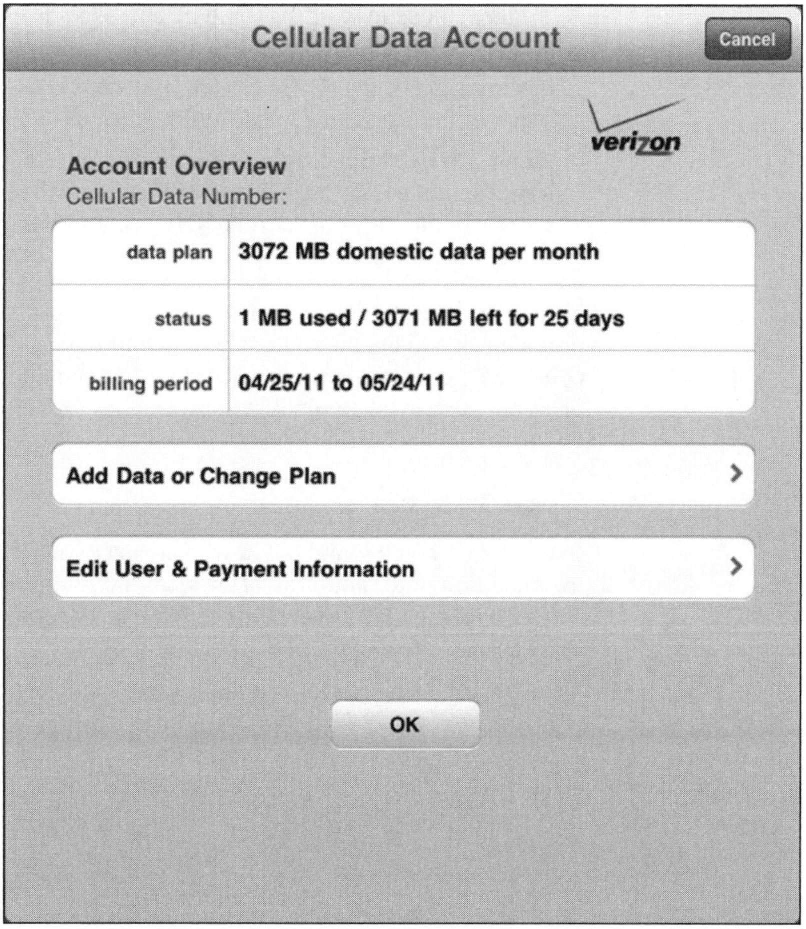

Troubleshooting Connectivity

There will be times when connectivity may not quite work as hoped. Different WiFi routers can be configured wrong or have some problems in the network that might limit your connection. These types of things are usually beyond your control.

But there are some things you can try if you are experiencing unexpected WiFi issues.

❋ **Be sure you're on the correct network.** If you have joined a network that's really far away, try joining one that's closer.

❋ **Look around.** If you are in a public place with lots of laptops and Internet devices going, the wireless router may simply be overworked. You may need to wait for some machines to drop off the network.

❋ **Interference is present.** Radio signals can fall victim to any kind of electromagnetic interference. Metal objects, exposed cables, microwave ovens… these can all degrade WiFi signals.

❋ **The router dropped you.** Sometimes wireless routers can be flaky. Try tapping the Settings app, then WiFi, and then the network you're currently on. Tap Forget this Network and then follow the steps to rejoin the network.

Your iPad is pretty adaptive for WiFi conditions, so if you are having problems, it's likely the router and not your device. If WiFi problems are consistent no matter where you try to join, it could be a hardware issue. Seek out your local Apple service specialist for help.

Conclusion

In this chapter, you found out how to connect your iPad to a local iTunes-installed computer and how iTunes can help you manage your device. You also learned how to connect to the Internet quickly and easily using WiFi access or cellular 3G connectivity.

In Chapter 4, "Fourth Step: Using the iPad Apps," you'll delve into how iPad apps can be acquired, managed, and configured.

Chapter 4
Fourth Step: Using the iPad Apps

Since the popularity of the iPhone, the advertising catchphrase "there's an app for that" has become synonymous with the iPhone and now the iPad. From games to productivity to content—with the thousands of apps available, and more coming every day, there almost is an app out there for any solution you may need.

As part of the "walled garden" approach Apple has toward content, all applications are only available through the iTunes Store. This central-store method means that ideally all applications will be checked for stability, appropriateness, and malicious behavior before they are ever exposed to the general public. By and large, that has been true to date, although not every app is necessarily checked for quality and usability.

This is where customer feedback comes into play. Users are able to quickly rank applications based on a five-star system, as well as provide detailed reviews on what they liked (and didn't like) about the app. This review system is a great way to narrow down the really good applications for your iPad.

In this chapter, you will discover how to

* Open and rearrange apps on your Home screen.
* Switch between apps.
* Close apps that are having problems.
* Download free and purchase commercial apps from iTunes.
* Configure app settings.
* Remove an app from the iPad.

Opening and Arranging Apps

Apps come in all shapes and sizes, but they all share a common feature: how they are started. From any Home screen, just tap the app's icon once. No matter what app you are using, that one action will get the application started.

The presentation of app icons on the Home screens is initially determined by the iPad, but you can quickly shuffle them around to the configuration you want.

Moving Apps

To move app icons, long-press any icon on any Home screen. In a brief moment, you will see the icons start to shake in their positions (see Figure 4.1).

Figure 4.1

Shaky apps, ready to move.

Look again at Figure 4.1, and you will note that some apps now have black X icons. These are apps that can be removed from the iPad. Note that in this sample configuration, the apps in the Favorite area cannot be removed. That's because they are system apps, put on the iPad by Apple, and not able to be removed.

Regardless of their removability, all apps can be moved to any other part of the screen. To move an app:

1. Long-press any icon on the Home screen. The icons will begin to shake.
2. Tap and drag the icon you want to move to another part of the Home screen.
3. Click the Home button. The apps will stabilize, and the app will reside in its new position.

Moving an app icon to another Home screen is just as easy. In fact, when you long-press an icon, notice the Home screen status indicator: it will have added another empty Home screen to your collection as a potential destination for any moved app. If you don't make use of the empty Home screen, the Home screen indicator will display the same number of screens you had before the move operation.

1. Long-press any icon on the Home screen. The icons will begin to shake.
2. Tap and drag the icon you want to move toward the edge of the Home screen adjacent to the Home screen to which you want to move the icon. After a pause, the next Home screen will slide into view.
3. Drag the app icon to the desired spot on its new Home screen.
4. Click the Home button. The apps will stabilize, and the app will reside in its new position.

Storing Apps in Folders

You can also store apps within folders on the iPad screen. This feature lets you store more apps on a particular screen, and even better, organize your apps into something that makes a bit more sense. For instance, if multiple children are using the iPad, you can store each child's set of apps within a folder with his or her name on it, so the apps are easy to locate and use. To create a new folder and name it, do the following:

1. Long-press any icon on the Home screen. The icons will begin to shake.
2. Tap and drag the icon you want to store in a folder so it is on top of another icon you want to store in the same folder. After a pause, the icons will superimpose on one another, and a new folder window will appear (see Figure 4.2).

Figure 4.2

Creating a new folder.
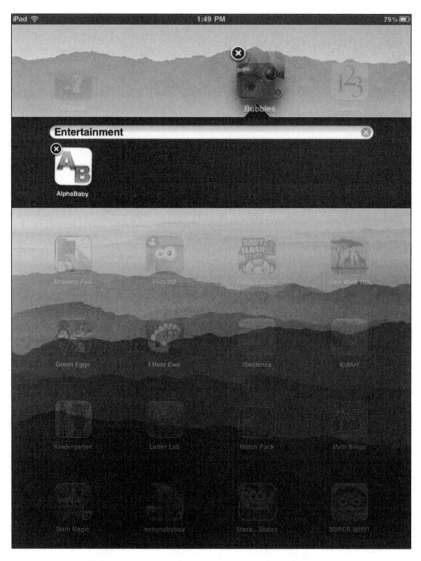

3. Drag the app icon to the desired spot within the folder window, as seen in Figure 4.3.

Figure 4.3

*Positioning apps
in the folder
window.*

4. The iPad will attempt to guess at a suitable folder name, but if it needs changing, tap the name field and use the keyboard to enter a new name.

5. Tap Done on the keyboard. The Folder will be renamed, as seen in Figure 4.4.

Figure 4.4

A new folder, set and named.

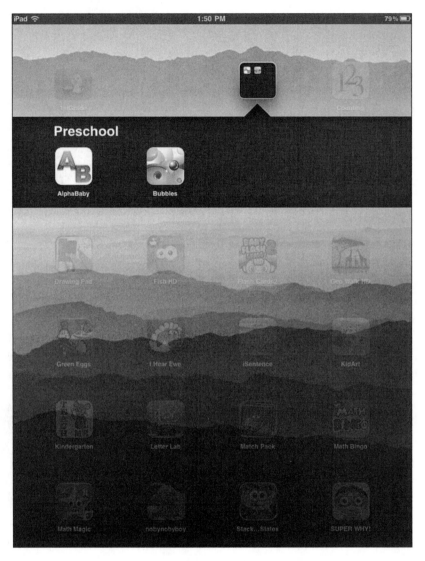

Folders, like app icons, can be moved around to any iPad location, including the Favorite area, located on the bottom of every Home screen. The Favorite area will house up to six app icons or folders. Move any icon to the Favorites by long-pressing it and dragging it to the Favorite area.

Moving Apps with iTunes

You can also, should you want, use iTunes to move your app icons or folders around. This is especially useful if you want to do a lot of reorganizing.

1. With the iPad connected to your iTunes-equipped computer, click the name of the iPad in the Devices section. The iPad's Configuration window will appear.

2. Click the Apps tab. The Apps page will be displayed (see Figure 4.5).

Figure 4.5

The iTunes Apps configuration page.

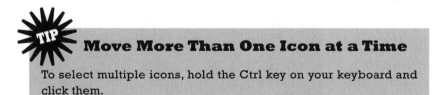

3. Click the Home screen you want to modify. The Home screen will appear.

4. Click the app or folder icon you want to move. The icon will be selected, and the X icon will appear.

Move More Than One Icon at a Time

To select multiple icons, hold the Ctrl key on your keyboard and click them.

5. Click and drag the icon(s) to the destination Home screen.

6. Click and drag individual icons to the desired locations on the new Home screen (see Figure 4.6).

7. Click Apply. The iPad will be synced with the new changes in place (see Figure 4.7).

Figure 4.6

The reconfigured Home screen in iTunes.

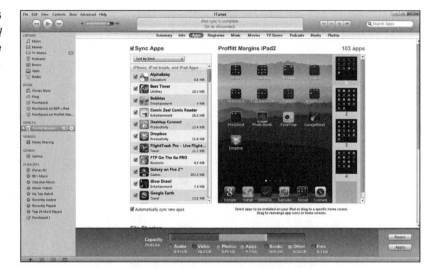

Figure 4.7

The reconfigured Home screen on the iPad.

Get Your Apps

Getting apps for the iPad, whether free of charge or something you pay for, is always done through the iTunes Store. Fortunately, you can get to the iTunes Store through your iTunes application on your computer or over the air using the App Store app on your iPad.

The real trick to getting any app in the first place is finding the right one. While Apple has made sure that apps in the Apps Store are free of malware and relatively stable, don't assume that every app in the App Store will be the greatest thing since sliced bread, even if it's in a featured spot within the App Store.

When you hear about a new app on the Internet or from a friend, read more than one review about the app from reputable sources. Use your favorite search engine to locate such reviews or blog entries about the app.

If you still want to try the app, or you're looking for apps in the App Store, the next place to check is the review section of the app itself. Look at the number of positive versus negative ratings, but also read the reviews. Sometimes disgruntled users will blast an app for some feature (or lack of feature) you don't even need. "It won't scramble eggs!" they cry. Okay, that's notable, but you're just looking for a cool new game for your kids, so the lack of scrambled eggs is not a problem.

NOTE App Review Sites for Kids

Best Kids Apps (*www.bestkidsapps.com/*) is a very good app review site for young ones' apps. Gizmodo (*http://gizmodo.com/*) and Engadget (*www.engadget.com/*) are also good for general iPad app reviews.

If there is a free version of the application available, definitely try that one first. It may have limited features, but it should give you a feel for how the app is put together and if (with the added features) the paid version will be a good fit.

One thing to watch out for is the iPhone apps that can run on the iPad. It doesn't take too much coding to get an iPhone app to run on the iPad, but such quick changes will result in an application that's clearly not configured for the iPad (see Figure 4.8).

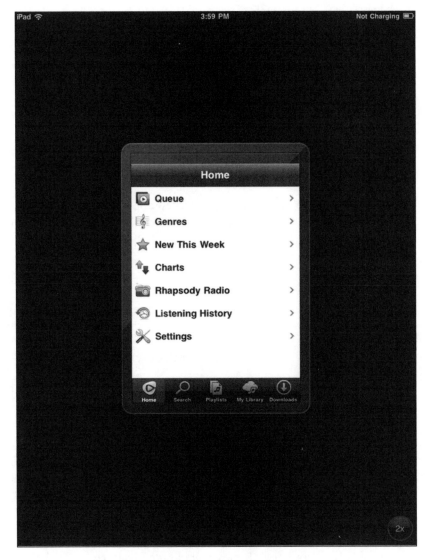

Figure 4.9 displays the 2X effect applied to the Rhapsody app. More readable, but still not great quality. For this kind of app, the issue is not a major concern, but for a kid's game, iPhone-specific apps can be a little off-putting.

Figure 4.9

*Rhapsody in
2X view.*

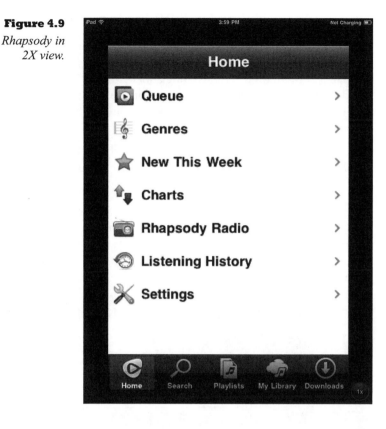

You may like the app so much that you will live with this configuration (at least until the developers come out with a true iPad version). One way to know if you are getting an app like this is to look for a small "+" symbol in the app's download button. This symbol indicates the app was developed for the iPad *and* the iPhone. Look at the screenshot of the app on the app's download page—many of these dual-platform apps are getting configured properly for iPad display, even if they will also run on the iPhone.

Each version of the App Store (whether in iTunes or the App Store app) will have different categories to organize apps. Most of these categories overlap, but if you are having trouble finding something, try browsing both stores.

Finally, the Search bar in both versions of the App Store is a powerful tool for locating apps. This tool will search app titles, keywords, and descriptions to help you find the appropriate application.

Given all of these ways of looking, it's going to be relatively simple to find your app.

Using the iTunes Application

Though the content of the iTunes version of the App Store is identical to its iPad counterpart, the iTunes application is best to use when you are planning on finding and installing a lot of apps. It's not a question of speed, but rather organization. You can find, download, and install apps with the iTunes application and then use the same application to quickly organize the apps on your iPad.

Here's how to use the iTunes application to find the popular Netflix app, which is great for watching kids' movies and TV programming.

1. Start iTunes on your PC or Mac; then click the iTunes Store link. The iTunes Store window will appear.

2. Click the App Store tab. The App Store window will appear.

3. Click the iPad button to shift the App Store to iPad apps (see Figure 4.10).

Figure 4.10

The iPad section of the App Store in iTunes.

4. Click in the Search Store field, type Netflix, and press Enter. The results will be displayed, as shown in Figure 4.11.

Figure 4.11

Tracking down Netflix.

5. Click the Netflix app. The Netflix app page will open (see Figure 4.12).

Figure 4.12

The Netflix app page.

6. To read more about the app, click the More link below the Description paragraph.

7. To find out how other users liked the app, read the Customer Ratings section.

8. When satisfied you want to download this app, click the Free App button. A login dialog box will appear (see Figure 4.13).

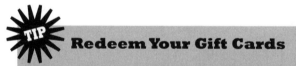

9. Enter your ID and Password information for the iTunes Store and click Get. The app will be downloaded.

10. The next time you sync with the iPad, the new app will be loaded onto the iPad.

TIP Redeem Your Gift Cards

If you have an iTunes Gift Card or Gift Certificate, click the Redeem link on the home page of the iTunes Store; then provide your gift card information. If you purchase an app, you will be given the choice to use the redeemed gift card amount or the payment method associated with your iTunes account.

Using the App Store App

Finding and installing an app from the iPad is just as easy as using the iTunes application. Let's track down the Discover app, which is a creative way to view Wikipedia articles in magazine format.

1. Tap the App Store icon to start the App Store (see Figure 4.14).

2. Tap the Search bar, type Discover, and tap Search. The results will be displayed, as shown in Figure 4.15.

Figure 4.15

Tracking down Discover.

3. Tap the Discover app. The Discover app page will open (see Figure 4.16).

Figure 4.16

The Discover app page.

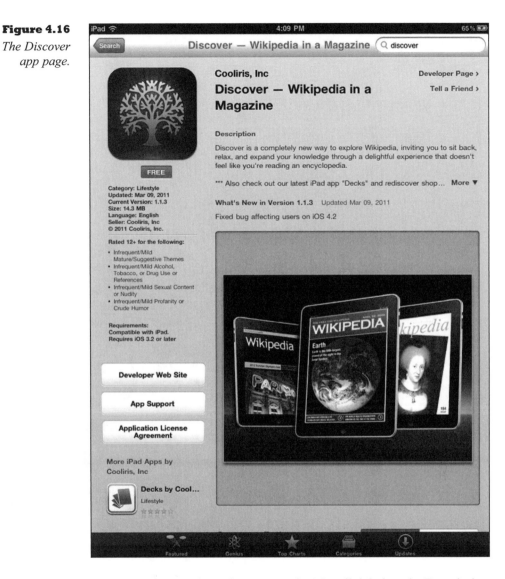

4. To read more about the app, tap the More link below the Description paragraph.

5. To find out how other users liked the app, read the Customer Ratings section.

6. When satisfied you want to download this app, tap the Free button below the large app icon. The button will change to a green Install App button.

7. Tap the Install App button. A login dialog box will appear.

8. Enter your iTunes Password information for the iTunes Store and tap OK. The app will be downloaded (see Figure 4.17).

Figure 4.17

*An app being
installed.*

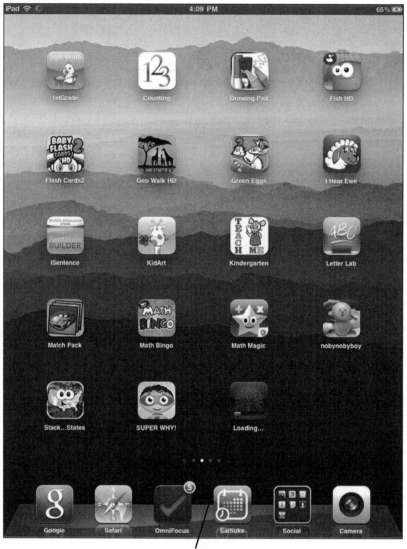

Installing App

Updating Apps

As improvements and fixes are made to the applications installed on
your iPad, the App Store will keep track of any new versions for your
installed software, and when they arrive, the App Store app will notify
you with a little red number on the App Store icon (see Figure 4.18).

Figure 4.18

The number indicates the number of apps to be updated.

Numeric Indicator

1. When such an indicator is visible, tap the App Store icon. The App Store will open.

2. Tap the Updates icon on the tab bar. The Updates page will open.

3. Tap the Update All button. The App Store will close, and any apps in the Updates list will be downloaded and installed.

Configuring Apps

Applications in the iPad vary in how they can be configured. Some apps have just a few configuration settings, if any, so the tools to configure them will be found in the App itself.

But some iPad apps will send their configuration settings into the iPad Settings app. If you can't find configuration settings in your app, check the Settings app. For this example, let's configure the Discover app.

1. Tap the Settings app icon. The Settings app will open.
2. Tap the Discover setting. The Discover setting pane will open (see Figure 4.19).

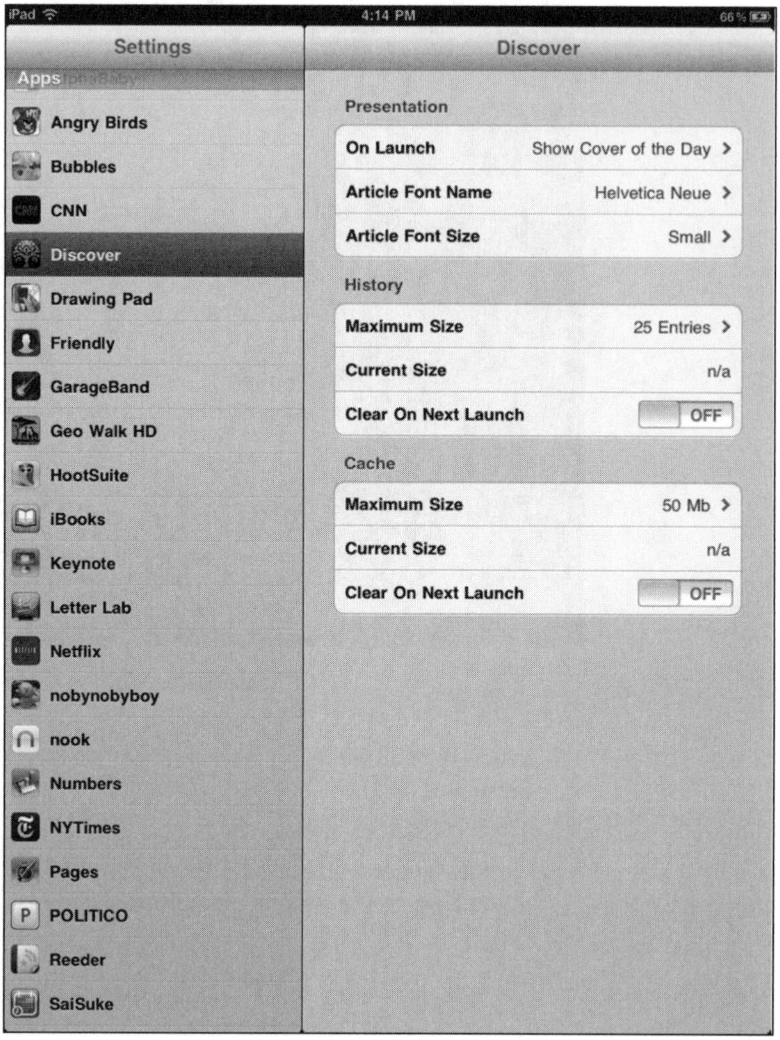

Figure 4.19

An example of an app's configuration settings.

3. Tap Article Font Name. The Article Font Name pane will open.

4. Tap the font you would like Discover to use. The font will be selected.

5. Tap the Discover back arrow to return to the Discover setting pane.

6. When your configuration is complete, click the Home button. The settings will be made in Discover.

Removing Apps

If you find you're not using an app, you can easily opt to remove it from your iPad. In this example, let's remove the Netflix app because you're too busy working to use this cool service.

1. Long-press the app you would like to remove. The apps will begin to shake, and removable apps will be indicated by a black X indicator.

2. Tap the Netflix app. A confirmation dialog box will appear (see Figure 4.20).

Figure 4.20

Confirm you want to delete an app.

3. Tap Delete. A rating dialog box will appear.

4. Tap the stars to set the rating (see Figure 4.21) and then tap Rate. The dialog box will close, and the app will be removed from your iPad.

5. Click the Home button. The app icons will stabilize.

Figure 4.21

Give your outgoing app a fair rating, which will show up in the iTunes Store.

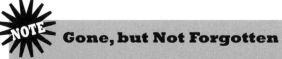

Gone, but Not Forgotten

When an app is removed from the iPad, it will still be maintained in the iTunes Library on your computer. To completely remove the app, click the Apps link in iTunes, select the app, and press Delete. You will be asked to confirm the action, and whether or not you want to keep the app's files or move them to the Recycle Bin. Select the option you want, and the app will be completely removed from your Library.

Conclusion

In this chapter, you've learned how to acquire, manage, and configure new apps for the iPad. In Chapter 5, "Work the Web: Safari," you'll explore the Internet with the iPad's powerful Safari browser.

Chapter 5
Work the Web:
Safari

There's a lot of jargon coming up. But follow along and soon you will know more about the Internet than you ever thought you could—or wanted to.

Browsers have actually been around for a long time, but were never really called browsers. Instead, they were called *text readers* or *read-only applications*, because what these programs did was open simple files of text and let someone read them—like a book. These programs were on computers called *dumb terminals*.

It seems odd to call a computer *dumb*, but compared to the computers used today, these computers weren't very smart. All they did was display information from big, monster servers called *mainframes* that were the size of an average living room. These servers weren't all that smart either, but they were good enough to take a lot of information and help people make sense of it.

The problem was that all these dumb terminals could only talk to the servers they were connected to. There was an Internet back then, but there was no World Wide Web. Internet traffic was mainly limited to message and file transfers, using arcane tools such as Usenet, Archie, or Gopher. If you know what those are, and don't work with computers full time, go audition for *Jeopardy*. Now.

The Secret Origins of the Web

In 1990, a scientist in Switzerland, Sir Tim Berners-Lee, got a brilliant idea. What if you could read files on any computer connected to the Internet anytime you wanted? You could put those files on a special server with just one job: showing those files to anyone who asked for them. Sir Berners-Lee, who was knighted for his work at the CERN institute, knew this idea would only work if all of these files were made readable by any computer.

So Sir Berners-Lee suggested that people use HyperText Markup Language (HTML) files. Because they are essentially plain old text files, HTML files could be read by any computer, would let people create any content they wanted, and would have hyperlinks—something that would revolutionize the way people absorbed material, since hyperlinks would let you jump around from file to file without having to remember file names.

Here Come the Browsers

Browsers were built to read all of these new HTML files. As with the dumb terminals, Sir Berners-Lee just wanted people to read information quickly in files—not change their content. So he and his colleagues figured out a way to make a program that did nothing but read and display HTML files. Other people got involved and made the application read more complicated HTML code.

People began calling the information on the Web page and calling the process of reading those pages *browsing*—and that's where the *browser* name comes from. Later, when the general public started using the Web and skipping from file to file quickly, the verb *browsing* got morphed into *surfing*. The name *browser* stuck, though, because it still describes more accurately what this type of application does. You can call any program like this a browser, of course. A program that does nothing but show pictures could be a picture browser. But these days the name is more synonymous with Web browsers, such as the iPad's Safari.

As the Web grew more popular, organizations and schools were quick to see the value of the Web—first, as a way to communicate more robustly with customers; then as a platform to get work done. Web browsers became useful not just for looking at the Web, but also as tools to learn and teach across every part of the world.

In this chapter, you will find out how to

* Navigate Web sites.
* Manage bookmarks and history.
* Use multipage browsing.
* Search for content.
* Customize your browser experience.

Navigating Web Sites

Browsing is more than just tapping through a collection of hyperlinked files. What really makes the whole thing work is the Uniform Resource Locater (URL). URLs are pseudo-English labels that make it possible to find and retrieve resources across the Internet in a consistent, predictable, well-defined manner. Every Web server has an IP address, but that's just a big collection of numbers. URLs make it easy for regular folks to type an address into the Address bar of Safari and bring up a page.

Of course, when you look at URLs such as *www.llanfairpwllgwyngyll gogerychwyrndrobwllllantysiliogogogoch.co.uk/,* using the IP address might actually be a blessing, but for the most part, URLs are easier.

NOTE: I Can't Make This Stuff Up

Llanfairpwllgwyngyllgogerychwyrndrobwllllantysiliogogogoch is a village on the Isle of Anglesey in North Wales that currently holds the Guinness record for the longest English place name. The village's Web site holds the record for the longest valid URL. Try to get your kids to pronounce *that* one. I'll let you know when I can.

Ready, Set, Browse

You can begin browsing with Safari as soon as you start the app. If the iPad is not connected to the Internet yet, Safari will prompt you to make that connection.

1. Tap the Safari icon. Safari will start (as shown in Figure 5.1).

Figure 5.1

The Safari browser.

2. Tap the Address bar and then the clear field icon so the URL in the field is removed and the keyboard appears.

3. Type the URL for the Web site you want to visit in the Address bar.

A Helping URL Hand

You do not have to type the URL identifier http:// before a Web site address. Safari will fill it in for you.

You also don't have to type in the full address every time you visit a Web site, thanks to the AutoFill feature in the Address bar. Just start typing the URL, and Safari will display a list of similar URLs for you to choose from.

4. Tap Go to visit the new page.
5. Long-press a highlighted or underlined hyperlink. An action menu will appear, giving you the options to open the link, open the link in a new page, or copy the link (see Figure 5.2).
6. Tap Open to go to the new page.

Figure 5.2

A hyperlink action menu.

Navigating the Web

After you have been browsing for a while, you may need to go back to a Web page you visited earlier in your current browser session. Two controls, the Back and Forward icons, will enable you to navigate through the pages you have visited.

Note, however, that navigation through Web pages is not tracked for *every* Web page you visit during a session. Safari uses a sequential navigation method that tracks only the pages along a particular path. For instance, assume you were browsing Page A, then Pages B, C, and D. On Page D, you found a hyperlink back to Page B and clicked it to visit that page. Now, from Page B again, assume you went off and visited Pages E and F. If you were to use the Back icon in this session, the order of pages that would appear for each click of the Back icon would be F to E to B to A. Pages C and D, because they were on another "track" of browsing, would no longer be a part of the browser's navigation, even if you were to cycle forward through the same pages again using the Forward icon.

One of the nicer features of the iPad is its capability to call up Safari whenever any hyperlink or Web page shortcut is tapped—in any app. That capability is particularly handy when using the Mail app, where you often receive URLs from colleagues.

Another useful feature in Safari is its capability to zoom in on any Web page. There are two ways to go about this while browsing.

The first method is the reverse pinch, or fanning, technique. To zoom in, simply tap the section of the page you want to enlarge and move your fingers apart. The page will zoom in as long as you move your fingers out. Reverse the move to a pinch and zoom back out.

The second method is double-tapping on a particular section of the page. Safari will automatically zoom in to have that section of the page fill the screen. This is particularly useful when visiting a page with a section of useful content surrounded by images and ads. To zoom back to the full-page view, double-tap again.

Managing Bookmarks and History

You and I are creatures of habit, and often we find ourselves clinging to the familiar as we move through our workday. Safari accommodates this trait with its Bookmarks feature. Bookmarks are markers that, when selected in a menu or clicked in the Bookmark toolbar, will take you directly to the Web page you want—without typing the URL address.

You can create a bookmark very easily in Safari. Then, when you need to, you can open up a page with just a couple of taps.

To open a bookmark, tap the Bookmark icon and select the bookmark you want from the action menu (see Figure 5.3). If there is a bookmark within the Bookmark bar, all you need to do is tap it.

Figure 5.3

The Bookmarks action menu.

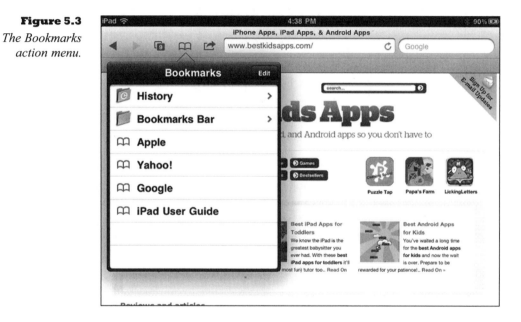

When you find a page you want to save, you can bookmark it and add it to your bookmark collection.

1. From a page you want to save, tap the Share icon. The Share action menu will open (see Figure 5.4).

Figure 5.4

The Share action menu.

2. Tap Add Bookmark. The Add Bookmark pop-over will appear (see Figure 5.5).

Figure 5.5

The Add Bookmark pop-over.

3. Confirm or edit the name of the bookmark you want to use.

4. Tap the Bookmarks control if you want the bookmark to appear somewhere other than the main Bookmark menu and then tap a new location.

5. Tap Save. The bookmark will be added to the desired location (see Figure 5.6).

New Bookmark

Figure 5.6

The new bookmark in the Bookmark bar.

Organizing Bookmarks

As time goes on, you may find your collection of bookmarks has grown quite a bit. Safari includes a way to organize bookmarks in a way that makes the best sense for you.

1. From any page, tap the Bookmark icon. The Bookmark action menu will open.

2. Tap the Edit button. The action menu will shift to Edit mode.

3. Tap and drag the Move icon on any item to move it up or down the list of bookmarks. The Move icon is denoted by three horizontal lines.

4. Tap the New Folder button. The New Folder pop-over will appear.

5. Type a Title for the new folder and tap Bookmarks. The new folder will appear in the Bookmarks action menu.

6. Tap a bookmark's Delete icon; then tap the Delete button. The bookmark will be removed.

7. Tap Done. The menu will reflect the changes you made.

Bookmarks on the Home Screen

You can also put bookmarks on any of the Home screens. When they appear on a Home screen, bookmarks are referred to as *Web Clips*.

1. From a page you want to save, tap the Share icon. The Share action menu will open.

2. Tap Add to Home Screen. The Add to Home popover will appear (see Figure 5.7).

3. Edit the name of the Web Clip icon and tap Add. The Web Clip icon will be added to a Home screen.

Figure 5.7

The Add to Home popover.

If you've been browsing around a while, and just can't seem to remember that site you visited a couple of days ago (and naturally forgot to bookmark), you can use Safari's History feature to track that site down.

1. From any page, tap the Bookmark icon. The Bookmark action menu will open.

2. Tap the History folder. The History action menu will open (see Figure 5.8).

3. Tap the page you want to revisit. The page will open in Safari.

Figure 5.8

The History action menu.

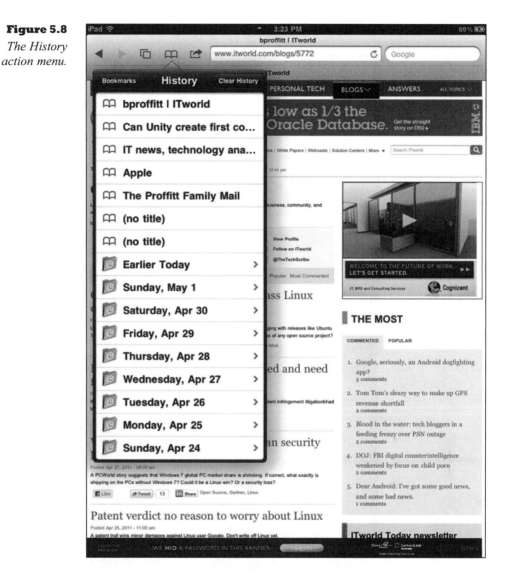

If you want to clear the history in Safari, the fastest way to accomplish this is through the History action menu.

1. From any page, tap the Bookmark icon. The Bookmark action menu will open.

2. Tap the History folder. The History action menu will open.

3. Tap the Clear History button. The Safari history will be erased.

Browsing Many Pages at Once

Many PC and Mac-based browsers have a feature known as *tabbed browsing*, which enables the user to access multiple pages at once.

Safari on the iPad doesn't feature tabs *per se*, but it does include a multiple page tool that will let you handle up to nine pages at the same time.

1. From any page, tap the Multiple Page icon. The multipage view will open, as shown in Figure 5.9.

Figure 5.9

The multipage view.

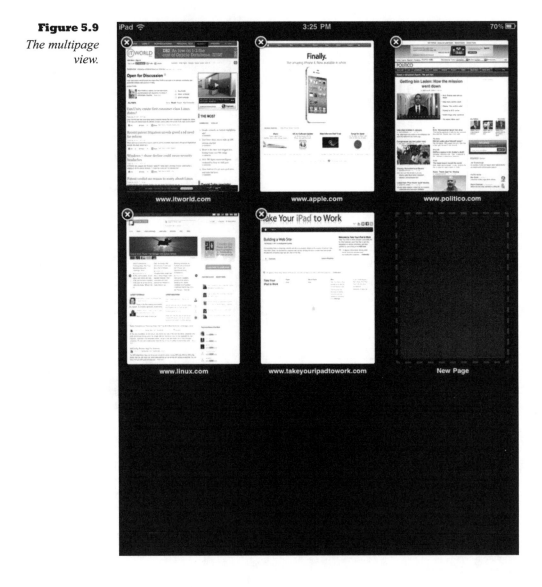

2. Tap any page. The page will open in full view within Safari.

3. Tap the Multiple Page icon again. The multipage view will open.

4. Tap the New Page rectangle. Safari will open without a page loaded (see Figure 5.10).

Figure 5.10

Safari ready to open a new page.

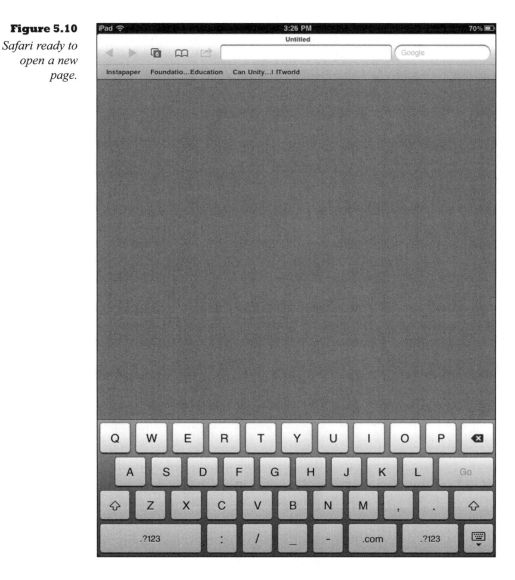

5. Type a URL in the Address bar or tap a bookmark. The page will open.

If you tap the Multiple Page icon once more, you will see the page displayed as one of the minipages. To remove a page, tap the black X icon to remove the page.

Searching for Content

Finding things on the Web used to be very easy; with only 500 or so Web sites in existence in the early '90s, you could almost index them by hand. It's true, I remember those days.

Today, there are billions of Web pages and finding useful things can be daunting sometimes, even with a good search tool. Safari has a Search bar that uses the most powerful search tool around, and also enables you to choose the search engines you prefer.

Using the Search bar is easy: just type in what you are looking for and press Enter. By default, the Search bar connects to the Google search engine, and it will display the results of your search in a new tab.

TIP   Suggestive Searches

Safari will suggest search terms similar to what you type, in an effort to save you time. If you see the term you were looking for in the menu, tap it to start the actual search.

To change search engines, you need to use the Settings app.

1. Tap the Settings app icon. The Settings app will open.
2. Tap the Safari setting. The Safari settings pane will open (see Figure 5.11).
3. Tap the Search Engine setting. The Search Engine pane will open.
4. Tap one of the three available options. The selected search engine will be indicated by a check mark.
5. Click the Home button. The new search engine will be used in Safari.

Figure 5.11

*The Safari
settings.*

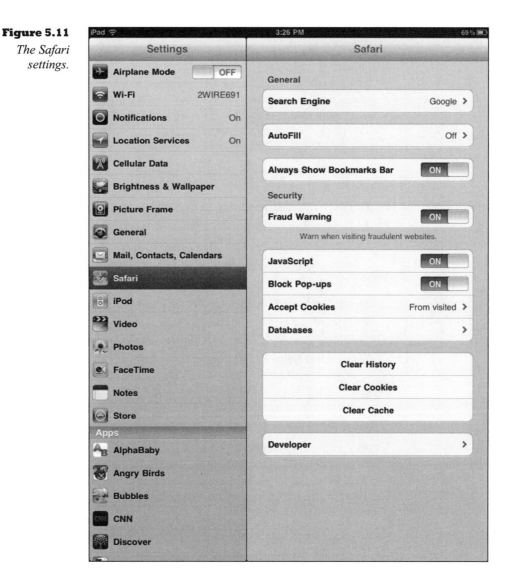

Customizing Your Browser

Whenever you travel extensively on the Internet, you're bound to run across a few common bumps in the road that could slow you down. Fortunately, Safari has some settings that will smooth out the ride.

One such feature is the AutoFill tool. AutoFill's job is to help you fill in those registration or payment information forms you might run into while surfing the Web. AutoFill uses your own Contact information to provide information for those forms when you come across them.

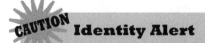 **Identity Alert**

Using AutoFill is handy, but be aware that if your iPad falls into someone else's hands, Safari could fill in your personal information, including passwords for sensitive data. It's something to keep in mind when
deciding whether to use AutoFill.

To activate AutoFill, follow these steps:

1. Tap the Settings app icon. The Settings app will open.
2. Tap the Safari setting. The Safari settings pane will open.
3. Tap the AutoFill option. The AutoFill screen will appear.
4. Slide the Use Contact Info control to On. The My Info control will activate.
5. Tap the My Info control. A menu of your contacts will appear.
6. Tap the contact that represents you. That contact will appear in the My Info control.
7. Slide the Names and Passwords controls to On. This will keep track of any login names and passwords as you enter them.
8. Click the Home button. The changes will be saved.

Stop Playing Whack-a-Mole

Pop-up windows can be the bane of your Web experience or a vital tool.
Disreputable sites can use them as forced advertising, but legitimate sites
also have a use for them. Depending on your Web habits, you may or
may not want pop-ups blocked, which is Safari's default setting. Here's
how to turn blocking off:

1. Tap the Settings app icon. The Settings app will open.
2. Tap the Safari setting. The Safari settings pane will open.
3. Slide the Block Pop-ups control to Off.
4. Click the Home button. The change will be saved.

Come to the Dark Side, We Have Cookies

Cookies are another piece of Web technology that can help or hinder
your Web experience. Cookies are little bits of tracking code that Web
sites will "hand" you when you visit. They can enhance your surfing,
because when you return to the site, it will "remember" you and your
preferences because of the cookie your browser has received from the
earlier visit.

The problem is that cookies can represent a security threat because any site can use a cookie to track where you have been on the Web even after you leave the site. Cookies can also be used as delivery mechanisms for some pretty nasty malware. Safari will give you the options not to accept cookies, pick them up just from sites you've visited, or pick them up from any site at all.

Of all of these options, the visited site option is probably the best compromise, but it's a matter of personal preference. To change the cookie setting:

1. Tap the Settings app icon. The Settings app will open.
2. Tap the Safari setting. The Safari settings pane will open.
3. Tap the Accept Cookies control. The Accept Cookies pane will open.
4. Tap the option you prefer. The selected option will be denoted by a check mark.
5. Click the Home button. The change will be saved.

Conclusion

In this chapter, you learned some of the finer points of operating the Safari browser, a flexible and fast window to the Internet.

In Chapter 6, "iBooks for Reading," you'll find out how the iPad performs as an electronic book reader, which will let you and your child read whole libraries of books and magazines wherever you go.

Chapter 6

iBooks
for Reading

It's a bit embarrassing for a writer to admit, but my kids didn't used to like to read. Their mother and I tried everything: rewards, cajoling, positive reinforcement—the works. Nothing really seemed to click. They could read; they just didn't want to.

But then our oldest discovered some books about wizards. And later our middle daughter found some other books about vampires and wolves. I know, wholesome fare this was not. But it got them hooked, and it made them see there was a whole world of imagination inside those pages, not just boring words.

We're still waiting for the lightbulb to come on for our youngest, who is learning English as her second language. But we know it will come. We may hope it will be something great, like stories about a little pioneer girl on a lonely prairie. But it could just as well be books about a kid who runs around in his underwear as a super-hero.

Great literature is just that: great. But before a love of literature, kids need to learn to love the process of reading, and the joy of discovering something new inside those pages. It helps when they see their parents reading, too, because reading can be a shared experience.

The iPad's form factor makes it an ideal device for reading electronic books—something we all figured out as soon as the iPad was announced. And these books can be for your child or you, because there's no official end to when you can learn something new.

Although access to buying books is limited to WiFi or a paid 3G plan, it's still very easy to get a copy of the latest bestselling kid's book, educational reference, or a nice novel for the parents on the iPad in seconds.

In this chapter, you will learn how to use the iBooks app to

* Find electronic books in the iBooks Store.
* Purchase books for the iPad.
* Read your purchased books.

Finding Your Reading Material

Finding good books for kids is often a challenge for parents. The best place to go isn't online at all: it's your local library. It may seem a little odd to mention a place that doesn't offer eBooks (yet), but your public library is an incredible source of information on the best books, because they aren't trying to push one book's sales over another. A good local bookstore is another wonderful resource, too, but sadly those are hard to find.

Your child's teacher can also help, because she may see the one book your kid always grabs in the book corner or school library.

Once you find a book, there are some great apps on the iPad to deliver the book to you in just a few seconds.

iBooks is the free app from Apple that, while not included with the iPad, is strongly suggested as your first downloaded app when you first connect to the iTunes Store with the iPad. If you didn't download it then, you should go ahead and download it to start your iPad reading experience.

1. Tap the iBooks icon to start the iBooks app. The first time it starts, you will be asked to sync your reading progress and bookmarks (see Figure 6.1).

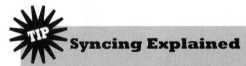 **Syncing Explained**

As you read your books, iBooks will keep track of your progress, as well as any bookmarks you might have inserted in your books. If you plan to read your book on another iBooks-equipped device, such as an iPhone, synchronization will enable the other device to pick up right where you left off on the iPad and copy your bookmarks. If you don't have other iBooks devices, tap Don't Sync.

Figure 6.1

Syncing iBooks.

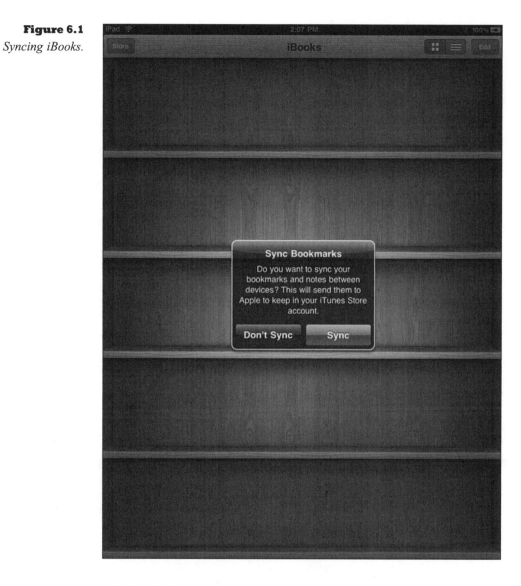

2. Tap the Sync option you want. The primary iBooks screen (an empty bookshelf) will appear.

3. Tap the Store button. The Store screen will appear (see Figure 6.2).

Figure 6.2

The iBooks Store.

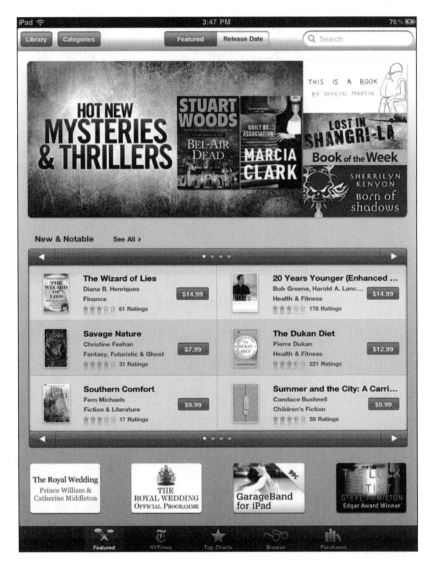

4. Tap the Search button bar and type the title or author name you're looking for. Suggested options will be displayed in the Suggestions menu as you type.

5. Tap the book or author name that matches your search. The results will be displayed on the Search screen, as shown in Figure 6.3.

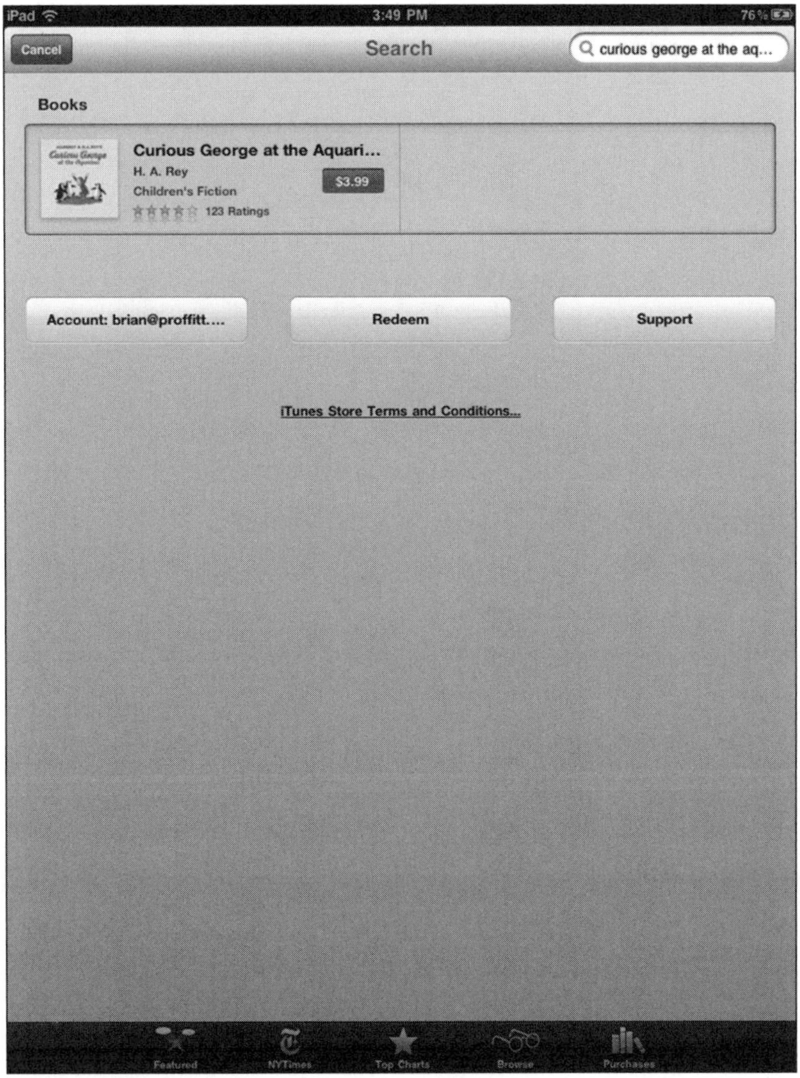

Figure 6.3

Finding the book you want.

6. Tap the book you want to view. The book's pop-over window will open (see Figure 6.4).

Figure 6.4

The book's window.

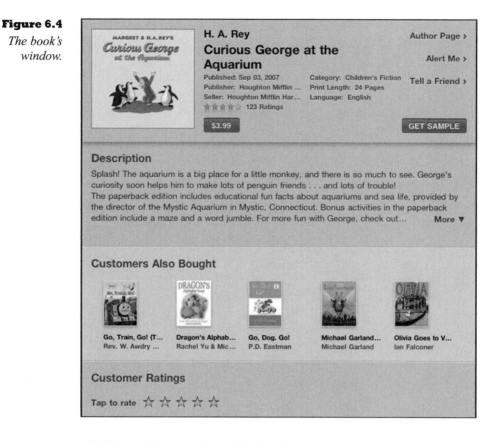

Description

Splash! The aquarium is a big place for a little monkey, and there is so much to see. George's curiosity soon helps him to make lots of penguin friends . . . and lots of trouble!
The paperback edition includes educational fun facts about aquariums and sea life, provided by the director of the Mystic Aquarium in Mystic, Connecticut. Bonus activities in the paperback edition include a maze and a word jumble. For more fun with George, check out...   **More ▼**

Customers Also Bought

Go, Train, Go! (T...   Dragon's Alphab...   Go, Dog. Go!   Michael Garland...   Olivia Goes to V...
Rev. W. Awdry ...   Rachel Yu & Mic...   P.D. Eastman   Michael Garland   Ian Falconer

Customer Ratings

Tap to rate ☆ ☆ ☆ ☆ ☆

7. To read more about the book, tap the More link below the Description paragraph.

8. To find out how other users liked the book, read the Customer Ratings section.

9. When satisfied you want to buy this book, tap the price button at the top of the window. The button will change to a green Buy Book button.

10. Tap the Buy Book button. A login dialog box will appear.

11. Enter your iTunes Password information for the iTunes Store and tap OK. The book will be downloaded, with the progress shown on the main iBooks screen (see Figure 6.5).

Figure 6.5

*Downloading a
book.*

Redeem Your Gift Cards

If you have an iTunes Gift Card or Gift Certificate, tap the Redeem button on the bottom of most pages in the iBooks Store and then provide your gift card information. If you purchase music or videos, you will be given the choice to use the redeemed gift card amount or the payment method associated with your iTunes account, which is used by iBooks.

Reading in iBooks

After you have a book downloaded, reading it is simply a matter of tapping the book on the iBooks shelf to open it (see Figure 6.6).

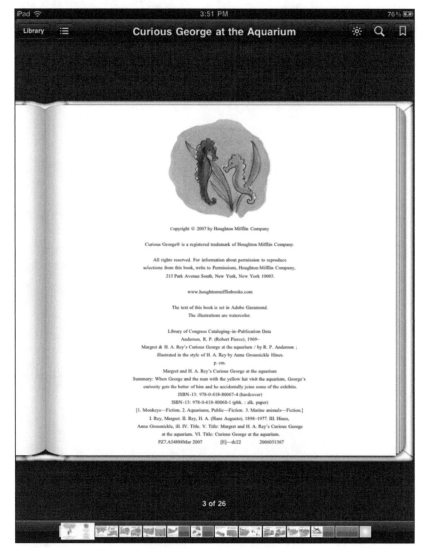

To turn the page of a book forward, flick your finger to the left (as if you were flipping a paper page). You can also tap the right edge of the page.

To flip back a page, flick your finger to the right or tap the left edge of the page.

Navigating beyond one page at a time can be done a couple of ways. Tap anywhere on the page to bring up the page controls seen in Figure 6.6. Then tap the Table of Contents button to view the Table of Contents page.

To move to another location in the book, tap any of the chapter or section headers that are visible. The book will be opened to that spot.

If you have any bookmarks inserted in the book, you can use the Bookmarks page to navigate to that bookmark. Tap the Table of Contents button and in the Table of Contents page, tap the Bookmarks button. Any bookmarks in the book will be listed, as shown in Figure 6.7. Tap the bookmark to view that page.

Figure 6.7

The Bookmarks page.

You can also use the page turner control found on the bottom of every page when you tap the page. Tap and drag the rectangular control to move to the page number you want. When you lift your finger, the desired page will open.

You can use the Brightness and Text controls to adjust the text size and display properties of the iBooks app.

If this seems simple, that's because it was designed to be that way. iBooks is meant to be simple, so you can do the thing you really need to do—read.

Conclusion

When you first opened your iPad box from the Apple Store, you were probably delighted with the ease-of-use and power contained in this handheld tablet device. The possibilities seemed endless, and reading books is just one fundamental example.

The iPad can also be a great source of multimedia content to make learning so much easier and more fun. In Chapter 7, "Multimedia Learning," we'll take a look at one of the most central iPad apps, iTunes, and find out how to listen to music and watch movies that can increase the opportunities for your child's learning experiences.

Chapter 7

Multimedia
Learning

In Chapter 1, "First Step: Introducing the iPad," you learned about the origins of the iPad and its relationship with earlier Apple devices, such as the iPod, iPhone, and iPod Touch.

In some circles, the iPad is mocked as a giant iPod Touch, and in some ways that description has some truth to it. The interfaces are similar, and there's quite a bit of shared functionality. If that's the case, then like the iPod Touch, the iPad should be able to display multimedia files with relative ease.

And that is right up the iPad's alley. Since the screen is much larger than its iPod and iPhone cousins, the iPad does a superior job of showing the latest movies and television shows with the Videos app. There is also the YouTube app, which taps into the vast community of video content on the YouTube Web site. It is also a great music player, thanks to the iPod app.

From an educational perspective, you might not think such apps are worth much, beyond welcome diversions from a busy day. Okay, there's some truth to that, since diversions with the iPad might not be what you're looking for. But it's not all fun and games; being able to listen to audio books on learning topics or watch informative videos on YouTube or Videos apps is a great way to teach your child new stuff.

In this chapter, you will learn how to

* Purchase multimedia content in the iTunes Store.
* Acquire an audio podcast.
* Play back multimedia content on the iPad.
* Find and view YouTube content.

Getting Multimedia: iTunes

As you learned in Chapter 4, "Fourth Step: Using the iPad Apps," the content of iTunes on your desktop machine is identical to its iPad counterpart in terms of apps. This is also the case with music and movies in the iTunes Store.

Finding and installing multimedia content with the iPad are just as easy as using the iTunes application. To get an idea of how you can purchase content for the iPad, here's how to find and purchase a music album with the iTunes app.

1. Tap the iTunes icon to start the iTunes app (see Figure 7.1).

Figure 7.1

The iTunes app.

2. Tap the Music button on the iTunes toolbar if it's not on the Music page already.

3. Tap the Search bar and type in the artist or album name you're looking for. Suggested options will be displayed in the Suggestions menu as you type.

4. Tap the artist or album name that matches your search. The results will be displayed on the Search screen, as shown in Figure 7.2.

Figure 7.2

Tracking down music.

5. Tap the album or song you want to view. The album's popover window will open (see Figure 7.3).

Figure 7.3
The album's window.

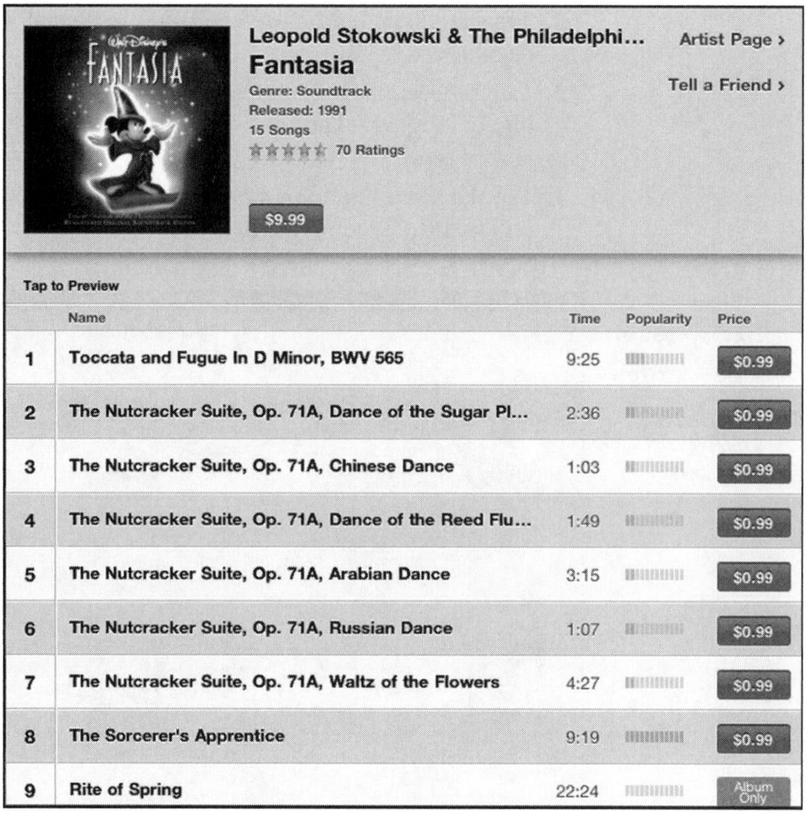
Leopold Stokowski & The Philadelphi...
Artist Page ›
Fantasia
Tell a Friend ›
Genre: Soundtrack
Released: 1991
15 Songs
70 Ratings
$9.99
Tap to Preview
Name
Time
Popularity
Price
1
Toccata and Fugue In D Minor, BWV 565
9:25
$0.99
2
The Nutcracker Suite, Op. 71A, Dance of the Sugar Pl...
2:36
$0.99
3
The Nutcracker Suite, Op. 71A, Chinese Dance
1:03
$0.99
4
The Nutcracker Suite, Op. 71A, Dance of the Reed Flu...
1:49
$0.99
5
The Nutcracker Suite, Op. 71A, Arabian Dance
3:15
$0.99
6
The Nutcracker Suite, Op. 71A, Russian Dance
1:07
$0.99
7
The Nutcracker Suite, Op. 71A, Waltz of the Flowers
4:27
$0.99
8
The Sorcerer's Apprentice
9:19
$0.99
9
Rite of Spring
22:24
Album Only

6. To read more about the album, tap the More link below the iTunes Notes paragraph.
7. To find out how other users liked the music, read the Customer Reviews section.
8. When satisfied you want to buy this album, tap the price button at the top of the window. The button will change to a green Buy Album button.
9. Tap the Buy Album button. A login dialog box will appear.
10. Enter your iTunes Password information for the iTunes Store and tap OK. The album will be downloaded, as shown on the Downloads page (see Figure 7.4).

Figure 7.4

*Downloading
music.*

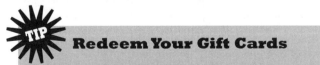

Redeem Your Gift Cards

If you have an iTunes Gift Card or Gift Certificate, tap the Redeem button on the bottom of most pages in the iBooks Store and then provide your gift card information. If you purchase music or videos, you will be given the choice to use the redeemed gift card amount or the payment method associated with your iTunes account, which is used by iBooks.

The procedure for buying video content, be it movies or TV shows, is identical to acquiring music. With music, you can buy whole albums or individual songs (though getting the whole album is typically less expensive per song). If you buy TV shows, you can get one episode at a time or entire seasons' worth of content.

Getting audio books also uses a similar process, although usually you can only buy the entire book. Many audio books have a Preview feature that allows you to hear some of the content before you purchase it.

iTunes also enables you to download audio or video podcasts, which are free programs, usually episodic, that cover a huge variety of topics: parenting, technology, news, music—if you can think of a topic, someone's likely to have done an episode or an entire series of podcasts about it. To get podcasts for your iPad, follow these steps:

1. Tap the Podcasts button on the iTunes toolbar. The Podcasts page will open (see Figure 7.5).

Figure 7.5

Tracking down a podcast.

2. Tap the Search bar and type in the topic or program name you're looking for. Suggested options will be displayed in the Suggestions menu as you type.

3. Tap the podcast that matches your search. The results will be displayed on the Search screen.

4. Tap the podcast you want to view. The podcast's popover window will open (see Figure 7.6).

Figure 7.6

The podcast window.

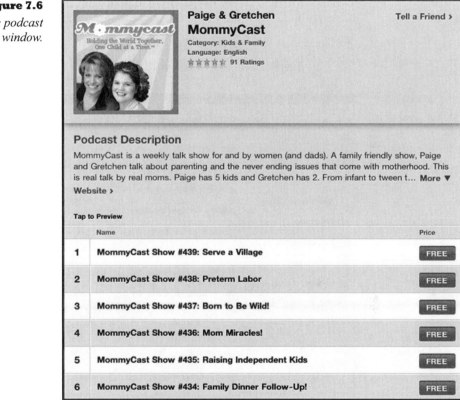

Paige & Gretchen
MommyCast
Category: Kids & Family
Language: English
★★★★☆ 91 Ratings

Tell a Friend >

Podcast Description

MommyCast is a weekly talk show for and by women (and dads). A family friendly show, Paige and Gretchen talk about parenting and the never ending issues that come with motherhood. This is real talk by real moms. Paige has 5 kids and Gretchen has 2. From infant to tween t... **More ▼**
Website >

Tap to Preview

	Name	Price
1	MommyCast Show #439: Serve a Village	FREE
2	MommyCast Show #438: Preterm Labor	FREE
3	MommyCast Show #437: Born to Be Wild!	FREE
4	MommyCast Show #436: Mom Miracles!	FREE
5	MommyCast Show #435: Raising Independent Kids	FREE
6	MommyCast Show #434: Family Dinner Follow-Up!	FREE

5. To read more about the podcast, tap the More link below the podcast's Description paragraph.

6. To find out how other users liked the podcast, read the Customer Reviews section.

7. When satisfied you want to listen to one of the podcast's episodes, tap the episode's Free button. The button will change to a green Get Episode button.

8. Tap the Get Episode button. A login dialog box will appear.

9. Enter your iTunes Password information for the iTunes Store and tap OK. The podcast will be downloaded.

Multimedia Playback: iPod and Videos

One major difference between the iPad version of iTunes and the desktop version is that the desktop version allows you to play back videos and music right from within the iTunes application.

On the iPad, this functionality is not within the iTunes app but instead is handled by other specialized apps. Any audio files (music, audio podcasts, and audio books) can be listened to via the iPod app, and video content (movies, TV shows, and video podcasts) can be viewed by the Videos app.

To listen to audio content in the iPod app:

1. Tap the iPod app icon. iPod will open, as seen in Figure 7.7.

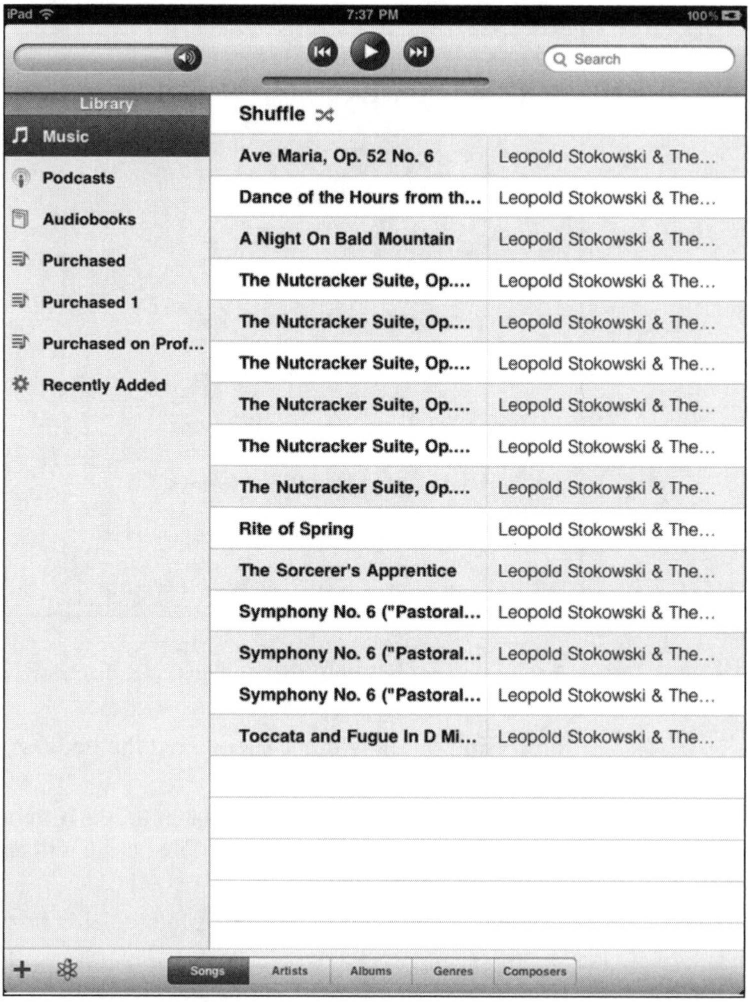

Figure 7.7

The iPod app.

2. To view the music content by album, tap the Albums button. The Albums page will appear, as seen in Figure 7.8.

3. Tap the album to play. The album's popover window will appear.

4. Tap any song in the album. The album will begin to play from that point.

5. To stop or otherwise control the playback, tap the album cover. The playback controls will appear, enabling you to fast forward, reverse, control volume, and so on.

6. To return to the iPod screen, tap the Back arrow in the lower-left corner of the screen.

Listening to an audio book or podcast is similar, although these categories are not as organized as the Music section of the iPod Library, since typically you will have a lot more songs to organize than podcasts and audio books. Simply find the book or podcast to listen to and tap it to start playback.

Watching videos is a very similar experience.

1. Tap the Videos app icon. Videos will open, as seen in Figure 7.9.

Figure 7.9

The Videos app.

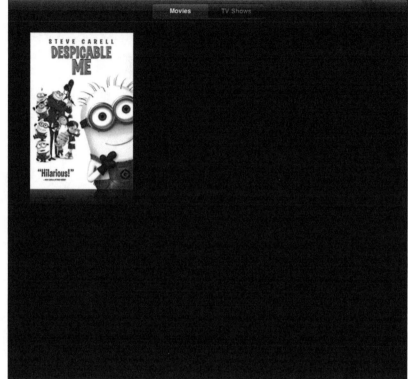

2. To view a movie, tap the Movies button. The Movies page will appear.

3. Tap the video to play. The video's playback information screen will appear (see Figure 7.10).

4. Tap the Play control. The video will begin to play.

5. To stop or otherwise control the playback, tap the video. The playback controls will appear, enabling you to fast forward, reverse, control volume, and so on.

6. To return to the playback information screen, tap the Done button.

7. To return to the main Videos screen, tap the Podcasts button.

Figure 7.10

The video's playback information screen.

Internet Video: YouTube

When YouTube first started, it was a site where people with perhaps too much time on their hands would upload home videos to share with friends and family. Some of these videos were interesting to more than the intended audience, and quite soon a community started developing to produce videos of higher quality and substance than creative wedding videos.

Today, YouTube is an Internet powerhouse, and nearly everyone realizes its potential as a platform for sharing knowledge. For the cost of making a decent video, parents and children can share marketing content with friends and family on public or private YouTube channels. There's no need to worry about distributing these videos because the distribution platform is already there.

To view YouTube videos on the iPad, you need to use the YouTube app because they won't appear within the Safari browser. If you click on a YouTube link in a Web page, however, the YouTube app will immediately open and begin playback, so the functionality is, while slower, still seamless.

Internet Required

YouTube videos require an active Internet connection to work, so plan your viewing time accordingly.

If you want to look for and view videos from within the YouTube app, follow these easy steps:

1. Tap the YouTube app icon. The YouTube app will open (see Figure 7.11).
2. Tap the Search bar and type in the topic you're looking for.
3. Tap the Search key. The results will be displayed on the Search screen.
4. Tap the video you want to view. The video's information screen will open.
5. Tap the Play control to start the video, or wait a few moments and the video should start automatically.

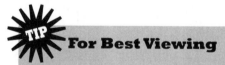

For Best Viewing

For the best viewing of any video content, whether with YouTube or Videos app, turn the iPad to the landscape position.

Figure 7.11

The YouTube app.

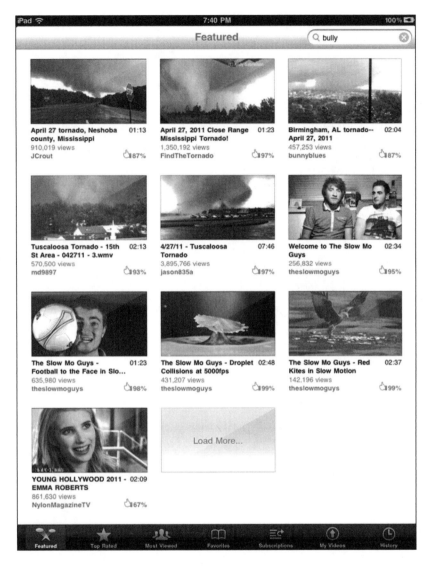

Figure 7.11

The YouTube app.

Conclusion

As video and audio content becomes easier for people to create, having a mobile platform to view or listen to such content is a big advantage. The iPad will connect you to a myriad of useful content, as well as more entertaining content to keep everyone engaged.

In Chapter 8, "Virtual Field Trip: FaceTime," you will learn about a brand-new multimedia feature for iPad 2 users called FaceTime. FaceTime uses the dual cameras on the iPad 2 to enable full videoconferencing capabilities with any other FaceTime user, free of charge, from any Internet-connected location in the world.

Chapter 8
Virtual Field Trip: FaceTime

In the 21st century, we were all supposed to have flying cars. And instant-cook kitchens. And video phone calls. So far, it hasn't been a great century for futurists who based their ideas on episodes of *The Jetsons*.

But the new century hasn't been a complete bust for technology that once seemed too fantastical to believe: videoconferencing has become a not-so-rare fixture for boardrooms and high-end school technology centers. This technology, which uses the ubiquitous Internet to connect dedicated video-conferencing devices to one another, is a definite step toward the future.

And there is a cost, usually a literal one: such devices are costly and typically out of the reach of most schools and certainly out of reach for most parents.

Webcams have been a fair substitute, but they are usually tied down to stationary machines and are not very portable. They are also typically not high-quality devices, with configuration sometimes being a challenge.

One of the more innovative features available for the iPad 2 is Apple's FaceTime app, which finally delivers the promise of affordable, portable, and decent quality videoconferencing for individual users. In this chapter, you will learn how to

* Set up FaceTime.
* Connect to FaceTime users you know.
* Make a FaceTime call.

What Is FaceTime?

FaceTime is not something new to the iPad 2, although the new iPad is the first model that can actually use it, thanks to the new on-board front- and rear-facing cameras. FaceTime was actually created for the iPhone 4 in the summer of 2010, the first device from Apple to feature a dual-camera setup.

It's this double-camera configuration that makes FaceTime work so well. Until recently, most mobile devices, when they had a camera, used a photo/video capture lens that was located on the back of the device—in other words, the side of the device that was on the opposite side of the device's video screen. Think about a two-video call, and you can quickly imagine such a situation becoming very awkward, very quickly.

With the iPhone 4, and now the iPad 2, FaceTime can enable you and your kids to easily engage in video calls with any FaceTime-enabled device in the world.

But in that statement alone, there are hidden limitations. Note that connectivity is limited to other FaceTime-equipped devices. Right now, that includes all iPad 2 devices, any iPhone 4 (and beyond), fourth-generation iPod Touch devices, and any desktop or laptop with Mac OS X 10.6.6 or higher, so we're not exactly talking about a small user base.

Still, as of press time, Windows and Linux users were not able to use FaceTime, and don't look for FaceTime on the Android mobile platform anytime soon, either, given the animosity between Apple and Google over their respective mobile platforms.

This means that as you seek out possible connections for your student, you will need to deliberately search for other students and classrooms that have the correct devices.

Another, perhaps more well-known, limitation is the inability for FaceTime devices to send their signals over any cellular network. This is likely due to the sheer amount of data each video call creates: upwards of 3MB per minute. That number may seem a bit abstract, but think about your own cellular data plan and any financial caps that might exist with it, and you will quickly see why pushing a FaceTime call of any significant length could be a very expensive proposition.

That expense is incurred by the cellular carriers, too. Increasingly, data carriers in North America, Asia, and Europe are learning that unlimited data plans will quickly jam their networks with traffic, and they have taken great pains to limit data traffic to keep their networks clear. This is why, to date, Apple has been unable to negotiate a plan with any cellular carrier.

The result of this behind-the-scenes technical discussion means that anyone who is using FaceTime must connect over a wireless network (or, for Mac users, a wired Ethernet connection will also work). This WiFi-only limitation has gotten quite a bit of knocking in the media, but to be honest, even 3G iPad owners can typically find a wireless network somewhere. Your student, too, is more likely to be at home or school, where such WiFi networks are common.

The good news is, once you find such a network, it is very simple to set up a FaceTime connection. But first, you need to configure FaceTime to be ready to receive and send calls.

Setting Up FaceTime

When you first use your iPad, FaceTime will likely be disabled by default. That's because you must register your contact information with the FaceTime app so callers can reach you. This contact information is in the form of an email address, one of which must be added to FaceTime.

1. Tap the Settings icon on the Home screen. The Settings app will open.
2. Tap the FaceTime setting. The FaceTime sign-in pane will open, as seen in Figure 8.1.

Figure 8.1

The FaceTime sign-in pane.

3. Type the email address or user name for your Apple ID into the user name field.

4. Type your Apple ID password into the password field.

5. Tap the Sign In button. The address confirmation screen will appear (see Figure 8.2).

Figure 8.2

Confirm the address you want to use for FaceTime.

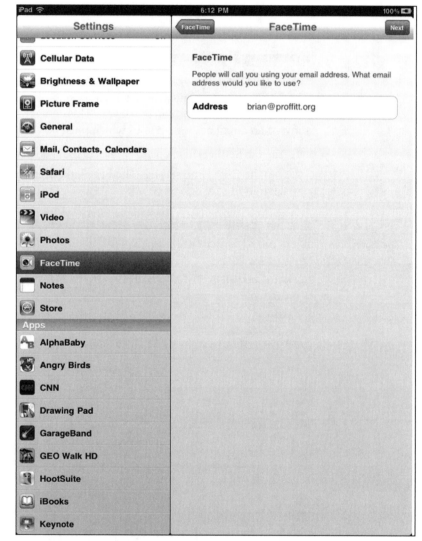

6. Tap the Next button. The address will be accepted, and the FaceTime settings pane will appear (see Figure 8.3).

Figure 8.3

The FaceTime settings pane.

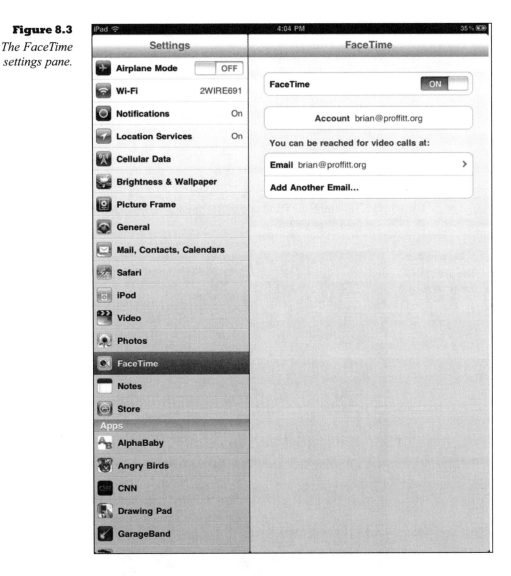

If you ever decide to disable your FaceTime app, you can use the Settings app to manage this.

1. Tap the Settings icon on the Home screen. The Settings app will open.

2. Tap the FaceTime setting. The FaceTime settings pane will open.

3. Slide the FaceTime control to Off. FaceTime will be disabled on your iPad.

Once FaceTime is initially configured, you can give the email address you entered to associates to use to contact you with their FaceTime devices.

Making a FaceTime Call

Very likely the hardest part of making a FaceTime call is finding someone with whom to connect. If your circle of friends and colleagues are dedicated Apple users, this problem is a bit easier to manage.

To date, there is no app or online directory that enables you to find out which of your contacts has FaceTime capabilities. You will need to find them using the old-fashioned way: ask them.

After you identify someone with whom you or your student can connect, the rest is a breeze.

1. Tap the FaceTime app icon. The FaceTime Home screen will appear (see Figure 8.4).

Figure 8.4

The FaceTime Home screen.

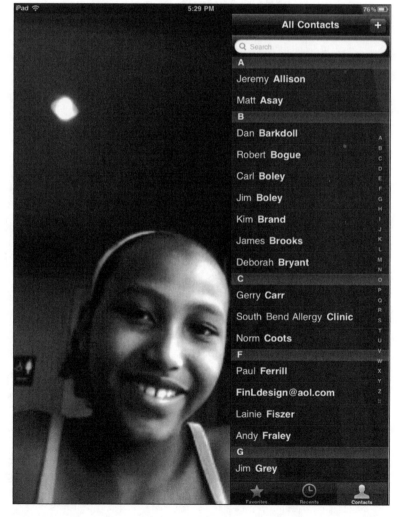

2. Tap a contact with whom you want to connect. The call will immediately start.

3. When the recipient answers, his image will appear in the large screen and your image will appear in the smaller picture-in-picture, as shown in Figure 8.5.

Figure 8.5

A call in progress.

4. When the call is complete, tap the End Call button. The call will end, and the Home screen will appear.

That's pretty much it; nothing fancy is needed. The quality settings are all automatic, though it's always good to have plenty of light available when making any video call.

When a call comes into FaceTime, a trilling tone will sound, and you will be given the choice to Accept or Decline the incoming call. Tap Accept and the call will begin, as shown in Figure 8.6.

Figure 8.6

An incoming call.

Another feature of FaceTime makes use of the rear-facing camera, so you can show callers something else while still being able to view them on the iPad screen. For instance, a student who wants to share an art project could use the rear camera to show off her work, while still watching her caller onscreen.

To use this feature, simply tap the camera switch button during a call. To reactivate the front-facing camera, tap the camera switch button again.

Video Mirroring with FaceTime

Another new hardware feature of the iPad 2, which hasn't gotten a lot of attention yet, is its capability to send the screen content from the device to another screen, such as a monitor or television screen.

Known as *video mirroring*, this is very useful if you ever want to run a demonstration of an iPad app for a class, and it's ideal for broadcasting FaceTime calls to many people at once. The iPad could do this, but only to Apple-compatible devices. The iPad 2 allows video mirroring to a much larger set of monitors.

To use video mirroring, all you need to do is purchase the correct video adapter for your iPad 2. If you want to connect to a computer monitor or TV with a VGA input, you should get the VGA adapter. To connect to an HDTV, purchase the Digital AV connector. Both of these connectors are available for purchase online at the Apple Web site or at any Apple retail outlet.

If you have a widescreen monitor, you can set the iPad 2 to feed to it by following these instructions.

1. Tap the Settings icon on the Home screen. The Settings app will open.
2. Tap the Video setting. The Video settings pane will open, as seen in Figure 8.7.
3. Slide the Widescreen control to On.

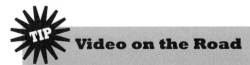

Video on the Road

If you are connecting to a TV from somewhere other than North America, you may want to switch the video output to PAL in the Video settings pane.

Figure 8.7

*The Video
settings pane.*

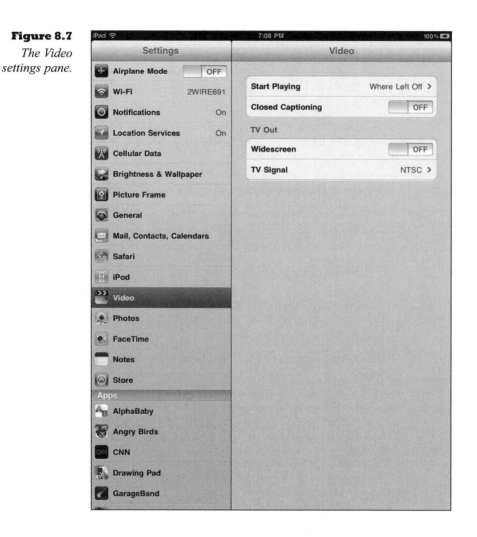

Conclusion

In this chapter, you learned about the newest iPad feature, FaceTime, and how easy it is to set up and use to contact any other FaceTime user.

The FaceTime app is a great way for kids and students to interact with friends and family, and even communicate with other students anywhere in the world. Using the video-out feature, you can send the video feed from your call to a larger screen or monitor, which will enable a whole group to view the call easily.

We've now reviewed the basics of using the iPad and iPad 2, and now it's time to start looking at the apps geared towards children of all ages. And as you will see in Chapter 9, "Apps for Toddler Learning," you're never too young to start using the iPad.

Chapter 9
Apps for
Toddler
Learning

From about their first second of life, children can communicate. Any parent will tell you that babies can usually get their intentions known through crying, gestures, and facial expressions. As they grow, they will pick up a vocabulary of hundreds of words, which they will employ to get what they need or want, express their feelings, or simply make conversation. Sometimes, lots and lots of conversation.

It's well known that kids' brains are sponges for languages. As parents, we see this every single day. But they can't do it on their own, nor should they. We, as adults, have a key role in early speech development. This is why interacting with our children and having them watch us interact with others is so important. This is true of both verbal and written language.

It's not about sitting down with them and practicing reading and writing (though that helps): parents have to convey to their child that such activities can be fun. Skills are all well and good, but in order for children to accomplish their best, they need to embrace these activities. Parents can help make this happen by reading aloud, singing songs, and playing games with language—anything that can bring the spark of interest to a child's mind will help.

At the same time, a whole other set of concepts is being developed in children's brains as they are learning language: the building blocks of math.

It starts small, of course: children figure out the differences between quantities of objects and start to discover patterns in the world around them. Later, they will start to use these basic foundations to begin working out problems with those objects.

This stems from a basic need of children to start looking around and getting a sense of order about their world. If the world is in order, then all is right with said world. Breaking things down into discrete objects and actions is the beginning of mathematical concepts. The good news is that just normal everyday activities will nurture the development of these mathematical concepts.

Of course, there's no reason parents can't help this along, by introducing activities that can increase a child's mathematical growth.

Art, particularly visual arts, is also a key aspect of early childhood development. Parents all marvel at the pretty scribbles our children lovingly hand us, perhaps not realizing that any creative effort a child undertakes has great benefits. Imaginations are stimulated, hand-eye coordination is improved, and overall expression of concepts is markedly improved. This is why parents are encouraged to provide as many opportunities as possible to explore the artistic process.

Such opportunities, really, are what many iPad apps can help you do. Whether art, language, or math, the right iPad apps will expose a child to activities designed to gently reinforce concepts parents are also demonstrating to their children. Using an iPad won't make your child a super-genius, but it will give that child a variety of activities that will help build a love for language, math, and art, even at this early age.

In this chapter, you will learn how to

* Learn the fundamentals of the alphabet, numbers, and shapes with Alpha Baby.
* Build vocabulary with Baby Flash Cards.
* Start math skills with Toddler Counting.
* Explore nature with I Hear Ewe.
* Get creative with Noby Noby Boy and Bubbles.

AlphaBaby: The Joy of Discovery

 Cost of Alpha Baby: $0.99

One of any child's favorite early games has to be the classic "peek-a-boo." Adults love to play this game because they can immediately evoke a positive reaction from a young child and amazingly, it can be played for a while without the child losing much interest.

The reason peek-a-boo works so well is that very young children have an underdeveloped sense of object permanence. You reveal yourself from behind a blanket or your hands over your face and, for the child, he is seeing you all over again. Throw in a funny face and a silly voice, and you're pure entertainment gold for the child.

Of course, as the child gets older, and the brain starts forming more permanent connections, she can figure out that Mommy and Daddy haven't really left—they're just behind the blanket, being silly. A little bit older, and the child may just look at you as if she's thinking, "Really, Daddy?"

But there's another element to the fun of peek-a-boo: the joy of discovering that familiar face all over again. That excitement is something that carries forward as the child grows older, and indeed can become the driving force behind much of his behavior as he moves into toddler and preschool age. That's why he'll empty out the cookware cabinet onto the kitchen floor, because he has discovered a whole new playground of shiny, noise-making objects that (bonus points!) usually bring the parents running.

AlphaBaby is a remarkably simple app that taps into that excitement of discovery within a more structured format. Toddlers will experience the thrill of discovering new and random objects on the screen (they never know what they'll see next), with the repetition that will slowly build connections between the letter, number, or shape displayed and the word for that object.

Playing with AlphaBaby

As I describe how to play AlphaBaby, please note that it isn't meant to be the only way to play with this app. Truthfully, for games like this, it's probably best for you to set your child down with the iPad and let her learn it on her own.

The point of this section is to let you know what the app can do, so if you sense the child is ready for a new challenge, or is just getting a bit bored, you can subtly intervene and demonstrate some feature she hasn't discovered yet. You shouldn't have to do that, because the interface on AlphaBaby is engaging enough that the child should be able to find these features on her own.

Which is pretty much the whole point.

☀ CAUTION **Safety Always First**

Even though the iPad and the iPad 2 each weigh less than two pounds, there's still the issue that these devices are essentially hard pieces of metal and glass. Because of this, here are some important precautions to take:

- ☀ Always supervise the use of the iPad by a small child.
- ☀ Set the child on the floor when she plays with the device.
- ☀ If you don't have a case for the iPad, get one and use it. A soft case will blunt the hard edges.
- ☀ Do not allow small children to play with iPads in moving vehicles unless the device is anchored.
- ☀ Don't throw the iPad.
- ☀ Never use an iPad near water.

As you can probably tell, not only will these tips protect the child, but they will also extend the life of the iPad itself.

Play on AlphaBaby is very simple: when the app is first opened, the child is presented with a completely blank screen, though a hint for adults appears on the bottom of the screen in teeny, tiny print (see Figure 9.1).

Figure 9.1

The initial AlphaBaby screen, with hint.

Press and hold the upper left corner to change settings

When the player taps the screen once, a random object will appear on the screen with a voice describing the object. Objects can be a letter, number, or basic shape (such as a heart, square, or triangle).

As the child continues to tap on the background screen, new objects will appear. To prevent cluttering, only a set number of objects will appear on the screen. Once that limit is reached, then the object that appeared least recently will disappear (see Figure 9.2).

Figure 9.2

AlphaBaby is set to display just six objects by default.

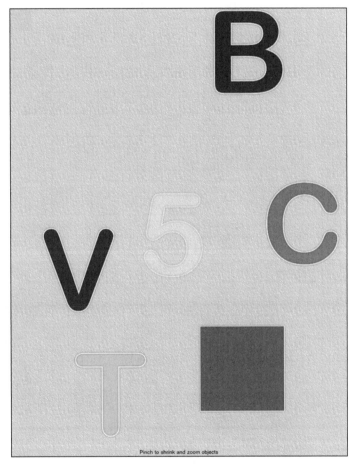

Pinch to shrink and zoom objects

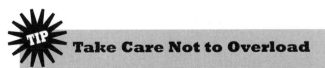

Take Care Not to Overload

When you first introduce this game to little ones, you may want to use just one or two object types, not all three. Using all of the objects could put a young child into overload.

As children continue to play with AlphaBaby, they may discover that additional gestures will cause the objects on the screen to do interesting things (as seen in Figure 9.3). Here's a list of these gestures for adults.

* **Double-tap.** Double-tapping on any object will expand it to its largest size. Double-tapping the object again will shrink it to its smallest size.

* **Pinch.** Pinching an object will shrink the object. Pinching multiple objects will bring them closer together.

* **Fan.** Fanning an object will expand the object. Fanning multiple objects will move them farther apart.

* **Tap and Hold.** Tapping and holding an object for a few seconds will shrink and rotate the object in a cycle, until the object is released.

* **Rotate.** Pinching and rotating an object will reorient it on the screen.

* **Swipe.** Swiping an object will send it bouncing around the screen. The object will not, however, interact with other objects.

Figure 9.3

Objects can be manipulated quite a bit.

Pinch to shrink and zoom objects

As you can see, there's a lot for children to do in AlphaBaby, since they can discover new objects to play with, and then manipulate these objects to their heart's content. One nice feature is that every time an object is touched or moved or resized, the app's voice will describe it again. This reinforces the connection between language and the object described.

Given the extensive range of actions found in AlphaBaby, it's clear that children will be able to find plenty to do with this app. As a parent or caregiver, you should have little need to help them along. You may, though, want to customize the app with additional options... including adding your own voice to the mix.

Setting Up AlphaBaby

As easy as it is to play, AlphaBaby comes with an abundance of settings for adults to configure. You can customize nearly every aspect of the application—from the colors of the background and objects to the types of objects displayed.

To access the settings for AlphaBaby, just tap and hold the upper-left corner of the AlphaBaby screen for three seconds. When the corner color changes to green, release the screen, and the Preferences popover menu will appear (see Figure 9.4).

Figure 9.4

The Preferences popover menu.

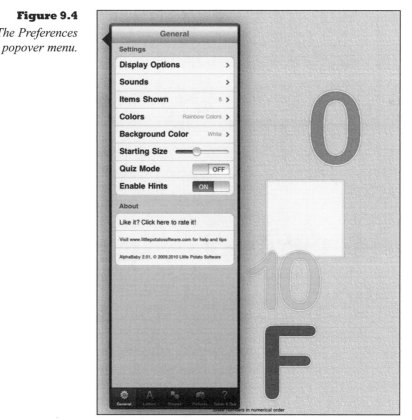

Using this menu, you can configure things easily in AlphaBaby. For example, there are two distinct narrators available in AlphaBaby: an adult voice, which is the initial voice heard when the app is first run, and a kid's voice. To change the voice, follow these steps:

1. Tap and hold the upper-left corner of the AlphaBaby screen for three seconds. The corner will flash green.
2. Release the screen. The Preferences popover menu will appear.
3. Tap the Sounds setting. The Sounds menu will appear (see Figure 9.5).

Figure 9.5

The Sounds popover menu.

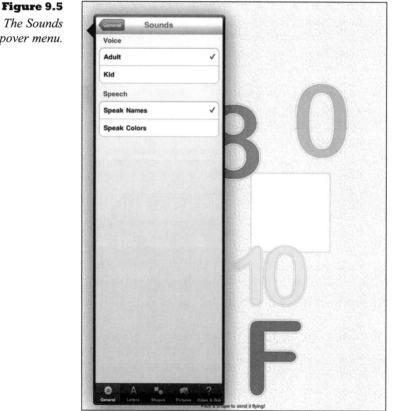

4. Tap Kid. The setting will be selected.
5. Tap outside the popover menu to close the menu and have the new setting take effect.

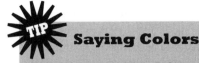

Saying Colors

If you would like AlphaBaby to say the color of the object instead of its name, navigate to the Sounds popover menu and tap the Speak Colors setting in the Speech section.

Show More Object Types

Although AlphaBaby starts off with letters, numbers, and shapes, that's not the limit to the objects it can display. It can also show colors as objects, as well as pictures you have stored on your iPad.

1. Tap and hold the upper-left corner of the AlphaBaby screen for three seconds. The corner will flash green.

2. Release the screen. The Preferences popover menu will appear.

3. Tap the Display Options setting. The Display Options menu will appear (see Figure 9.6).

Figure 9.6

The Display Options popover menu.

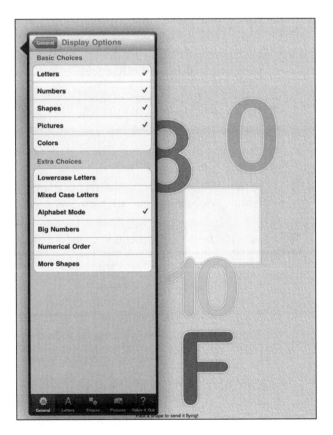

4. In the Basic Choices group, tap the object types you want AlphaBaby to use. Tapping a selected item will deselect it.

5. In the Extra Choices group, tap the options you would like to use. The options are

   ＊ **Lowercase Letters.** All letter objects in AlphaBaby will appear in lowercase.

   ＊ **Mixed Case Letters.** Letter objects will appear in lower- and uppercase.

   ＊ **Alphabet Mode.** When letters appear, they will be in alphabetical order.

   ＊ **Big Numbers.** Number objects from 11 to 20 will be added to AlphaBaby play.

   ＊ **Numerical Order.** When numbers appear, they will be in numerical order.

   ＊ **More Shapes.** Nine more shapes will be added to AlphaBaby play.

6. Tap outside the popover menu to close the menu and have the new settings take effect.

Showing More Objects

When AlphaBaby is first played, the app displays six objects at a time. This is easily changed in the Preferences.

1. Tap and hold the upper-left corner of the AlphaBaby screen for three seconds. The corner will flash green.

2. Release the screen. The Preferences popover menu will appear.

3. Tap the Items Shown setting. The Number of Items Shown menu will appear (see Figure 9.7).

4. Swipe the picker to select the number of items you want AlphaBaby to display. AlphaBaby can display 1–8 objects or 10, 15, or 20 objects.

5. Tap outside the popover menu to close the menu and have the new setting take effect.

Figure 9.7

The Number of Items Shown popover menu.

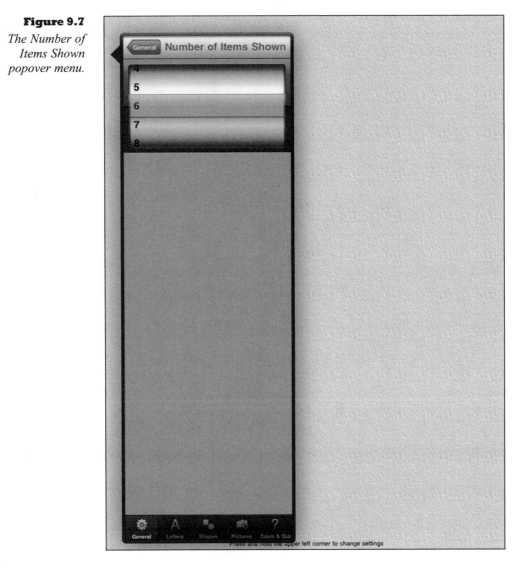

Educators and scientists have demonstrated that certain colors, such as red, black, and white, elicit more visual responses in younger children. Adults who want to take advantage of this can change the app's color scheme or just change the colors to the child's preferences. Either way, it's a simple matter.

1. Tap and hold the upper-left corner of the AlphaBaby screen for three seconds. The corner will flash green.

2. Release the screen. The Preferences popover menu will appear.

3. Tap the Colors setting. The Colors menu will appear (see Figure 9.8).

Figure 9.8

*The Colors
popover menu.*

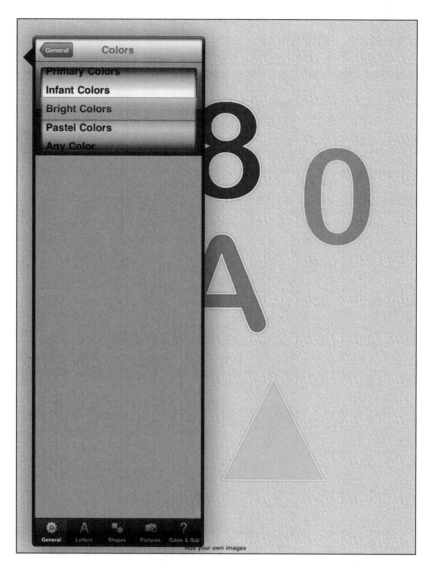

4. Swipe the picker to select the color scheme for AlphaBaby to display.

5. To select a single color, select the Choose a Color option to reveal the Choose a Color popover menu and select the color there.

6. Tap the General back button. The Preferences popover menu will appear.

7. Tap the Background Color setting. The Choose a Background menu will appear (see Figure 9.9).

Figure 9.9

The Choose a Background popover menu.

8. Swipe the picker to select the background color for AlphaBaby to display.

9. Tap outside the popover menu to close the menu and have the new setting take effect (see Figure 9.10).

Figure 9.10

A new color scheme (red, in this case) is easy to configure.

Starting a Quiz

As a child becomes more familiar with the objects in AlphaBaby, adults can set up an easy challenge/response game for the child.

AlphaBaby calls this a "quiz," but it's nothing so formal. A set of objects will appear on the screen, and the narrator will ask the player to find a certain object. If the child correctly touches the right object, a verbal cue celebrates the success. If not, the child is gently encouraged to try again.

There's no tracking or grading going on here; this is just a mild challenge for players, which is why it's optional in AlphaBaby. When adults think their child is ready to try it, here's how to turn on the quiz option:

1. Tap and hold the upper-left corner of the AlphaBaby screen for three seconds. The corner will flash green.
2. Release the screen. The Preferences popover menu will appear.
3. Slide the Quiz Mode switch to On.
4. Tap outside the popover menu to close the menu and have the quiz start.
5. Tap the screen once to start the quiz.

Recording Your Voice in AlphaBaby

The narrator voices in AlphaBaby are good and should appeal to most children. Adults, however, can add their own voices to the app, replacing the narrators' voices. Many parents can see the appeal in this option, since younger children will respond more positively to a familiar voice.

To record any new voice into AlphaBaby, you will need to record a sound clip for each AlphaBaby object with which you want to associate your voice. You should set aside a little time to do this, since there are 86 objects in AlphaBaby, not counting any additional pictures you might choose to add to the app. I'd recommended that you find a quiet space before you record the voiceovers; iPad microphones are good, but not outstandingly great.

1. Tap and hold the upper-left corner of the AlphaBaby screen for three seconds. The corner will flash green.
2. Release the screen. The Preferences popover menu will appear.
3. Tap the object icon on the bottom of the popover menu that you want to record. The object menu will appear (see Figure 9.11).

Figure 9.11

The Letters popover menu.

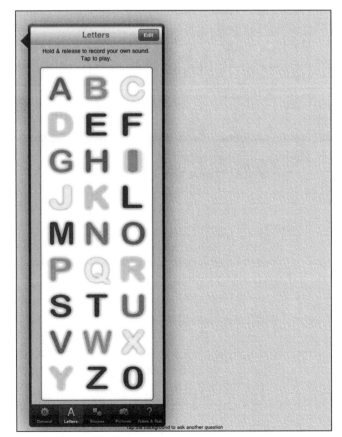

4. Press and hold the object for which you want to record a voiceover. The Release to Record status indicator will appear at the top of the menu, as shown in Figure 9.12.

Figure 9.12

Preparing to record.

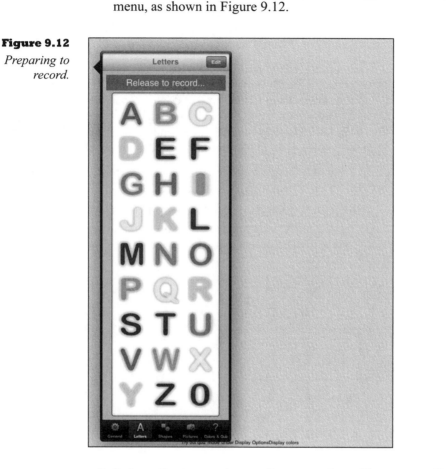

5. Release the screen. A recording status bar will appear and begin to progress.

6. Before the status bar is finished, clearly speak the object's name. Your voiceover will be recorded, which will be denoted by a small audio icon on the object.

7. Tap the object to hear your voiceover and confirm its accuracy and clarity.

8. Repeat as needed for other objects.

9. To remove a voiceover from an object, tap the Edit button at the top of the object popover menu. All recorded objects will have a delete overlay on their audio icons.

10. Tap the icon you want to remove from the voiceover.

11. Tap Done. The voiceover changes will be made.

12. Tap outside the popover menu to close the menu and have the new settings take effect.

Adding Pictures

Besides the objects that come in AlphaBaby, you can also add your own personal objects, in the form of pictures stored on your iPad. This is a great way to deeply personalize the AlphaBaby app, since you can insert images of people and objects the child is familiar with and help her make the language connections that much faster.

TIP

Managing iPad Images

This section will assume you have either taken pictures with the iPad 2 or imported them onto either iPad model. For more information about working with pictures on any iPad, see the "Shutterbugging 101" section in Chapter 16, "Art Class Without Smocks."

There really isn't any limit to the number of pictures you can use in AlphaBaby; just the amount of memory storage on your iPad will limit you. Whatever pictures you choose to use, be sure the pictures are clear in what they represent. You wouldn't necessarily want to show a picture of a man on the deck of a boat and have the voiceover describe that picture as "ocean."

1. Tap and hold the upper-left corner of the AlphaBaby screen for three seconds. The corner will flash green.

2. Release the screen. The Preferences popover menu will appear.

3. Tap the Pictures icon on the bottom of the popover menu. The Pictures menu will appear (see Figure 9.13).

Figure 9.13

The Pictures popover menu.

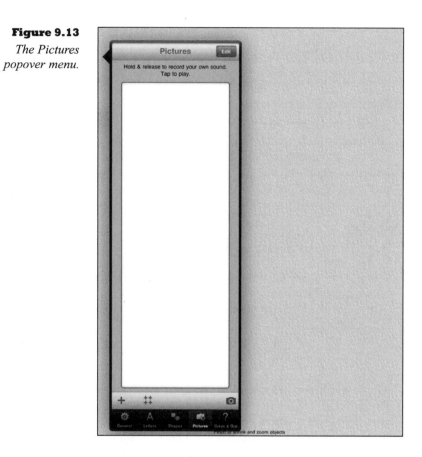

4. To add a single picture, tap the single "+" Add icon. The Photo Albums popover menu will appear (see Figure 9.14).

Figure 9.14

The Photo Albums popover menu.

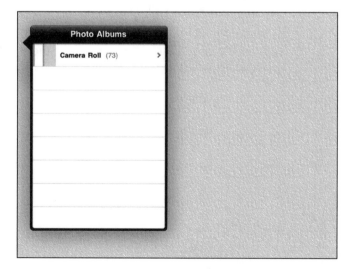

5. Tap the album option you want to browse. The album's contents will be displayed.

6. Tap the image you want to use. The image will appear in the Choose Photo popover menu (shown in Figure 9.15).

Figure 9.15

The Choose Photo popover menu.

7. Drag, pinch, or fan the image in the menu to size the image so the main object fills the frame.

8. Tap Use. The properly cropped image will appear in the Pictures popover menu.

9. Repeat as needed for other pictures.

10. Tap outside the popover menu to close the menu.

Adding Multiple Images

You can also add multiple images into AlphaBaby, so you don't have to pull images in one at a time.

1. Tap and hold the upper-left corner of the AlphaBaby screen for three seconds. The corner will flash green.

2. Release the screen. The Preferences popover menu will appear.

3. Tap the Pictures icon on the bottom of the popover menu. The Pictures menu will appear.

4. To add a photo library, tap the multiple "+" Add icon. An alert box will appear (see Figure 9.16).

Figure 9.16

*Since photo
libraries can
contain location
information,
AlphaBaby must
warn you
properly.*

5. Tap OK. The Use Your Current Location alert box will appear.

6. Tap OK. The Photo Albums popover menu will appear.

7. Tap the album option you want to browse. The album's contents will
be displayed in the Tap to select popover menu.

8. Tap the images you want to use. The images will be selected.

9. Tap the Add button. The images will be resized and will appear in
the Pictures popover menu.

10. Tap outside the popover menu to close the menu.

Adding a Camera Image

If you want, you can use the iPad 2's onboard camera to capture an
image directly for AlphaBaby.

1. Tap and hold the upper-left corner of the AlphaBaby screen for three seconds. The corner will flash green.
2. Release the screen. The Preferences popover menu will appear.
3. Tap the Pictures icon on the bottom of the popover menu. The Pictures menu will appear.
4. To take a picture, tap the Camera icon. The Camera app will open (see Figure 9.17).

Figure 9.17

The Camera app.

5. Tap the Camera icon. The iPad 2 will take the picture, and it will appear in a Move and Scale window (shown in Figure 9.18).

Figure 9.18

Moving and scaling a camera snapshot.

Retake   **Move and Scale**   Use

6. Drag, pinch, or fan the image in the window to size the image so the main object fills the frame.

7. Tap Use. The properly cropped image will appear in the Pictures popover menu.

8. Repeat as needed for other pictures.

9. Tap outside the popover menu to close the menu.

Once images are loaded into the AlphaBaby app, you will have to record a voiceover for each new image object. AlphaBaby cannot assign voice narration to an object when it doesn't know what the image is. Follow the steps in the "Recording Your Voice in AlphaBaby" section earlier in this chapter to accomplish this task. Say "pineapple."

Expanding Language: Baby Flash Cards

 Cost of Baby Flash Cards: Free

While AlphaBaby is an excellent app for getting across the basics of letters, numbers, and shapes, all of the language connections involved are visual and auditory in nature. The child sees the object and hears the description.

Other apps go a bit beyond this type of connection and introduce written language connections, too. One such app is Baby Flash Cards.

Despite the name, Baby Flash Cards is actually fairly appropriate for children from one to four years old, though by age four, children may find this app a bit repetitious.

There are many similarities between Baby Flash Cards and AlphaBaby: both feature randomized selections of different objects for the child to see and hear. Baby Flash Cards, however, features many more objects in several categories, ranging from animals to musical instruments to foods.

Baby Flash Cards also differs from AlphaBaby in the way that players interact with the objects. Like the name suggests, Baby Flash Cards presents the objects solely in flash-card format. This means there is less opportunity for interaction with the objects.

New objects can't be added to Baby Flash Cards, but given the sheer number of objects within the latest version of Baby Flash Cards, there are more than enough to keep children busy for quite some time.

Playing with Baby Flash Cards

There are two modes for playing Baby Flash Cards, which are clearly indicated on the Home screen of the app (see Figure 9.19): Play and Quest.

Figure 9.19

The Baby Flash Cards Home screen.

 An Interesting Look

You can see that Baby Flash Cards has a far different look and feel than most other iPad apps. That's likely due to the cultural differences of the Hong Kong-based developers and artists who worked on the app. For this book's purposes, we will try to explain the interface in as familiar terms as possible.

In Play mode, the child is presented with a range of flash cards (randomized or otherwise), which advance whenever the player touches the screen. Audio and written descriptions of the object are given simultaneously when the flash card appears in Play mode (see Figure 9.20).

Figure 9.20

A typical Baby Flash Cards object.

In Quest mode, play is similar; although when the flash card is initially presented, no descriptions are given—the child is encouraged to name the object first himself. Touching the object again will reveal the written and audio descriptions.

If, at any time, the child wants to go back to the previous card, he can tap the back arrow button in the upper-left corner of the screen. To hear the audio description of the object again, he can just tap the speak icon in the lower-left corner of the screen.

To return to the Home screen, tap the return icon in the upper-right corner of the screen.

Setting Up Baby Flash Cards

As with other learning games, the real power of Baby Flash Cards is how it can be configured. Adults can set up Baby Flash Cards to meet the needs of the child playing the game.

Tapping on the Settings icon on the Home screen (which looks like a gear) opens the Settings screen (see Figure 9.21)

Figure 9.21

The Baby Flash Cards Settings screen.

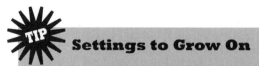

Settings		Categories	
Random Order	ON	Animals	ON
Voice	ON	Colors	ON
User Voice	ON	Food	ON
User Text	ON	Fruits	ON
Quick Touch	OFF	Letters	ON
Card Theme	Blue Red	Musical instruments	ON
Autoplay OFF		Numbers	ON
		People	ON
		Plants	ON
		Shapes	ON
		Transportation	ON
		Others	ON

PLAY   QUEST

Many of the settings are fairly self-explanatory. The switches control various aspects of both Play and Quest modes of Baby Flash Cards: you can randomize the order of flash cards, specify the categories that will appear, and activate program and user voice settings.

TIP

Settings to Grow On

If a younger child is starting to use Baby Flash Cards, you might consider shutting off various categories to keep the game simpler. As children mature, adults can activate categories and add to the game's repertoire. Just don't go crazy: little ones may not know what an accordion is, for instance.

Self-Describing Objects in Baby Flash Cards

Baby Flash Cards has the feature that lets adults record their own voices to describe each Baby Flash Cards object. It also enables the written descriptions to be edited as well.

You might wonder at this last statement, since an airplane (for instance) is always going to be described as an airplane. True, but what if your family refers to such an object as a plane? You can change object descriptions to match your family's personal preferences.

Another reason to edit written descriptions: second-language practice. So instead of "airplane," it could be "Flugzeug" or "Avion" or "Aeroplano." The possibilities are certainly very intriguing, since this gives Baby Flash Cards the capability to be a perfectly useful foreign language training device.

Here's how to set an object's written and audio description:

1. In the Baby Flash Cards Home screen, tap the Rec icon. The Rec screen will appear (see Figure 9.22).

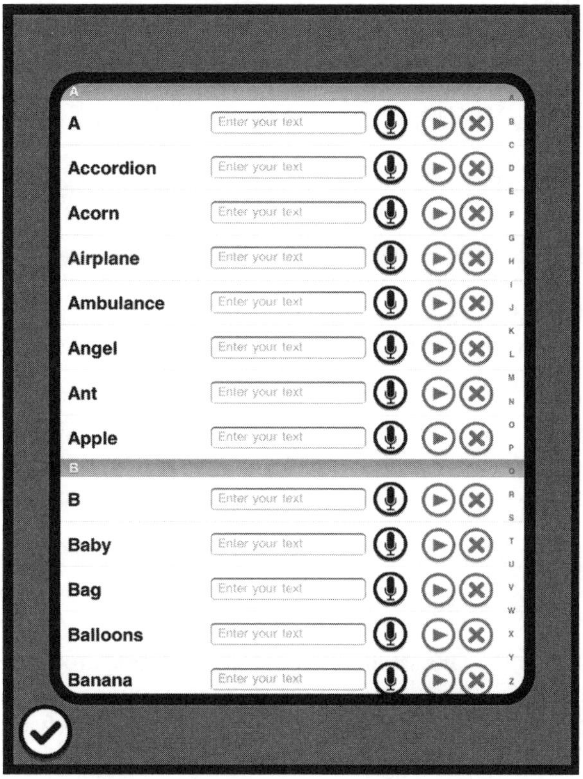

Figure 9.22

The Baby Flash Cards Rec screen.

2. Tap the first letter of the object you want to edit. The listing will move down to that section.

3. Tap the Enter your text field for the object you want to edit. The cursor and iPad keyboard will appear.

4. Type the new description for the object.

5. To record a description in your own voice, tap the Microphone icon for the object. A recording status bar will appear and begin to progress.

6. Before the status bar is finished, clearly speak the object's name and tap the Stop button. Your description will be recorded, and the object's Play and Delete icons will be activated.

7. Tap the Play button to hear your description and confirm its accuracy and clarity.

8. Repeat as needed for other objects.

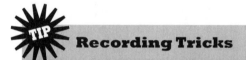

Recording Tricks

Unlike AlphaBaby, Baby Flash Cards doesn't auto-edit audio recordings to remove silent spaces before and after the word being recorded. Use the Stop button after describing the object so you don't have long pauses in game play.

9. To remove an audio description from an object, tap the Delete button next to a recorded object. The recording will be removed.

10. To remove a written description from an object, tap the Delete button inside the written description field. The description will be removed.

One Counting iPad App! Ah Ha Ha Ha!

Cost of Toddler Counting: $0.99

As children conceptually organize the world around them, one of the earliest and easiest ways to organize is through counting. A big reason for this is the built-in counting equipment we all carry around with us: those dangly 10 digits at the end of our hands. Younger children have it even better: with bare feet, they get a bonus 10 toes with which to count.

You may laugh, but the reason why we use base-10 math is purely because of the construction of our hands.

There are, naturally, drawbacks to this approach. When children use fingers to count, they may not properly understand that they're counting other objects. The fingers are just a proxy. Nor do fingers and toes really match amounts with Arabic numbers.

Toddler Counting is a very simple app that helps children make those connections. It lets them count objects on the screen at their own pace, giving them the opportunity to hear and see numbers as they count.

Playing Toddler Counting is easy. There are two modes of play: Easier and Harder, as shown in Figure 9.23.

Figure 9.23

The Toddler Counting Home screen.

Both modes will depict various objects on the screen and ask the child to count them. When the child taps on each object, the game will highlight the object with the next number in the sequence, while the audio narration will speak the number. Once all the items are counted, the app will deliver an encouraging audio message, and the screen will display a new set of objects to count.

Toddler Counting will continue to cycle through object sets indefinitely, unless the app is exited with the Home button, or the app's Home screen is requested by shaking the iPad a couple of times.

The Harder mode is identical to the Easier mode, except that the Easier mode displays sets of up to 10 objects, with Harder mode displaying up to 20 (see Figure 9.24).

Figure 9.24

Counting hamburgers and other fun objects.

Hearing the Sounds of the World

 Cost of I Hear Ewe app: Free

Those of us who were children in the 1960s will appreciate the I Hear Ewe app, if only because it will bring back memories of a toy from our childhood: the old Mattel See 'n Say. You remember them, particularly the Farmer Says model: point the arrow at the animal on the round face of the toy, pull the string and "The ducks says… quack, quack, quack."

Classic.

I Hear Ewe works in much the same way: the app presents 24 animals and 12 vehicles in a straightforward grid (shown in Figure 9.25).

Figure 9.25

The I Hear Ewe screen.

When the child taps an animal or machine, the object expands to fill the screen, and the voice narrator will introduce the sound the object makes, followed by the sound itself.

There's no skill to this app, nor is it expandable. It is, however, multi-lingual: English is one of four languages available in I Hear Ewe. You may not want to swap out for a different language, but if you are in a multilingual home, and want to reinforce another language, this is not a bad feature. To change the language to Spanish, German, or Chinese, just follow these steps:

1. Tap the Information icon on the Home screen. The Settings action menu will appear (see Figure 9.26).

Figure 9.26

The Settings action menu.

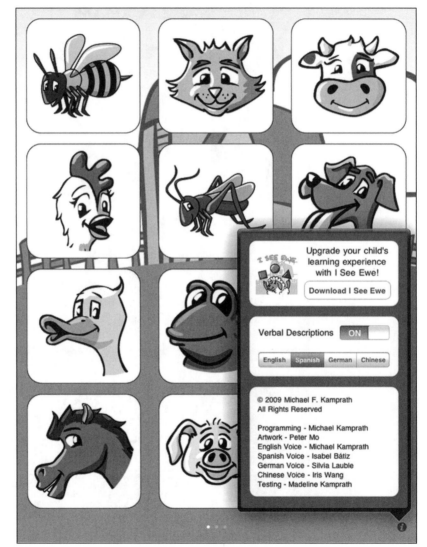

2. Tap the desired language setting. The setting will be selected.

3. If you just want the app to play an object's sound, slide the Verbal Descriptions control to Off.

4. Tap outside the action menu to close the menu.

Play for Creativity's Sake

Sometimes you just need to play.

Since a large number of apps available for the iPad are games and entertainment apps, this is not exactly sharing anything new. With the right application on the iPad, you can accomplish pure play while also getting some developmental growth out of the game as well.

Forever Blowing Bubbles

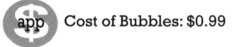 Cost of Bubbles: $0.99

Bubbles is one such game.

There is very little point to Bubbles. But if you are one of those people who love to pop the bubble-wrap packaging (and you are, aren't you?), then the enjoyment of Bubbles will definitely not be lost on you. For children, it's pure entertainment.

There are two things you can do in Bubbles: drag your finger(s) across the screen to create bubbles, then tap the bubbles to pop them with a satisfying, well, pop!

That's all there is to it. The bubbles on the screen will orient themselves with gravity, depending on how you are holding the iPad. Eventually, all of the bubbles will pop on their own (typically in about 8–10 seconds, depending on the size of the individual bubble), which will return to the Home screen, until the child creates more bubbles again (see Figure 9.27).

Figure 9.27

*Bubbles. C'mon,
you know you
want to pop
them.*

This is a pretty little game that should appeal to very young children (and their parents) while improving hand-eye coordination. If you or your child's tastes run a little darker, the game also has the option of displaying claymation bubbles with odd-looking faces on them. They're kind of creepy, so really young children might not need to see them. If you have older kids who want to try them out, follow these steps:

1. Tap the Settings icon on the iPad Home screen. The Settings app will open.

2. Tap the Bubbles option. The Bubbles pane will appear.

3. Tap the Bubble Style option. The Bubble Style pane will appear.

4. Tap the Claymation option to select it.

The next time you start Bubbles, they will look very different, as shown in Figure 9.28.

Figure 9.28

These guys are just a wee bit creepy.

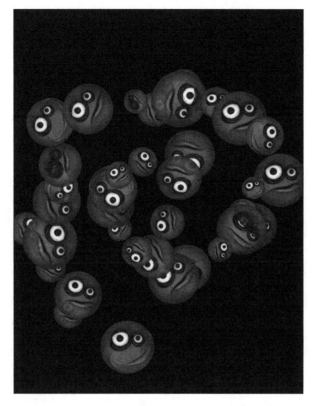

Stretch Out with Noby Noby Boy

 Cost of Noby Noby Boy: $0.99

Slightly more complex (and just a bit stranger) is Noby Noby Boy, the game from Japanese developer Keita Takahashi that breaks the paradigm of what typical game play is about.

In the game, Boy is a four-legged caterpillar-like creature who can be stretched, pulled, shrunk, and essentially manipulated as much as you want on the screen. And that's pretty much it. As a sort of afterthought to the game, the more a player stretches Boy, the more hearts are accumulated. These hearts can be transferred to a similar and much larger creature known as Girl. Girl sits on the planet Earth and as more hearts are given to her from players all over the world in real time, the more she grows. Girl has stretched to the Moon, Mars, Jupiter, and as of January 2011, Saturn. As of this printing, Girl was on her way to Uranus.

The collaborative effort of the hundreds of thousands of Internet play-ers affecting the length of a single game element has its appeal for adults, but it's the basic play with Boy that will mostly appeal to children.

There's a lot to do with Boy, since he can interact with (very) random objects on the screen and be stretched and pulled pretty indiscriminately. Tapping on any object or screen edge will immediately snap either the head or tail end of Boy to that object, where he will stick until either tapped again or pulled hard enough away (see Figure 9.29).

Figure 9.29

Boy can be stretched to a child's imagination.

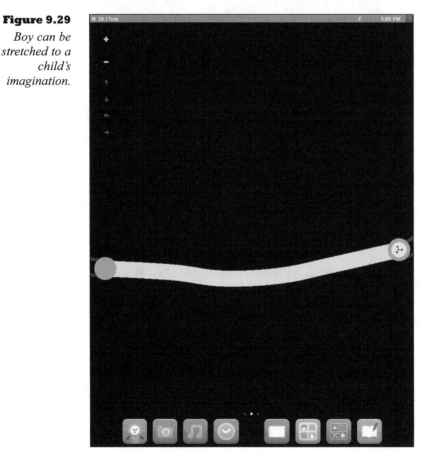

There is a drawing mode for Noby Noby Boy, where Boy (or you) can draw lines and shapes on the screen. This is found by swiping the lower icon bar to the right and tapping the purple drawing button.

If you carry your iPad 2 around, you can even use the onboard GPS system to attach one end of Boy to your location on a Google map and let the other end stretch with you as you travel (as shown in Figure 9.30).

Figure 9.30

Traveling with GPS and Boy.

For the best benefit, players are simply invited to play with the app, since the usual goal seeking of most games is very much absent in Noby Noby Boy. Let your child discover the fun things in Noby Noby Boy. If you want to follow along and give some guidance, a tap on the Help icon in the upper-right corner of the screen will reveal a somewhat apathetic Fairy with some hints.

Conclusion

As you can see, there are quite a few educational and developmental iPad apps out there for toddlers. Too many to be covered in a single chapter, that's for sure. When you explore the app store looking for more apps for your young child, be sure to look for apps that have as much interactivity as possible. Also, avoid apps that want you to pay for extras—there's little sense in that. Finally, don't use apps that are strictly educational. Fun is important, because that will hold the child's attention longer.

Moving on to Chapter 10, "Apps for Pre-Kindergarten," we'll look at apps that are designed to work well with children who are just a couple of years away from their first day of school. Apps that will ideally get them better prepared for that first day.

Chapter 10

Apps for Pre-Kindergarten

Until recent years, literacy meant the ability to read the printed word. Kind of like what you're doing now.

But as technology became more pervasive in our daily lives, the definition of literacy expanded a bit, to include not only reading the printed word, but also finding the best way to get the printed word.

Thanks to the Internet, the printed word can be found nearly everywhere, from millions of online sources. In some ways, this is good: as more and more children seek online experiences, their overall literacy increases, if only because so much Internet content needs to be read when consumed. But it brings many people another, new challenge: discerning what's worth reading.

Because of this, it's more important than ever for children to get an early start on their reading skills

Meanwhile, mathematical concepts continue to expand as children approach kindergarten. Beyond just the basics of numbers, size, volume, length, area, shapes, space, and time are concepts that are completely appropriate for children this age to learn. Having these building blocks well in hand enables future students to move right into formal math learning later.

The best part about learning at this age is that learning is almost all completely fun. Repetition is certainly key, but done within the context of a fun app on the iPad, it makes the repetition so much easier to handle.

The apps in this chapter are appropriate for three- to five-year-old children, though some—like Fish School and the Dr. Seuss books—are geared for the younger end of that age range, with others like What's the Difference and Math Magic being flexible enough to use even beyond this set range and into kindergarten.

In this chapter, you will learn how to

✳ Practice the alphabet, numbers, and shapes with Fish School.

✳ Explore read-aloud story apps from the mind of Dr. Seuss.

✳ Enhance pattern and visual acuity with What's the Difference?

✳ Build math skills with Math Magic.

Fish School: Catching Some Knowledge

 Cost of Fish School: $1.99

Put children in front of an aquarium, and they will be mesmerized by the bright, quick colors darting through the shimmering water. That's a big part of the draw of Fish School, the educational app from the uniquely named company Duck Duck Moose.

Fish School approaches learning through a more traditional method: letters, numbers, and shapes are presented in sequential fashion, enabling children to see and hear the words for these objects as they play. What differentiates Fish School from similar apps is the superior animation and the incorporation of music within the play—a staple of Duck Duck Moose apps.

The animation within Fish School is a real draw: fish may swim around in specific patterns, but the water motion as they move and hold in place is visually quite eye-catching for children.

There are eight modes of play within Fish School to entertain and teach a child. Within each mode, schools of various fish will swim around and interact based on the mode of play.

✳ **ABC.** Fish will swim to form the letters of the English alphabet.

✳ **123.** Fish will group themselves into numbers from 1 to 20, with colorful fish eggs appearing for counting.

✳ **Play.** As fish casually swim around the screen, tapping them in various ways will cause them to react in unique ways. This is purely for entertainment, and not much learning is found here.

✳ **Shapes.** Fish will organize into one of seven basic shapes.

* **Musical ABC.** As "The Alphabet Song" is sung in the background, fish will swim into the letters of the alphabet in time with the music.
* **Colors.** Various fish will swim across the screen, and when a child taps one, all of the aquatic life in that color will appear on the screen.
* **Differences.** Fish will swim across the screen, with one being out of place. Tapping the different fish will yield a reward and reset the screen,
* **Matching.** Sixteen fish will appear on the screen for a game of matching.

When Fish School is first started, the initial screen shows a single fish laying colorful roe along the sandy sea floor. Tapping each one of the fish eggs will crack the egg open and let a little fry come swimming out (as shown in Figure 10.1). The fry will stay in place in an arc pattern, or will move offscreen when tapped.

Figure 10.1

The initial Fish School screen.

Tapping the large fish swimming back and forth will start the game, initially in ABC mode. Each mode of Fish School is entered by tapping the bubbles on the lower-left corner of the screen, as shown in Figure 10.2.

Figure 10.2

Fish School in ABC mode.

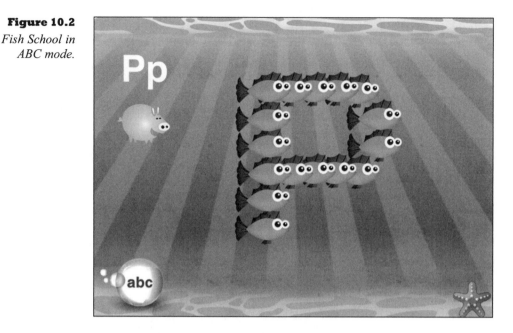

The bubbles act as the only game control interface. Parents might get interested in that sea star sitting in the lower-right corner, but alas, it's only a fun bubble generator.

To play the ABC mode, the child can tap the screen anywhere to advance to the next letter of the alphabet. Tapping on the displayed letter or object in the upper-left corner will have the narrator give a descriptive message, such as "A is for apple." If you want to step back to the previous letter, swipe from left to right across the screen.

The 123 mode mode is similar to ABC mode, in that the fish will swim out in sequential order to form the numbers from 1 to 20. To hear the number spoken, tap the number in the corner of the screen. Navigation between numbers is exactly the same as in ABC mode. What's different in 123 mode (other than the lack of the sea star) are the rows of roe that appear on the bottom of the screen that match the number shown. Tapping any fish egg lets the player hear a sequential count as the eggs crack open and a fry swims out (see Figure 10.3).

Figure 10.3

*Fish School in
123 mode.*

In Play mode, a whole ecosystem of fish swim around the screen to a classical rendition of "The Alphabet Song." Tap a fish to have it swim faster across the screen. Tap and drag a fish to move it onscreen. Tap and hold any fish to have it grow to rather enormous sizes (see Figure 10.4).

Figure 10.4

*Fish School in
Play mode.*

Shapes mode is identical to ABC mode, except now the fish are in one of seven basic shapes (see Figure 10.5).

Figure 10.5

Fish School in Shapes mode.

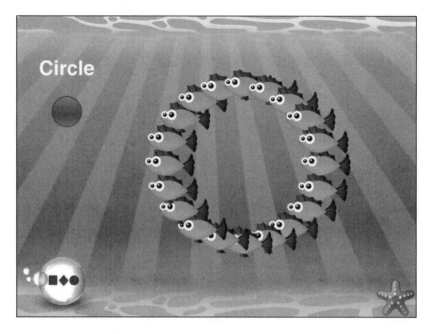

Musical ABC mode is the least interactive mode of the game, because fish will automatically swim into letter patterns to the tune of "The Alphabet Song." The only drawback here is that the song will repeatedly play until another mode is entered or the app is closed.

Colors mode returns the interactivity, with another set of varied fish swimming placidly along. But tap one of the fish and all of the fish will change to the initial fish's color; then the narrator will describe the color with a written description on the screen (see Figure 10.6). Tapping any part of the screen will return the multispecies schools.

Difference mode is an easy game of spot the oddball. As various identical fish swim around the screen, players must tap the fish that does not belong. If the tap is successful, a new set of fish will appear to play the game again (see Figure 10.7).

Finally, there's Matching mode, which is a simple game of Concentration, played with eight pairs of objects. On each turn, players can select two fish to see what's behind them. When a pair is matched, they will swim off, making the remaining matches easier to find (see Figure 10.8).

Figure 10.6

Fish School in Colors mode.

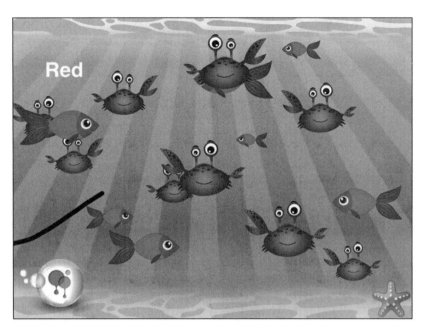

Figure 10.7

Fish School in Difference mode.

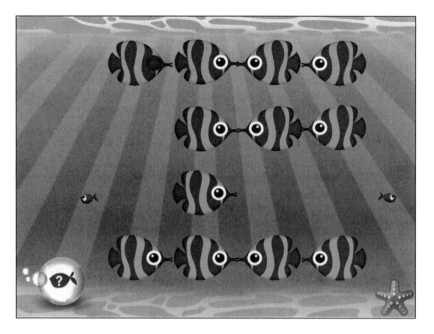

As you can see, the games within Fish School are very simple to play and understand, which makes it much more appropriate for younger children than those about to enter kindergarten. The fun animations and easy pace of the games should hold kids' interest while getting across basic language and math concepts.

Oh, the Apps You Will Use

Currently, there are 20 Dr. Seuss books offered by Oceanhouse Media, with prices varying from $2.99 to $4.99. This is, by app standards, a little pricey. Compared to the price of an actual book, though, these are rather reasonable. And these apps do much more than a book.

For children's literature, there are few writers who will instantly invoke the positive feelings that Theodore Geisel has for so many years.

No positive feelings yet? Then perhaps if we refer to Mr. Geisel by his more popular pseudonym, you'll have a better reaction: Dr. Seuss.

Until his passing in 1991, Geisel was the prolific creator of 44 children's books, most under the Dr. Seuss pen name, though others were used. His writing and artistic style are instantly recognizable and even today his stories are loved by children and adults everywhere.

So when Oceanhouse Media started offering iPad versions of Geisel's works, it was little surprise these apps, known as omBooks, would be among the most popular children's iPad apps offered.

Each app presents a Dr. Seuss book in a set framework.

* **Read to Me.** Readers are read the text of the book. Pages are not turned automatically, and readers can interact with the page as much as they want before going to the next page in the story.

* **Read It Myself.** Readers read the text of the book themselves. If they need help, they can tap individual words or whole passages to be read aloud. Pages are not turned automatically, and readers can interact with the page as much as they want before going to the next page in the story.

* **Auto Play.** Readers are read the text of the book and pages are turned automatically. Readers can interact with the page, but only before the next page in the story appear.

What's really interesting about any of these Dr. Seuss apps is how parents can set the level of interaction with the app. If you just want your child to read a great story, Auto Play is a good option, because the child can sit back and enjoy the story.

TIP Accept No Substitutes

Auto Play is convenient for those few situations where you can't read to your child directly, but by no means should it take the place of your reading to your child. Reading to your children is a great way to bond, practice your silly voices, and not-so-secretly enjoy the Dr. Seuss stories of your own childhood.

For very early readers, Read to Me is an excellent choice. The story is still read to children, but they have the benefit of exploring the environments of the book. Tap a word in the story to have that word read aloud. Tap and hold a paragraph to have the paragraph read aloud. Swiping across the screen will turn the page.

But what's really neat is what happens when you tap on any object in the story. The word for the object appears and is read aloud (sometimes with a sound effect), as seen in Figure 10.9.

Figure 10.9

That's one big cat.

This interactive setting is also available in Auto Play, but it has a time limit; eventually, the next page is going to appear. In Read to Me, children have all the time in the world to play with the elements of the story.

Read It Myself is the mode that will be the best challenge for up and coming readers. Everything is done by the reader: page turning, exploration, and, of course, reading. But, if readers get stuck on a particular word, all they need to do is tap the word to have it read. Or tap and hold the paragraph, and it will be read, too.

With over 20 books available now, and likely more on the way, there's a good range of reading levels available, from Dr. Seuss's ABC to Yertle the Turtle. Whatever the reading level of your child is, these are great apps to visit, over and over again.

One of These Things...What's the Difference?

 Cost of What's the Difference? HD: $3.99

One of the ways to practice the powers of observation is to observe. Watching the world around them is a natural way for kids to learn, since we are visual creatures by nature.

Of course, are they looking at the world, or *seeing* it? One fun app to help them build their powers of observation is What's the Difference?

What's the Difference? is an app with simple rules: two very similar pictures are displayed, side by side. Players must then find five things that are different in each photo within a certain amount of time. Sounds easy, right? But there's a catch: the pictures are highly detailed, and sometimes the differences are subtle, as seen in Figure 10.10.

Figure 10.10

Five differences? Go ahead, find them.

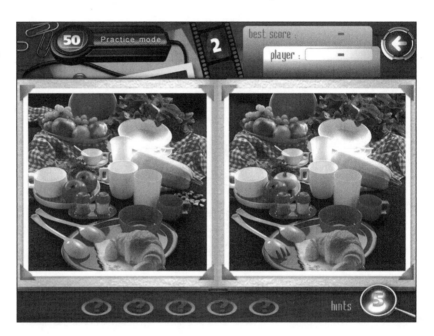

When What's the Difference? is first started, the Home screen will let you start a new game or continue with a game you left earlier, as shown in Figure 10.11.

Tap the How to Play option to reveal the simple instructions for the app. One way the game assists you is with hints. Tap the magnifying glass and a hint will flash on the photo. But be careful: there are only five hints per game played. Once you're out of hints, you're on your own.

To begin play, tap the New Game option, and the three modes of play for What's the Difference? will be shown (see Figure 10.12).

Figure 10.11

The What's the Difference? home menu.

Figure 10.12

Three ways to play What's the Difference?.

* **Survival.** Players get a time limit to find the five differences. If they don't find the differences in time, the game is over.
* **Challenge.** Players find differences as fast as they can, with bonus time added for speed.
* **Practice.** Sixty seconds are allowed for finding differences in every picture. This allows for slower play.

To pause any game, tap the red arrow button in the upper right of the screen to return to the Home screen.

Though the rules of What's the Difference? are very easy—especially in Practice mode—this is likely a game that older children will enjoy. That's because the pictures are incredibly detailed and the differences can be hard to find. You may want to play along with your children to assist them on some of the pictures, until they get the hang of how to spot differences.

If your children are visually oriented, this is one app that will sharpen their observational skills.

Abracadabra with Math Magic

 Cost of Math Magic HD: $0.99

By now, children are likely familiar with basic math concepts like counting, as well as rudimentary addition and subtraction. You can build on these concepts and start children practicing basic math with Math Magic.

Math Magic has a lot of interesting features that should make it attractive for parents. The first great feature is its ability to set up the application to be personalized for any child playing the app and also able to receive status reports on the child's progress in the app via email. This additional reporting service, plus the flexibility to increase the difficulty of the questions, makes Math Magic an app that can be used all the way from preschool to third grade.

Personalize Math Magic

When Math Magic is first started, a splash screen will appear inviting parents to sign up for the parent reporting service. To start the process, tap the Yes, I'm a Parent button and then enter your email address in the appropriate field.

If you are wondering if this is worth the effort, keep in mind that if you have more than one child at different ages or learning levels, tracking their efforts within Math Magic is key to accurate tracking. It also makes Math Magic flexible for a wider range of kids.

In a few minutes, an email will appear in your inbox. Using any email client, open the email message and click (or tap) the link included in the message from SmarTots. SmarTots is the third-party service that provides the reports for Math Magic, along with quite a few other apps. If you already have a SmarTots account, you can log in to the SmarTots Web site and the connection to the Math Magic app will be established.

If you are new to SmarTots, you will need to provide a new password to enable your SmarTots account.

After you create a SmarTots account, you can personalize the game for children playing the app, either within Math Magic or on the SmarTots site.

Keeping to Yourself

If you would rather not divulge your email to a third-party service, your child can still use Math Magic to its fullest extent. The only features missing will be reporting and any personalization of the app.

To customize Math Magic for a child:

1. Tap the Parents icon. A confirmation screen will appear (see Figure 10.13).

Figure 10.13

Math proves you're a parent.

2. Enter the answer to the given question within the time limit and tap Go. A SmarTots screen will appear (see Figure 10.14).

Figure 10.14

Other SmarTots apps.

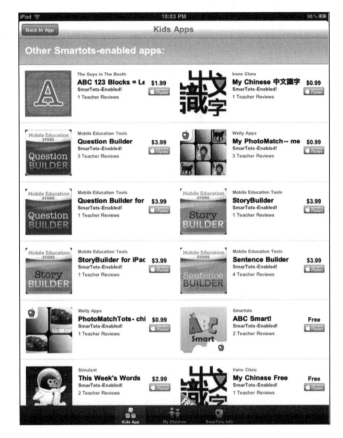

3. Tap the My Children option. The My Children page will appear (see Figure 10.15).

Figure 10.15

Adding a child.

4. If this is the first child to be added, tap the My Child listing. Otherwise, tap the Add Another Child button. The Edit Children screen will appear (see Figure 10.16).

![The Edit Children screen showing "Edit Children" title, "Personalize this App for your Child" heading, "Your Child's Name" with "Hello, My Child" field, "Get Age-Specific Recommendations (optional)" section, "Birthday Apr 14, 2011" field, and Submit/Cancel buttons.]

Personalize this App for your Child

Your Child's Name

Let your kids see their name and face whenever they play this app.

Hello,

My Child

(Edit Photo)

Get Age-Specific Recommendations (optional)

The SmarTots recommendation engine uses this info and usage data to send you custom app recommendations. This profile is not viewable by the public.

Birthday   Apr 14, 2011

[**Submit**]   [**Cancel**]

5. Enter the child's name.

6. If you have a picture of the child, tap the Edit Photo icon. The Choose image action menu will appear.

7. iPad 2 users can tap Take a picture. A small Camera action menu will appear, which can be used to take a photo of the child.

   or

7. iPad users should tap Camera Roll. The Camera Roll action menu will appear.

8. Tap the photo to use. The photo will appear in the Choose Photo action menu.

9. Resize the photo until the image of the child appears in the high-lighted box and then tap Use. The photo will appear next to the child's name.

10. To get age-oriented suggestions from SmarTots, tap the Birthday field. The Enter Your Child's Birthdate screen will appear (see Figure 10.17).

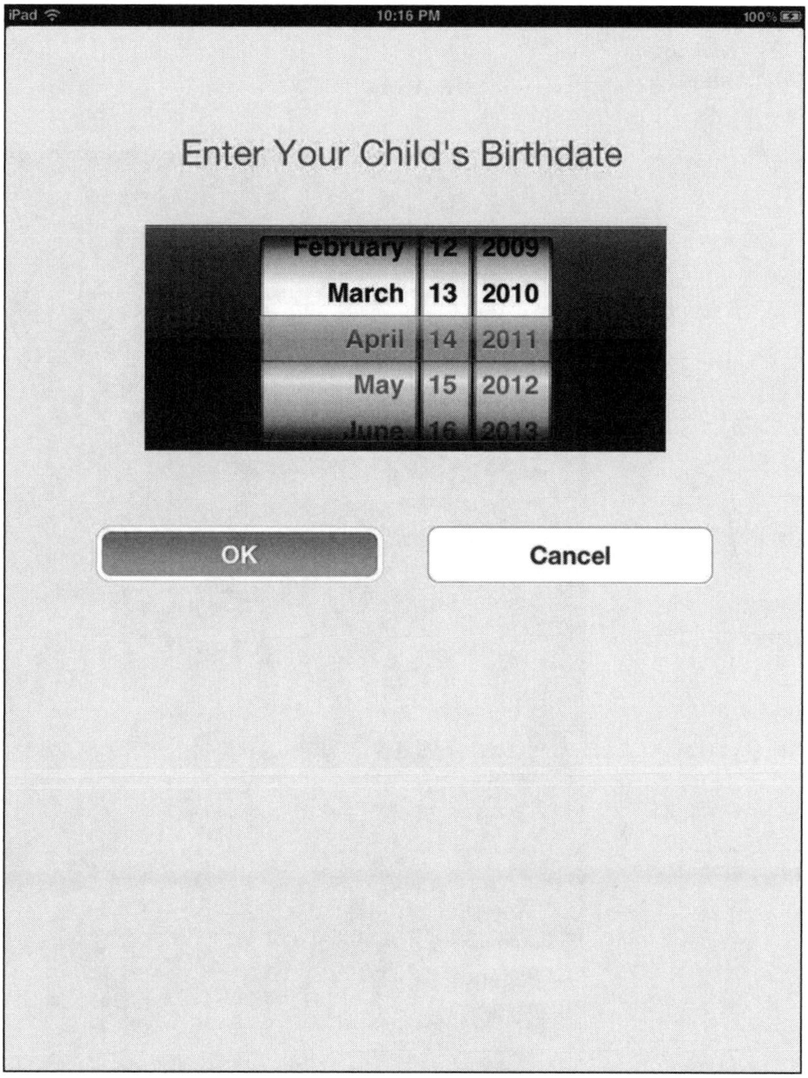

Figure 10.17

The Enter Your Child's Birthdate screen.

11. Use the picker controls to select your child's birth date and tap OK. The date will be entered.

12. Tap Submit. The My Children screen will appear.

13. Tap Back to App. The Math Magic screen will appear with a welcome message for the child (see Figure 10.18).

Figure 10.18

*The custom
Welcome screen.*

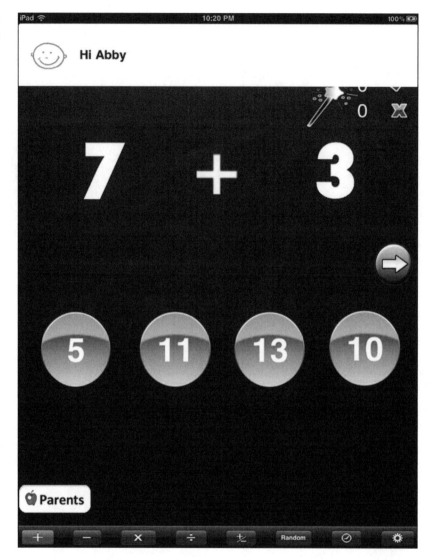

Once the SmarTots account is created, you can log on to the SmarTots site at any time from any browser and navigate to the Reports screen to see your child's participation with Math Magic or any SmarTots-enabled app (see Figure 10.19).

Figure 10.19

Viewing a child's report.

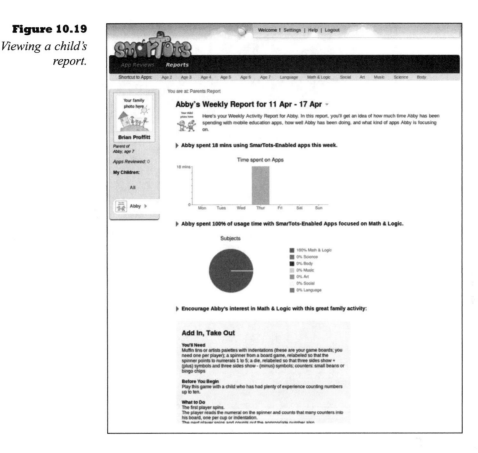

Play Math Magic

Math Magic can be played in one of two ways: Practice mode and Challenge mode.

Within practice mode, players can select what kind of math problems they want to solve: addition, subtraction, multiplication, and division. There is also an addition-subtraction combination option and a random option that will throw out any kind of question, based on the difficulty options set.

As children play the game, they will be given a math question and then can choose from one of four possible answers (see Figure 10.20). Correct and incorrect answers are tracked in the upper-right corner of the app. In practice mode, this tracking continues for as long as the child remains within a certain family of problems (such as addition). If the child switches to another family, then the tracking is reset.

Figure 10.20

*Answering
questions in
Math Magic.*

Once a question is answered correctly, the app will present the next question in the set. If a question is incorrectly answered, the problem will remain on the screen until it is answered correctly.

In challenge mode, questions are presented based on the options set by the parent in the Preferences screen. If challenge questions are set for subtraction, for instance, then those will be the types of questions presented, regardless of what family of questions the child was working with in practice mode.

Challenges are also to be done in a certain amount of time. The initial time is one minute, though this duration can be changed as well.

Once the challenge is completed, a Great Job splash screen will appear with the final tally of correct and incorrect problems. Tapping the splash screen will start another challenge. Challenges will continue until another type of practice mode problem is selected.

Customize Math Magic

As alluded to in the beginning of this section, Math Magic is a game that can be customized quite nicely for children with any level of math skills.

To customize Math Magic, tap the Preferences icon in the lower-right corner of the screen. The Preferences screen will appear, as seen in Figure 10.21.

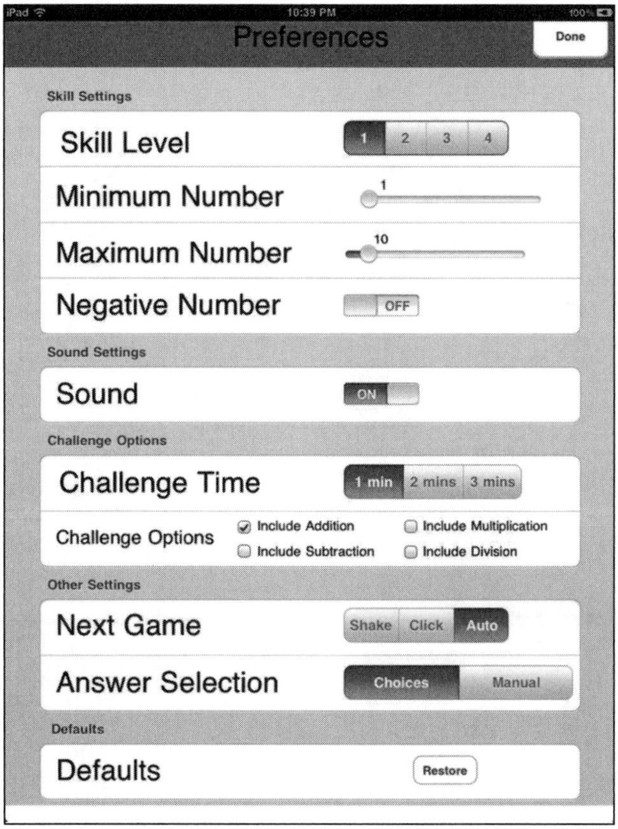

Figure 10.21

The Preferences screen.

In the Skill Settings section, you can set the difficulty for practice and challenge questions to a very exacting level. The Skill Levels will set the difficulty to predefined settings, but you can tap and slide the Minimum and Maximum Number controls to set the level of problems to be easier or harder than these preset levels. You can even add negative numbers to the mix of questions.

If you want to alter challenge options, tap the duration period you want for the Challenge Time and choose which sets of questions will be included in challenges.

By default, Math Magic is set to proceed to the next game when finished with a game. If you or your child would prefer to have the control in your hands, tap the Shake or Click button to determine how a new game will be started manually.

Another way of increasing the difficulty of the app is removing the multiple-choice answers for each question. Tap the Manual option, and players will need to enter their answers directly, as shown in Figure 10.22.

To return to the game, tap the Done button.

Figure 10.22

Answering questions directly.

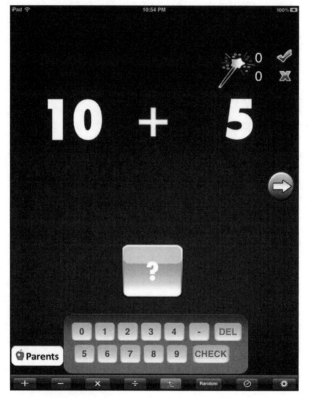

Conclusion

As children get ready for their first day of school, there's a lot to be said for preparing them before they walk into their first classroom. The apps in this chapter are among the best examples of apps that can make that preparation fun and rewarding.

But the learning with the iPad doesn't stop when they get to school. In Chapter 11, "Apps for Kindergarten," we'll explore the best apps for students in kindergarten and how they can supplement the learning they are starting to get in their first classroom.

Chapter 11

Apps for
Kindergarten

I t is, for many parents, a day yearned for and dreaded at the same time. The day when their precious child, who has been the center of their universe for the past five years, leaves home to explore the wide open world of school. And naptime.

In the United States, kindergarten is a familiar rite of passage for many parents and children in the fall of their fifth or sixth year, though curiously kindergarten is only compulsory in 12 states, even though every state-run school district offers it. For many families, kindergarten is an accepted part of the learning process, a celebration of their children's entry onto the educational path they will be walking for many years to come.

In recent years, kindergarten has moved from more of a transition year for students to one that acts as a head start for students to get ahead on their academic careers. Some would argue the thoughts behind these policies, but this seems to be the reality in many U.S. school districts. Because of these higher expectations, many parents and teachers are open to any tools that can help their kindergarteners acclimate.

Now that children are older, they are likely to be much more well versed in using the iPad, and will feel freer to explore topics and games independently. Parents should not worry about this; in fact, they should encourage a little more independent play. But hey, let's be clear: there's independent, and there's independent. Don't give kids so much free range that the iPad ends up out in the sandbox or in the swimming pool.

In this chapter, you will learn how to

* Build reading and spelling skills with Word Magic.
* Practice math and reading with TeachMe: Kindergarten.
* Create sentences and words with Super Why!.

Word Magic Hocus Pocus

 Cost of Word Magic: $0.99

Now that letters and phonics are becoming part of your child's regular education, it's a good time to start reinforcing those skills. The Word Magic app will let your child do just that.

If you have read Chapter 10, "Apps for Pre-Kindergarten," then Word Magic will immediately look very familiar to you, since Anusen also makes Math Magic. Word Magic is very similar to Math Magic in its look and feel, including the capability to personalize the app for any child playing it and to use the SmarTots service for status reports on the child's progress in the app via email. This additional reporting service, plus the flexibility to increase the difficulty of the words, makes Word Magic a flexible app that can be used beyond kindergarten.

Personalize Word Magic

When Word Magic is first started, a splash screen will appear inviting parents to sign up to the SmarTots parent reporting service (see Figure 11.1). For new SmarTots uses, tap the Yes, I'm a Parent button and then enter your email address in the appropriate field.

In a few minutes, an email will appear in your inbox. Using any email client, open the email message and click (or tap) the link included in the message from SmarTots. SmarTots is the third-party service that provides the reports for Word Magic, along with quite a few other apps.

If you are new to SmarTots, you will need to provide a new password to enable your SmarTots account. After you create a SmarTots account, you can personalize the game for children playing the app, either within Word Magic or on the SmarTots site.

If you have already signed up for a SmarTots account, within any game that uses the service, you will be shown a Connect to SmarTots popover screen that will enable you to simply connect Word Magic to the SmarTots service (as shown in Figure 11.2).

Figure 11.1

Establishing a SmarTots account.

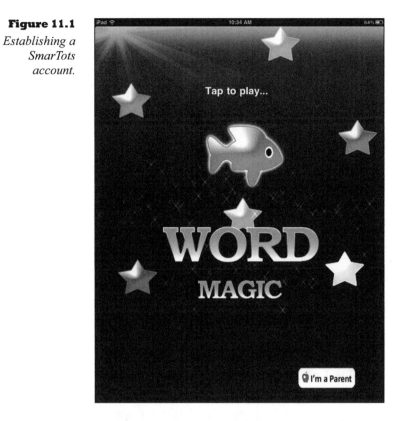

Figure 11.2

Connect to an existing SmarTots account.

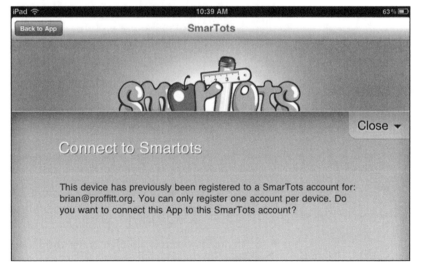

Tap Connect and Word Magic will be connected to the SmarTots system (see Step 3 and the next Tip).

To customize Word Magic for a child, follow these steps:

1. Tap the Parents icon. A confirmation screen will appear.

2. Enter the answer to the given question within the time limit and tap Go. A SmarTots screen will appear.

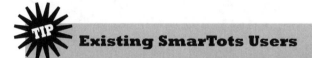

Existing SmarTots Users

If you already have a SmarTots account and tapped Connect when first starting the Word Magic app, you should start here at Step 3 to continue the process of customizing Word Magic for your child. If all of your children are entered, you can skip these steps, as SmarTots will have already supplied the information.

3. Tap the My Children option. The My Children page will appear.

4. If this is the first child to be added, tap the My Child listing. Otherwise, tap the Add Another Child button. The Edit Children screen will appear.

5. Enter the child's name.

6. If you have a picture of the child, tap the Edit Photo icon. The Choose image action menu will appear.

7. iPad 2 users can tap Take a picture. A small Camera action menu will appear, which can be used to take a photo of the child.

    or

7. iPad users should tap Camera Roll. The Camera Roll action menu will appear.

8. Tap the photo to use. The photo will appear in the Choose Photo action menu.

9. Resize the photo until the image of the child appears in the highlighted box and then tap Use. The photo will appear next to the child's name.

10. To get age-oriented suggestions from SmarTots, tap the Birthday field. The Enter Your Child's Birthdate screen will appear.

11. Use the picker controls to select your child's birth date and tap OK. The date will be entered.

12. Tap Submit. The My Children screen will appear.

13. Tap Back to App. The Word Magic screen will appear with a welcome message for your child.

Once the SmarTots account is created, you can log on to the SmarTots site at any time from any browser and navigate to the Reports screen to see your child's participation with Word Magic or any SmarTots-enabled app.

Play Word Magic

Word Magic is a flash-card game that can be played in one of two ways: Practice mode and Challenge mode.

Within Practice mode, players continuously step through the presented words, each pronounced by the narrator and with one or two letters missing.

As the child plays the game, he will be given a word with missing letters and can choose from one of four possible letters (see Figure 11.3). Correct and incorrect answers are tracked in the upper-right corner of the app. In Practice mode, this tracking continues for as long as the child plays. Tracking is reset when a new game is started.

Figure 11.3

Spelling in Word Magic.

Once a word is spelled correctly, the app will present the next question in the set. If a word is spelled incorrectly, the problem will remain on the screen until it is answered correctly.

In Challenge mode, words are presented based on the options set by the parent in the Preferences screen. If challenge worlds are set for the phonetics family, for instance, then those will be the types of words presented, regardless of what family of words the child was working with in Practice mode.

Challenges are also supposed to be done in a certain amount of time. The default time is one minute, although this duration can be changed as well.

Once the challenge is completed, a Great Job splash screen will appear with the final tally of correct and incorrect words. Tapping the splash screen will start another challenge. Challenges will continue until another type of Practice mode is selected.

There are two Game modes within Word Magic: Missing Letters and Phonetics.

In Phonetics mode, one or two letters will be missing from the words, in any position within the word. If two letters are missing, those letters will always be together: all letters must form a single sound, such as "gh," "ph," or "ee."

Missing Letters mode gives players a little more control over which letters are missing. Tap the buttons on the top of the screen to enable the different sets of words (see Figure 11.4).

* **_ord.** The first letter of each word is missing.
* **w_rd.** An interior letter of each word is missing.
* **wor_.** The last letter of each word is missing.
* **Random.** Any letter within each word could be missing.

In Missing Letters, only one letter at a time will be removed from any given word. Also, the tracking for each set of words will be reset whenever a new set of words is selected.

Figure 11.4

*Choosing
Missing Letters
modes in Word
Magic.*

Customize Word Magic

Like Math Magic, Word Magic is a game that can be customized for several levels of reading and spelling skill.

To customize Word Magic, tap the Preferences icon in the upper-right corner of the screen. The Preferences screen will appear, as seen in Figure 11.5.

In the Answers Selection section, you can choose the Game mode for the player.

In the Settings for Phonetics mode section, select the types of words you want to be included in the practice sets. You can even have the game provide multisyllabic words.

Choosing skills levels is a little more quantifiable in the Settings for Missing Letters mode section. Parents can select the Maximum Word length (from three to six letters), as well as one of two levels of difficulty.

If you want to change challenge options, tap the duration period you want for the Challenge Time, and choose which sets of questions will be included in challenges.

Figure 11.5

The Preferences screen.

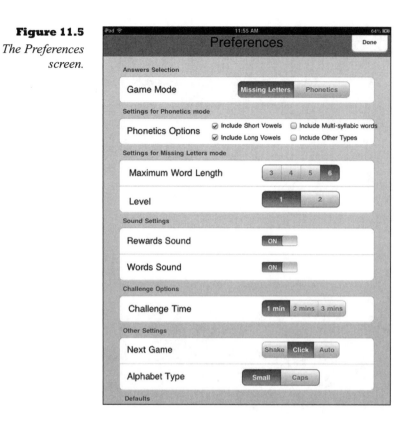

By default, Word Magic is set to proceed to the next word when finished with a word. If you or your child would prefer to have the control in your hands, tap the Shake or Click button to determine how a new word will be presented.

To return to the game, tap the Done button.

Build Skills with TeachMe: Kindergarten

 Cost of TeachMe: Kindergarten: $0.99

Word Magic and Math Magic are great games that target spelling and math skills for players, respectively, and the SmarTots reporting system makes these games even more helpful for parents interested in tracking their child's learning progress. They are not the only apps that will help children learn these basic skills.

Part of 24x7digital's TeachMe series of apps, TeachMe: Kindergarten combines learning of math and spelling with reading by adding Dolch sight words to the app. And, to make the game more fun for kids, a reward system is used in the app that gives players fun incentives as they go.

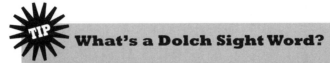

What's a Dolch Sight Word?

If you aren't familiar with Dolch sight words, they are an educational tool used in English-speaking countries to teach 220 of the most commonly used service words found in English text. Because these are so common, sight words can comprise anywhere from 50 to 70 percent of an average passage of text. You can see why learning them is a good idea.

Because some Dolch sight words are not intuitively sounded out, usually educators teach them by rote memorization, hence "sight" words. For kindergarten, these sight words include "all," "am," "are," "at," and "ate"... just for starters.

Configuring TeachMe: Kindergarten

Before your child can play TeachMe: Kindergarten, you will need to set the app for at least one of the children playing the game. This process begins from the initial splash screen, shown in Figure 11.6.

1. Tap one of the Empty child icons. The Add Player screen will appear (see Figure 11.7).

2. Type the child's name into the Name field.

3. If you have a picture of the child, tap the Photo icon. The Photo action menu will appear.

4. iPad 2 users can tap Take Photo. A small Camera action menu will appear, which can be used to take a photo of the child.

or

4. iPad users should tap Choose a Photo. The Photo Albums action menu will appear.

5. Tap the photo album where your photo is saved.

6. Tap the photo to use. The photo will appear in the Choose Photo action menu.

7. Resize the photo until the image of the child appears in the highlighted box and then tap Use. The photo will appear next to the child's name.

8. Tap Done on the keyboard. The TeachMe: Kindergarten Home screen will appear.

Figure 11.6

The initial TeachMe: Kindergarten splash screen.

Figure 11.7

Adding a player to TeachMe: Kindergarten.

To start playing TeachMe: Kindergarten, tap the player name to open the player's Home screen (see Figure 11.8).

Figure 11.8

A player's Home screen.

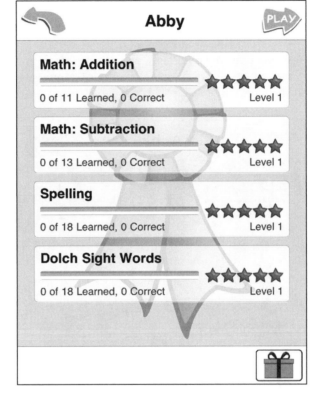

Paying for Extra Players

While TeachMe: Kindergarten is only $0.99 to purchase, any players beyond the first player must buy access to the game to play at a cost of $1.99 each. This should be noted if you plan to have more than one child play TeachMe: Kindergarten.

Playing TeachMe: Kindergarten

Once TeachMe: Kindergarten is started, each player's Home screen will display his individual progress in the four categories of learning used in TeachMe: Kindergarten.

Math: Addition. Simple addition problems.

 Math: Subtraction. Simple subtraction problems.

 Spelling. Filling in missing letters to complete spelling words.

 Dolch Sight Words. Multiple-choice questions that players use to identify one of the Dolch sight words.

To begin play, tap the Play icon in the upper-right corner of the screen. A random screen from one of the four learning categories will appear, as shown in Figure 11.9.

Figure 11.9

A sample spelling screen.

The animated Mini Mouse will tell the player the instructions for each screen, but essentially the math and spelling games are played by tapping and dragging the appropriate number or letter from the choices on the bottom of the screen to the blank line in the equation or word presented.

For spelling, that is pretty much the extent of the game play. If an incorrect answer is given, Mini Mouse will let the player know, and the player can try again. The player will not, however, have a successful retry counted for her score.

In the Math: Addition screens, players can get extra help by adding objects to the screen and then counting them individually. This is done by tapping the plus icon on the chute, shown in Figure 11.10. Once all the objects are added to the screen, they can be counted, thus helping the player get the correct solution.

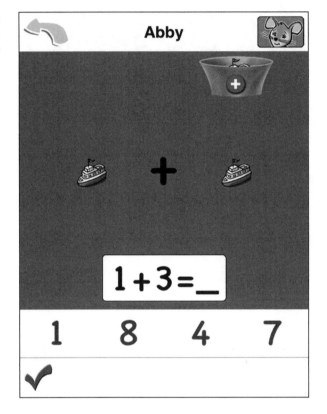

Math: Subtraction offers another way to help players get the problems solved. In Figure 11.11, you can see an example of a subtraction problem. If players get stuck, they can tap and drag the correct number of objects into the trash can. Players can then count the remaining objects by tapping each one individually. This will help them determine the correct answer to tap and drag to the solution line.

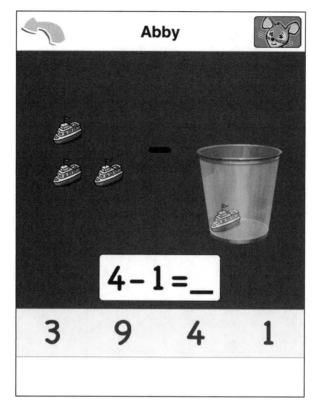

The Dolch sight words offer a completely different way to play. Mini Mouse asks the players to find a given word in the four choices presented (see Figure 11.12). Once the correct word is tapped, the problem is solved.

After three correct answers are given, TeachMe: Kindergarten players are awarded a single coin on the Coin screen, shown in Figure 11.13.

Once a certain number of coins are collected, players can start spending them on various items like stickers or food for a virtual aquarium's fishes. Tap the gift box icon to open the Rewards screen, shown in Figure 11.14.

Figure 11.12

Choose the right sight word.

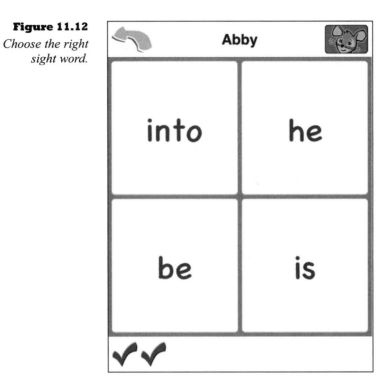

Figure 11.13

Earn coins for correct answers.

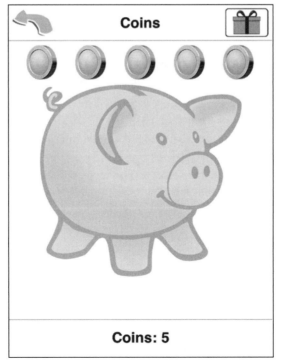

Figure 11.14

Spend coins for neat rewards.

To spend coins, swipe the Rewards screen to find the theme in which you want to purchase reward items. In the Stickers screens, players can buy theme-based stickers, following these steps:

1. Tap one of the sticker screens. The screen will open to the selected scene (see Figure 11.15).

2. Tap the grocery cart icon. A screen full of sticker objects will appear (see Figure 11.16).

3. Tap an object to select it. The scene will change to Mini Mouse ringing up the purchase on a cash register (see Figure 11.17).

Figure 11.15

An empty sticker scene.

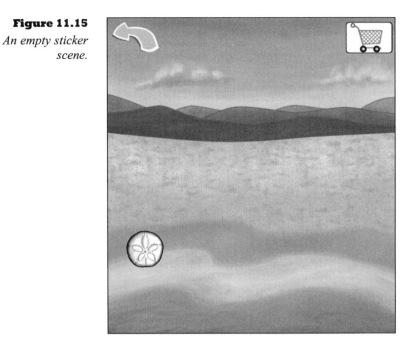

Figure 11.16

Sticker objects for a scene.

Figure 11.17

Purchasing a sticker.

4. Tap the coin-in-hand button. The sticker will be purchased for the stated amount and will then appear in the sticker scene.

5. Tap and drag the sticker to place it on the screen.

6. Tap the Exit icon to leave the scene.

Like many kindergarten classrooms, TeachMe: Kindergarten even gives you an aquarium where you can use your coins to buy sand, plants, food, and fish. The process is similar to buying stickers, but more coins are needed. Food can go for as little as one coin, but fish start at five coins.

Rather than the simplistic sticker albums, working with the aquarium actually gives kids a better feel for saving their funds to buy the various items for the aquarium, especially food, which doesn't last forever.

1. In the Rewards screen, tap the Aquarium screen. The screen will open to the aquarium (see Figure 11.18).

Figure 11.18

An aquarium to fill.

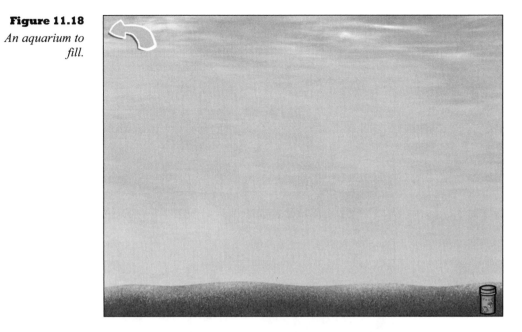

2. Tap the Food icon. The aquarium toolbar will appear (see Figure 11.19).

Figure 11.19

Shop or feed fish.

3. Tap the Fish Store icon. The Fish Store screen will open (see Figure 11.20).

Figure 11.20

Lots of things for sale in the Fish Store.

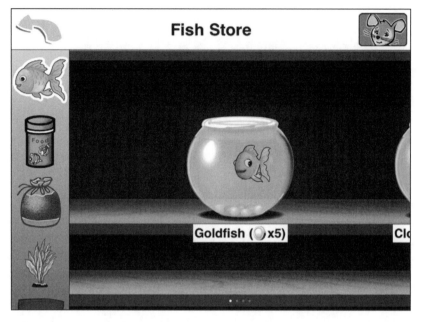

4. Tap the type of item you want to buy. The products for the type selected will appear.

5. Tap the item to buy. The shopping toolbar will appear.

6. Tap the grocery cart icon. The scene will change to Mini Mouse ringing up the purchase on a cash register

7. Tap the coin-in-hand button. The item will be purchased for the stated amount and will then appear in the aquarium toolbar (see Figure 11.21).

8. Tap and drag the item to the designated location on the screen. The item will behave as it would in an actual aquarium.

9. Tap the Exit icon to leave the aquarium.

Figure 11.21

*Get your fish
ready to swim.*

Configure TeachMe: Kindergarten

As a parent, you can manage TeachMe: Kindergarten in quite a few ways
to make it more or less challenging for your child.

As the app is played, math and word questions will be "learned" and not
repeated within TeachMe: Kindergarten for the level of play the child is
working with. This setting usually occurs after the question has been
answered correctly a predetermined number of times in a row (the
default is twice). You can control this setting and many more to match
TeachMe: Kindergarten to your child's pace. To reach the settings for
your child, follow these steps:

1. Tap the Players button on the TeachMe: Kindergarten Home screen.
   The Players screen will appear, as shown in Figure 11.22.

2. Tap the player to manage. The player's Settings screen will open
   (see Figure 11.23).

3. To adjust the number of times a question must be correctly answered
   to learn it, tap the # to Learn Question option. The # in a row to
   Learn screen will appear.

4. Tap the option suited for your child. The option is selected.

5. Tap the back icon. The user Settings screen will appear.

6. To change the number of correct answers a player must have to earn
   a coin, tap the # Correct to earn reward option. The # Correct for
   reward screen will appear.

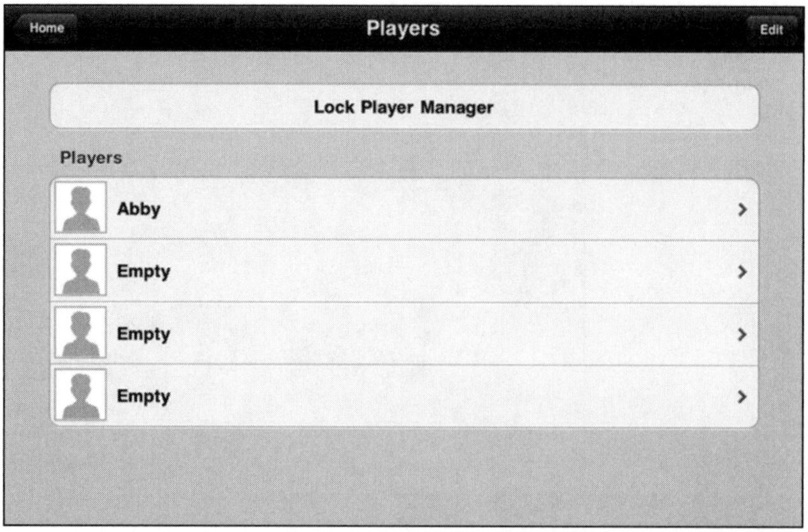

iPad for Kids

Figure 11.22
The main Players screen.

Home	Players	Edit

Lock Player Manager

Players

Abby   >

Empty   >

Empty   >

Empty   >

Figure 11.23
An individual player screen.

Players	Abby

Settings

Abby   >

Correct to earn reward   3 >

Rewards   >

Show Exit button   ON

to Learn Question   2 >

TeachMe Topics

ON   Math: Addition >
  Level 1

ON   Math: Subtraction >
  Level 1

ON   Spelling >
  Level 1

ON   Dolch Sight Words >
  Level 1

Reset

Reset Player

214

7. Tap the option suited for your child. The option is selected.

8. Tap the back icon. The user Settings screen will appear.

9. To customize the questions in a topic, tap the topic option. The Topic screen will appear (see Figure 11.24).

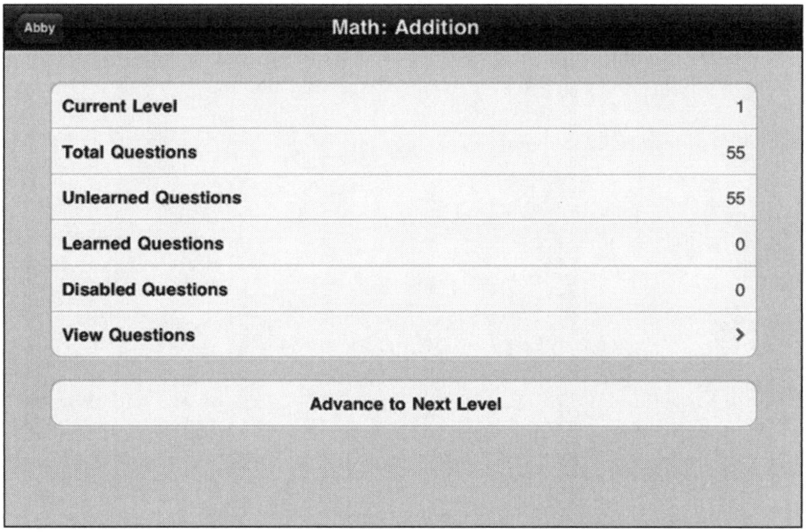

Figure 11.24

Configure topics.

10. To advance the player to a higher level, tap the Advance to Next Level button. A confirmation message will appear.

11. Tap Advance to confirm the change. The level will be increased by one, and a fifth of the questions will be learned.

12. You can see all questions for the topic by tapping the View Questions option. The topic questions screen will open (see Figure 11.25).

13. Tap on an individual question to change its status. The question's status screen will appear.

14. Tap the option suited for your child. The option is selected.

15. Tap the back icon. The topic questions screen will appear.

16. Tap the back icon. The Topic screen will appear.

17. Tap the back icon. The user Settings screen will appear.

18. Tap the back icon. The Players screen will appear.

19. Tap the back icon. The Home screen will appear.

Figure 11.25

Configure individual questions.

Math: Addition	Math: Addition		
Unlearned	Learned	Disabled	All
1 + 5 Last 3 Answers: None			Unlearned >
1 + 6 Last 3 Answers: None			Unlearned >
1 + 7 Last 3 Answers: None			Unlearned >
1 + 8 Last 3 Answers: None			Unlearned >
1 + 9 Last 3 Answers: None			Unlearned >
2 + 4 Last 3 Answers: None			Unlearned >
2 + 5 Last 3 Answers: None			Unlearned >
2 + 6 Last 3 Answers: None			Unlearned >
2 + 7 Last 3 Answers: None			Unlearned >
2 + 8 Last 3 Answers: None			Unlearned >
3 + 3 Last 3 Answers: None			Unlearned >
3 + 4 Last 3 Answers: None			Unlearned >
3 + 5 Last 3 Answers: None			Unlearned >
3 + 6 Last 3 Answers: None			Unlearned >
3 + 7 Last 3 Answers: None			Unlearned >
3 + 0 Last 3 Answers: None			Unlearned >
4 + 1 Last 3 Answers: None			Unlearned >
4 + 2 Last 3 Answers: None			Unlearned >
4 + 3 Last 3 Answers: None			Unlearned >
4 + 4 Last 3 Answers: None			Unlearned >
4 + 5 Last 3 Answers: None			Unlearned >

Super Learning with Super Why!

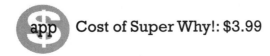 Cost of Super Why!: $3.99

Sometimes kids just need a hero to show them the way. The PBS children's show *Super Why!* reveals the adventures of a quartet of (very) young superheroes who use their literary powers to save the day and make reading fun.

PBS has expanded on its early childhood program with a great app by the same name. The app features the four heroes in separate adventures designed to boost reading, spelling, and sentence construction.

The four games are available from the game's Home screen (see Figure 11.26). Tapping on each character's icon will start the respective game. Each game has a very robust help system, so very little instruction or configuration is needed.

Figure 11.26

The Super Why! Home screen.

  ✻ **Super Why's Story Saver.** Sentences are read to the children and
    then they are to choose the missing word in the sentence by tapping
    it (see Figure 11.27).

Figure 11.27

Super Why's Story Saver.

❋ **Princess Presto's Wand Up Writing.** Players will listen to the phonetic sound of a letter and then tap the letter associated with that sound. Players can then trace the letter on the screen to write the letter on the screen, eventually creating a new word, as shown in Figure 11.28.

Figure 11.28

Princess Presto's Wand Up Writing.

❋ **Wonder Red's Rhyming Time.** Players can listen to a word and then tap on the rhyming word to progress in the game (see Figure 11.29).

Figure 11.29

Wonder Red's Rhyming Time.

✳ **Alpha Pig's Lickety Letter Hunt.** Players are given a letter to find and then must tap it to continue on the right path and eventually spell an entire word (see Figure 11.30).

Figure 11.30

Alpha Pig's Lickety Letter Hunt.

All of these games are enjoyable for kindergarteners and slightly younger children, and should provide a lot of enjoyment while learning.

Conclusion

Kindergarten is an exciting new time for children and parents alike, with lots of new experiences and learning to do. The apps featured in this chapter are specifically designed to aid kindergarteners practice the skills they are learning at school and prepare for concepts they will be learning later.

In Chapter 12, "Apps for First Grade," we'll explore the best apps for students in what is usually the first all-day school experience, where basic reading and math skills are still taught, as well as more diverse subjects.

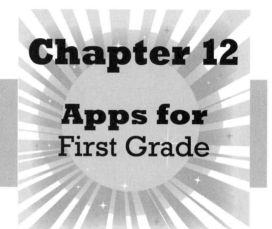

Chapter 12

Apps for
First Grade

For students in the United States, first grade is typically the start of "real" academic work. In many locations, it means a full day's worth of school and new subjects like social studies, science, and even history in some schools.

By now, students are well on their way to grouping and organizing 100 objects at a time, while also getting a handle on simple fractions, such as $\frac{1}{2}$ or $\frac{1}{4}$. They should also be working with addition and subtraction problems with numbers that can add up to 99.

In language, writing skills are starting to be polished up, with sentence structure and spelling at the top of the priority list. Story concepts and creation skills are being learned, and in reading, students are working on recognizing phonetic parts of words so they can blend the sounds together when they run into unfamiliar words.

Students exploring history and social studies are focusing on local and perhaps national history to some extent, and simple geography, such as directions and map reading. In the U.S., states might be covered as well.

Right now, children will be getting better equipped to separate games for fun and games for learning when they use the iPad. This is not meant to be discouraging, but it does mean that parents will need to pay attention to the apps their children use to be sure they are more engaging.

In this chapter, you and your student will learn how to

* Start creating sentences with Sentence Builder.
* Practice handwriting skills with Letter Lab.
* Enhance reading with Phonics Made Easy.
* Manage higher math concepts with Time, Money & Fractions.
* Learn about the United States in Stack the States.
* Explore the planet with Google Earth.

Formulating with Sentence Builder

 Cost of Sentence Builder: $3.99

Anyone who's ever written something down understands that there's a big difference between the process of verbal communication and written communication. In some ways, verbal communication is a lot easier: facial expressions and gestures can help get our point across faster, sometimes, than the written word.

Writing gets short shrift these days in a world where visual media is so easy. But writing is permanent, and when done correctly can inspire and inform readers for a long time.

In the first grade, children have started to read with a fair bit of confidence, and they are now able to put words together into sentences. That's the object of Sentence Builder, another SmarTots-enabled game designed to make sentence creation easy.

Personalize Sentence Builder

When Sentence Builder is first started, a splash screen will appear for players to enter their name. Parents can also sign up for or log in to the SmarTots parent reporting service (see Figure 12.1).

New SmarTots users can tap the Parents Center button and then enter their email address in the appropriate field. In a few minutes, an email will appear in your inbox. Using any email client, open the email message and click (or tap) the link included in the message from SmarTots. SmarTots is the third-party service that provides the reports for Sentence Builder, along with quite a few other apps.

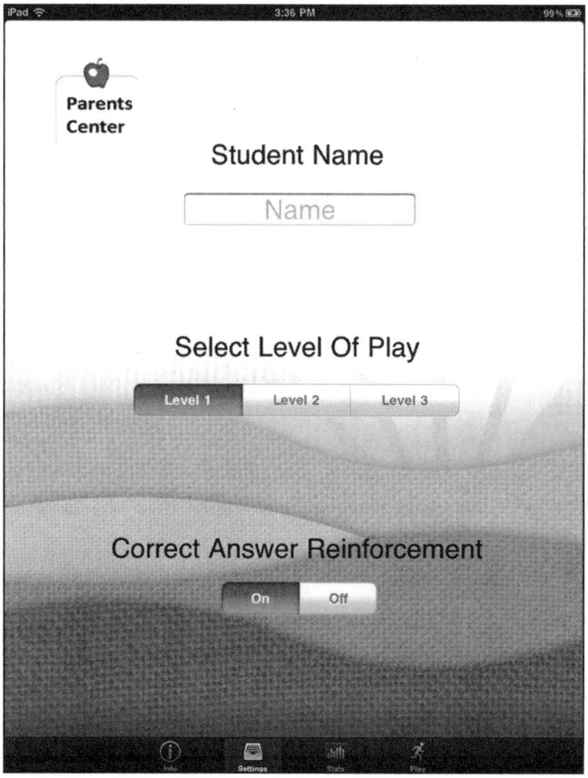

Figure 12.1

The Sentence Builder Settings screen.

If you are new to SmarTots, you will need to provide a new password to enable your SmarTots account. After you create a SmarTots account, you can personalize the game for children playing the app, either within Sentence Builder or on the SmarTots site.

If you have already signed up for a SmarTots account, within any game that uses the service, you will be shown a Connect to SmarTots popover screen that will enable you to simply connect Sentence Builder to the SmarTots service.

Tap Connect and Sentence Builder will be connected to the SmarTots system.

To customize Sentence Builder:

1. Enter the child's name in the Student Name field.
2. Tap the level of play.
3. Tap the desired setting for answer reinforcement.
4. Tap the Play icon. The Play screen will appear (see Figure 12.2), and the game will begin.

Figure 12.2

*Playing
Sentence
Builder.*

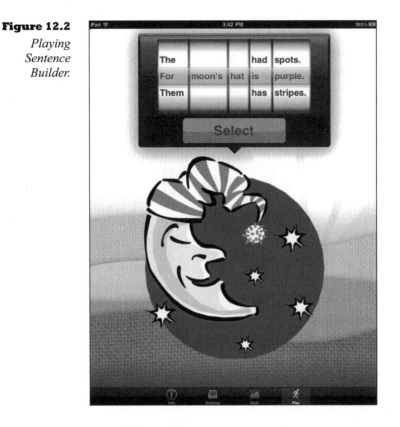

Once the SmarTots account is created, you can log on to the SmarTots site at any time from any browser and navigate to the Reports screen to see your child's participation with Sentence Builder or any SmarTots-enabled app.

Play Sentence Builder

Sentence Builder is designed to enable students to build sentences—hence the name. But not just any sentence: constructs must correctly and grammatically describe an image displayed on the screen.

There are three levels of play that can be used in Sentence Builder:

* **Level 1.** The subject and its adjective are fixed. Players must select the correct modifier and verb for the sentence.
* **Level 2.** Players select the adjective, modifier, and verb for a given sentence, but they may be given just two, three, or five choices for each sentence component.
* **Level 3.** The player chooses each component of the sentence, and has five choices for each component.

It is very important to start out at the beginning levels and not overwhelm your children. Watch as they learn to determine when they can advance to the next level.

Figure 12.3 shows a typical Level 1 sentence. "Fish" (the subject) and "silly" (the adjective) are fixed; players must use the picker wheels to create a proper sentence with the modifier and verb components.

Figure 12.3

A simple sentence to build.

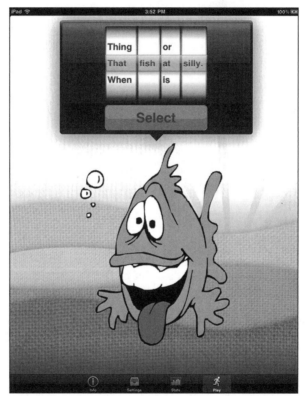

Once a sentence is constructed, the player taps the Select button. If the sentence is correct, then the app will congratulate the player and (if the answer reinforcement setting is activated) repeat the correct sentence back to the player.

If a sentence is incorrect, the app will encourage the child to try again.

When a sentence is completed, the player can tap the Next Sentence button to get another sentence to build.

To view the progress of your child, you can tap the Stats icon and view the Stats screen.

For a more complete report (that is properly spelled), tap the Settings icon and then the Parents Center to get a report from the SmarTots system.

As games go, there are not a lot of rules, but there is a lot to learn as sentences are formed.

Put It in Writing with Letter Lab

 Cost of Letter Lab: $0.99

There's another aspect of writing that's also getting pushed aside these days because of keyboards on computers and phones: handwriting.

In kindergarten and first grade, print, not cursive, is the rule of the day, and Letter Lab is a great way of applying the touch-screen technology of the iPad to practice the skills of handwriting. But first, you will need to get another piece of hardware for your iPad.

Moving Beyond Fingers

Thus far, every application in this book can be interfaced via the usual method: your fingers. Letter Lab, however, requires a bit finer control. Plus, there's the whole point of the app, which is teaching players to handwrite using a pen, crayon, or other writing implement. Yes, you can use Letter Lab with your fingers, but that sort of misses the point.

(Younger children, though, can try Letter Lab and trace letters with their fingers, just to get an idea of the shape of the letters.)

To get the most from Letter Lab, you will need to get a stylus for your iPad. A stylus is a pen-sized device that simulates writing on the iPad screen with a pen.

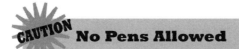 **No Pens Allowed**

This is very important: you may get tempted to use an actual pen on the iPad. Don't. First, it won't work: proper iPad styluses use a reactive surface that the iPad can detect. Second, you run a huge risk of scratching or otherwise damaging the glass on your iPad screen. Styluses are not terribly expensive, and they're a good investment to protect your screen.

There are a lot of stylus models on the market today, and you are encouraged to find one that meets your budget and feels good in your hand.

The Griffin line of styluses definitely bears investigating; they are well-regarded as solid devices at a mid-range price. Griffin even makes a kid-friendly stylus known as the iMarker, which fits well with smaller fingers.

Playing Letter Lab

The rules for Letter Lab are straightforward: players are presented with a page containing a letter of the alphabet, in both upper- and lowercase form (see Figure 12.4).

Figure 12.4

Writing practice.

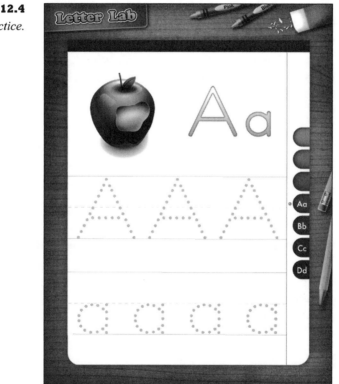

Using a stylus, the child can practice writing the letters by tracing over the letters as often as she likes. When the page is "full," tap the eraser in the top-right corner of the screen to clear what has been written on the screen.

Players can use two colors of "crayon" in Letter Lab: pink and blue. Tap on the desired crayon at the top of the screen to change the color. You might be attracted to the pencils on the right side of the screen, but they're purely decorative (see Figure 12.5).

Figure 12.5

Neatness counts.

To listen to the name of the letter, or the object representing the letter, again, simply tap it.

Practice is completely open—Letter Lab does not grade a child on her writing, nor set a time limit on how long she can practice. When the child wants to try a new letter, she can tap the next letter on the right side of the screen, or swipe the list of letters to navigate farther down the alphabet.

Start Writers Off Right

It is very easy for absolute beginner writers to make letters backwards or start writing in the wrong place. Parents should show their children how to begin and make a letter before turning them loose.

Settings in Letters Lab are also simple. The only real configuration setting is the audio part of the app.

To change your settings:

1. From the iPad Home screen, tap the Settings icon. The Settings screen will open.
2. Tap the Letter Lab option in the Apps section of the left pane. The Letter Lab screen will open, as shown in Figure 12.6.

Figure 12.6

Letter Lab settings.

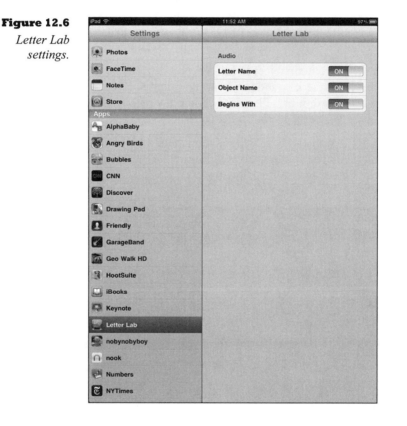

3. Tap the slider controls to adjust the audio settings as you desire.
4. Tap the Home button to exit Settings. The settings will be applied the next time you start Letter Labs.

Easing into Reading with Phonics Made Easy

 Cost of Phonics Made Easy Flash Action: $4.99

Phonics is one of those early school subjects that seems so simple to adults, who have forgotten how difficult it was at the time they were learning how to do it.

The phonetic method of learning to read is a time-tested way of figuring out the pronunciation of an unfamiliar word by breaking the word down into known sounds and then stringing them together into one cohesive word. In this way, students can figure out letter combinations that may not be familiar to them, such as "ph" or "qu" that actually sound like "f" or "kw," respectively, and then apply that knowledge to a new word.

Like any other subject in school, phonics takes a lot of practice, so kids can learn these sounds by heart and then pull them out as needed without much thought. Phonics Made Easy provides a game-like interface that gives students that practice.

When Phonics Made Easy is launched, the player is invited to type his name on the first screen (see Figure 12.7). The player is then taken to the first of four game categories.

Figure 12.7

Starting Phonics Made Easy.

There are no settings to configure in Phonics Made Easy, nor is there any tracking of how each player is doing. In each category, players are given a series of challenges, and when they reach a predefined number of correct questions, they will be awarded a play area associated with that category.

Figure 12.8, for example, shows the first category, Beginning and Ending Sounds, which requires nine correct questions in the Beginning Sounds question set to receive a play area and move on to the Ending Sounds question set.

Figure 12.8

Each question set features a variety of different challenges.

The instructions for each challenge are audibly given to players. If an instruction is missed, it will eventually be repeated, or the player can tap the Help icon and hear it again immediately.

After the player completes the task, tap the OK button in the lower-right corner. If the challenge was correct, the player will be rewarded with a marker on the left. Collect the required number of markers, and the play area will be opened on the right side of the screen, as seen in Figure 12.9.

Play areas feature a variety of activities. The Beginning and Ending Sounds area enables players to touch paint a picture of an object that uses a particular beginning sound by tapping on individual colors and areas of the picture (see Figure 12.10).

Tap on the controls to the left of the picture to change the background, music, and even animate the picture. Tap the back arrow in the lower-left corner of the play area to return to the main game.

Play Area Tab

Figure 12.9

Play areas are unlocked when question sets are completed.

Figure 12.10

The Beginning and Ending Sounds play area.

The four categories of Phonics Made Easy are designed to highlight different skills sets of phonics learning.

* **Beginning and Ending Sounds.** Players will learn a variety of beginning and ending sounds, and how they flow within certain words.

* **Long and Short Vowels.** "Ay?" Or "ah?" The differences between long and short vowel sounds are explored.

* **Rhyming Families.** Challenges are geared to emphasize words that rhyme.

* **Blends and Digraphs.** Consonant sounds that blend or form digraphs (two letters that form one sound) are featured in this category. This could be a bit advanced for first graders, so parents and teachers may want to give a little instruction on the differences between these two concepts.

While progress is not formally tracked within Phonics Made Easy, individual players' scores are kept separate, so as players move through the game, they can always see their own scores.

Get Counting with Time, Money & Fractions

 Cost of Time, Money & Fractions On-Track: $9.99

Another app from the makers of Phonics Made Easy is Time, Money & Fractions, which takes a similar approach to learning these mathematical topics.

There are different levels of Time, Money & Fractions apps available, so be sure to have the right one for your child's age level. In this chapter, Time, Money & Fractions for Grades 1–2 is examined.

As with Phonics Made Easy, when Time, Money & Fractions is launched, the player is invited to type her name on the first screen. The player is then taken to the place in the game she was in last (see Figure 12.11).

There are some differences between these apps, beyond just the subject matter. In Time, Money & Fractions, players proceed through more challenges in each category, and the challenges will have multiple answers in each one.

Figure 12.11

A Time, Money & Fractions money challenge.

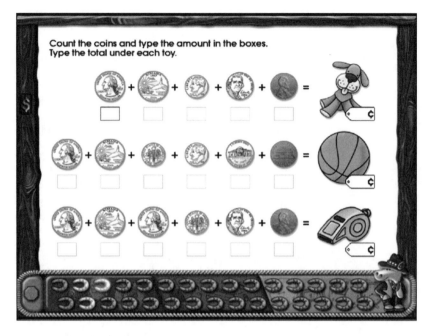

Count the coins and type the amount in the boxes.
Type the total under each toy.

While it initially appears that players must proceed through each of the categories sequentially, players can, if they want, tap on any one of the colored horseshoe sections along the bottom of the screen to move to another subject. From left to right, the topics are

* **Money.** Challenges are designed to enable players to count U.S. currency and add amounts correctly.
* **Fractions.** Children are asked to figure out fraction questions, based on the picture choices they are presented, as shown in Figure 12.12.
* **Time.** Players are asked to answer time-based questions, especially for analog clocks (see Figure 12.13).

The instructions for each challenge are given audibly to players. If an instruction is missed, it will eventually repeat, or the player can tap the Help icon on the top-left part of the screen and hear it again immediately.

After the player completes the task, he can tap the Horse character in the lower-right corner. If the challenge was correct, the horseshoe for the question will be displayed in green. Incorrect challenges are denoted with red horseshoes.

Time, Money & Fractions is not all about challenges, however. As the game progresses, mini-games will pop up for players to do before the next challenge (see Figure 12.14).

Figure 12.12

A Time, Money & Fractions fraction challenge.

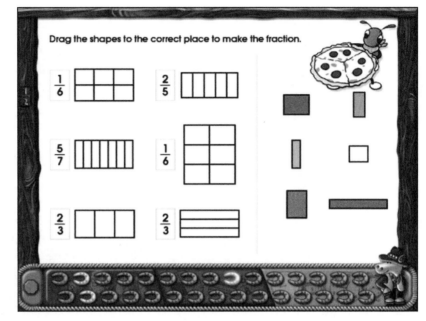

Figure 12.13

A Time, Money & Fractions time challenge.

Figure 12.14

One of the Time, Money & Fractions mini-games.

Progress is marked with the horseshoes, but parents can also get a more detailed report for the player. Tap the stop sign icon to reveal the game control screen, shown in Figure 12.15.

Figure 12.15

The Time, Money & Fractions control screen.

Tap the certificate to view the player's detailed progress. To return to the game, tap the game screen. Parents can also reset their child's challenges by tapping the blue reset icon.

Time, Money & Fractions is definitely an educational game, but it blends in some fun activities to keep players engaged.

Geography Made Fun

Geography, in the past, was something that a lot of first graders didn't really need to know too much about. Figuring out where school was in relation to their home and the nearest playground was more suitable to this grade level.

The advent of the Internet and instant communications with anyone in the world have changed that a bit. The capability to connect with anyone on the planet means that kids need to know more about where these people are more than ever.

There are two great apps for kids to use to learn geography. The first is Stack the States, a quiz-based game that lets players test their knowledge of U.S. geography and learn how to, well, stack U.S. states.

The second is not a straightforward learning app, but still a fantastic reference tool for all ages: Google Earth.

Learning with Stack the States

 Cost of Stack the States: $0.99

Of all the apps in this book, Stack the States certainly ranks as one of the most unique learning apps. The game itself is simple: players are given multiple-choice geographic questions and if they answer the question correctly, they can drop a state that's the answer to the question onto a small platform at the bottom of the screen.

Yes, seriously.

The idea of the game is that players should answer enough questions correctly to obtain enough states to stack them above a line set in the screen, like the one shown in Figure 12.16.

Figure 12.16

Answer the question, get a state.

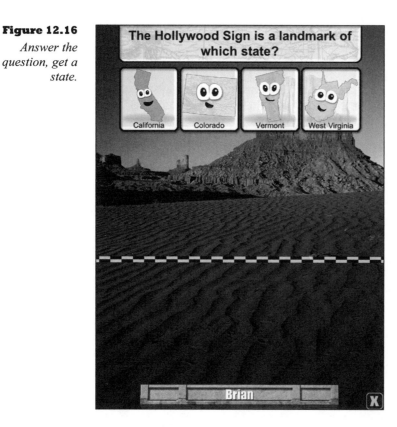

The questions may be challenging for first graders to answer alone, so this may be a game to play as a family activity until children get more familiar with U.S. geography. Once a player gets a state, it will appear above the line. Tap and drag the state to the position about the platform from which you want to try and drop it. Tap and rotate the state using the white controls surrounding the state to align it as best you can (see Figure 12.17).

There are some things to note. First, the states are all sized relative to each other, so smaller states will take longer to stack. Second, all the states bounce on landing, so dropping states from very high on the screen could cause the state to bounce off completely, like poor Arizona did in Figure 12.18.

You can alleviate the bounce problem by lowering the state on the screen before tapping the Drop It! Button.

Once the states are stacked high enough, the round is over, and players will be awarded a new random state on their status map, which is displayed when the My States button is tapped, as shown in Figure 12.19.

Figure 12.17

Align states carefully before dropping them.

Figure 12.18

Watch out for bouncing states.

Figure 12.19

Earn bonus games by acquiring enough states.

Stack the States is a very fun game that even parents might secretly start playing, too. When students are ready, they can also play the companion game, Stack the Countries.

Walk the World with Google Earth

Cost of Google Earth: Free

Google Earth is an app that, although introduced on desktop computers, was a perfect fit for iPad users.

The app is an incredibly rich reference tool that enables users to zoom in and see any part of the world, thanks to a huge database of maps and satellite photos. It is very similar to the Maps app that comes with every iPad, but Google Earth makes navigation around this virtual planet a much smoother experience.

Figure 12.20 shows a default opening view for Google Earth, high above North America, which is as good a place as any to start.

Figure 12.20

A view of the world.

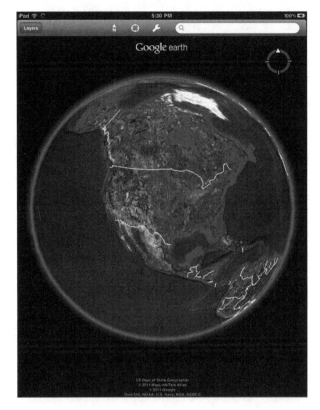

To zoom down to a lower altitude, use the fanning gesture on the iPad screen. As you get lower, more geopolitical details will become visible, if you have those details set for display (see Figure 12.21). To zoom up, pinch the screen.

If you want to zoom in to a specific spot, double-tap the spot on the globe. The globe will center on the selected region and zoom in closer.

Depending on how detailed the satellite photos are, you can get pretty close to whatever spot in the world you want to look at (see Figure 12.22). This is great for showing younger kids where places are located that are very close to home.

Tap in the Search bar and enter a name of a geographic place. If Google Earth recognizes it, the globe will instantly transport you to that spot (see Figure 12.23).

Figure 12.21

Getting closer to home.

Figure 12.22

Buildings can show up in fantastic detail.

Figure 12.23

Places near and far can be found.

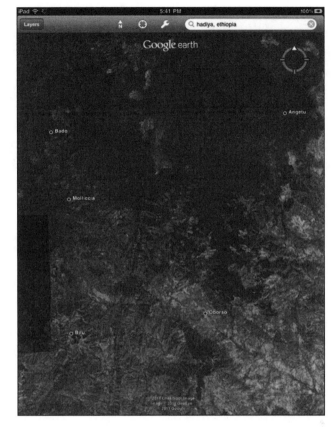

There are a variety of layers that can be applied to Google Earth: Wikipedia entries, photos from users of the group photo-sharing service Panoramio, and even local businesses. Tap the Layers button to see the available layers and tap one to view it in Google Earth. Figure 12.24 illustrates the Businesses layer.

Figure 12.24

Find places to eat and do business.

Conclusion

First grade will open up a lot of new learning opportunities for children, expanding their horizons in ways parents will marvel at. These apps will definitely help guide their way.

In Chapter 13, "Apps for Second Grade," we'll look at apps that take on even more new subjects, as well as strengthen existing knowledge.

Chapter 13

Apps for Second Grade

At this age, students are well on their way in their academic careers, and have moved beyond the basics of reading, writing, and 'rithmetic and into social studies and science. The challenges presented in school are now something that most students can take in stride. They have been there, done that.

This doesn't mean that they still don't need a little help along the way.

Students should understand the basics of reading, which means taking letter patterns on paper and translating them into spoken language by using the sounds of letter combinations, word parts, and syllables. That's what we call *phonics*. But sight words are part of the curriculum, to build their vocabulary, too.

Mathematically, students understand the relationship between numbers, quantities, and place value in whole numbers up to 1,000. They should be able to estimate, calculate, and solve problems involving addition and subtraction of two- and three-digit numbers and solve simple problems involving multiplication and division. And (believe it or not), the early precursors to algebraic modeling are being taught at this grade level.

In this chapter, your child will explore

* Grade-level sight words with Sight Words HD.
* Building math skills with Math BINGO and Tic Tac Math.
* The solar system and the entire visible universe with Star Walk.

Test Reading with Sight Words HD

 Cost of Sight Words HD: $3.99

As you may recall from Chapter 11, "Apps for Kindergarten," Dolch sight words are an educational tool used in English-speaking countries to teach 220 of the most commonly used service words found in English text. Because they are so common, sight words can comprise anywhere from 50 to 70 percent of an average passage of text.

Because some Dolch sight words are not intuitively sounded out, usually educators teach them by rote memorization, hence "sight" words.

This is the whole purpose of Sight Words HD, which supplies all of the Dolch sight words, from pre-primer to third grade, for parents and teachers to test their students' sight-reading skills.

Sight Words HD is a unique app in this book because it does not directly engage the student in game play. It is strictly used as a practice tool, and needs at least a second participant to accurately evaluate students in case they reach a word they can't read.

Play Sight Word HD

Working with Sight Word HD is very much a two-person activity. A set of words is displayed for a reader in a timed session. As the words are read aloud by the reader, the helper can tap the Next Word button (shown in Figure 13.1) and move to the next word.

Figure 13.1

Assessing with Sight Words HD.

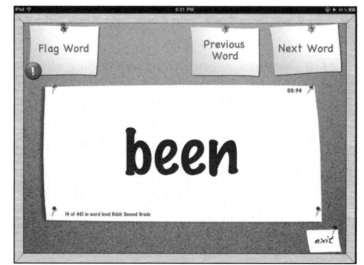

If a reader has a problem reading a word, then the assessor can tap the Flag Word button, which will save the word in the Flagged Words set so that it can be reviewed later. As words are flagged, a small indicator will display the number of flagged words in that session (see Figure 13.2).

Figure 13.2

Challenging words can be flagged for later review.

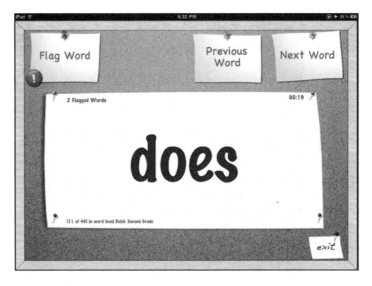

If a reader gets through the whole set without any flagged words, Sight Words HD will display a reward splash screen for the reader, as shown in Figure 13.3.

Figure 13.3

Good performance is definitely noticed.

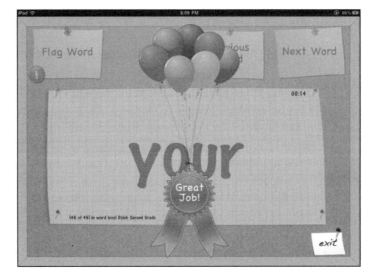

Starting any assessment is easily done from the Home screen (displayed in Figure 13.4), which lists just three options: Start Assessment, Flagged Words, and Setup Words. Tap Start Assessment to begin any new assessment. To review words that were flagged, tap the Flagged Words option to review that set of words.

Figure 13.4

The Sight Words HD Home screen.

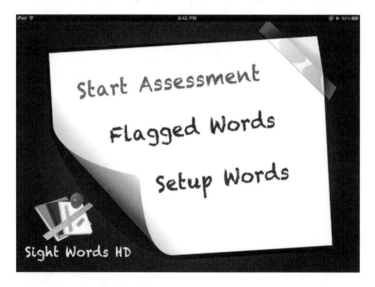

During any regular or flagged words assessment, tap the green Exit button to end the assessment and return to the Home screen.

Set Up Sight Words HD

Much of what makes Sight Words HD a valuable assessment tool is its capability to set the exact level of words to be tested. You can also add words for assessment, which greatly increases the flexibility of the app.

All of the configuration settings for Sight Words HD are handled from the Setup screen. Tap the Setup Words option on the Home screen, and the Setup screen will appear, as shown in Figure 13.5.

There are different sets of sight words provided by Sight Words HD, displayed in the Word Levels section of the Setup screen. To change the set of words to be provided in an assessment, tap the desired level. The level will be selected in the Word Levels section, and the contents of the word set will be shown in the Details section on the right side of the Setup screen (see Figure 13.6).

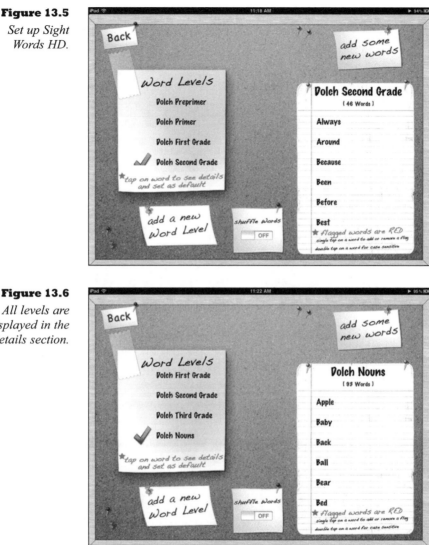

Figure 13.5

Set up Sight Words HD.

Figure 13.6

All levels are displayed in the Details section.

If any words have been flagged within a set of words, they will be listed in red type within the Details section. If you want to unflag the word, tap the word in the Details list. To reflag it, tap it again.

The capability to add new words to Sight Words HD is tremendously helpful, since you can have the child learn a particular set of words in addition to the standard Dolch words. These might include words that are culturally or spiritually based, words from a story your child has read recently, or even family names. To add words to Sight Words HD, you must first add a new word level to the app, because custom words cannot be added to the preprovided word levels in the app.

1. From the Setup screen, tap the Add a New Word Level control. The Create a New Word Level List popover box will appear (see Figure 13.7).

Figure 13.7

Define a new word level list.

2. Type a word level list title in the popover box and tap the Accept button. The new level will be added to the Word Levels section.

3. Tap the new word level. The level will be selected with 0 words displayed in the Details section.

4. Tap the Add some new words control. The Add New Words popover will appear.

5. Type a new word and tap the Add button (see Figure 13.8). The new word will be added to the list.

Figure 13.8

You've got to start sometime.

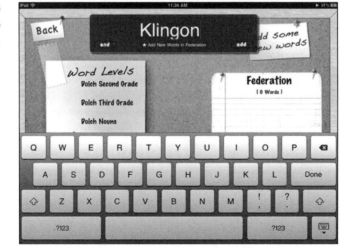

6. Add new words by repeating Step 5. When finished, tap the End button, and the word list will be displayed in the Details section.

By default, Sight Words HD displays words in assessments in the order in which they appear in the word list. You can change things up by tapping the Shuffle words slider on the Setup screen. This will scramble the order of words presented in an assessment, just in case the reader is memorizing the pattern of words presented.

Fun and Games with Math

Math in the second grade is very much an incremental step of learning, since many of the same skills learned in earlier school work are still being used—it's just that now students are working with larger groups of numbers.

This means that apps that enable as much practice as possible are important for students at this level. Two apps that fit the bill nicely are Tic Tac Math and Math BINGO.

Xs and Os with Tic Tac Math

 Cost of Tic Tac Math: $4.99

Starting Tic Tac Math, the initial screen lets players choose the type of math problems they want to solve, as well as if they are playing against the game or another player (see Figure 13.9).

Astute observers will also note the presence of the I'm a Parent button, which indicates that Tic Tac Math is another SmarTots-enabled game. You can choose to link to the free SmarTots parent reporting service if you want to track your child's progress with the math problems presented in the game. This is the only way you can customize the app for an individual child, because Tic Tac Math on its own does not provide a way for the app to follow certain users.

New SmarTots users can tap the I'm a Parent button and then enter their email address in the appropriate field. In a few minutes, an email will appear in your inbox. Using any email client, open the email message and click (or tap) the link included in the message from SmarTots. SmarTots is the third-party service that provides the reports for Tic Tac Math, along with quite a few other apps.

Figure 13.9

Starting Tic Tac Math.

If you are new to SmarTots, you will need to provide a new password to enable your SmarTots account. After you create a SmarTots account, you can personalize the game for children playing the app, either within Tic Tac Math or on the SmarTots site.

If you have already signed up for a SmarTots account, you will be shown a Connect to SmarTots popover screen that will enable you to simply connect Tic Tac Math to the SmarTots service.

Tap Connect and Tic Tac Math will be connected to the SmarTots system.

Once the SmarTots account is created, you can log on to the SmarTots site at any time from any browser and navigate to the Reports screen to see your child's participation with Sentence Builder or any SmarTots-enabled app.

There are three levels of play in Tic Tac Math: easy, advanced, and expert. The levels roughly correspond to the math standards of first, second, and third grade, respectively, for the addition and subtraction groups, and second, third, and fourth grade for multiplication and division problems.

Game play is simple: after selecting a family of problems with which to work, the number of players, and the level of difficultly, tap Play Now to start a game (see Figure 13.10).

Figure 13.10

Tic Tac Math game play.

To gain a square, a player taps that square, which opens the problem in an Answer This screen, as shown in Figure 13.11.

Players should type their answer to the problem and tap the Enter button. If the answer is correct, the players will be awarded an X (or O) in that square (see Figure 13.12). If their answer is wrong, however, they will lose their turn. In a single-player game, it is important to note that this means the computer player will effectively take that square for itself.

Figure 13.11

The Answer screen.

Figure 13.12

Filling the field of play.

One nice feature of the game is that players can use a stylus or finger to work through the problems before they answer. This is extremely useful for more complicated problems, where the answer might not jump right out, as shown in Figure 13.13.

Figure 13.13

Working through a problem.

Figure 13.14

Start over or move to another set of problems.

If a player makes an error, he can tap the Erase button to clear the work screen.

Game play will continue until the game is won, lost, or tied. The player's score of won games will be tracked in the Score status bar as long as that set of problems is being played. To stop a game, tap the Pause button, which will open the game dialog box, shown in Figure 13.14.

Start Over is a bit misleading—it does not return to the app's Home screen, but rather restarts the game the player is in now. Choose a Different Game will return to the Home screen.

B-I-N-G-O for Math

 Cost of Math BINGO: $0.99

Of the two math games in this chapter, Math BINGO is likely to engage players a little bit more, since BINGO is a bit more complex than Tic Tac Toe. This is purely a matter of preference, of course, so you can let your children decide which app they prefer.

Math BINGO is a time-based BINGO game that players win by getting five BINGO bugs in a row when answering math problems. The problems are not as complex as those presented in Tic Tac Math, because the players are playing against time, and problems that were too difficult would bog down game play.

The problems are presented randomly, so players will not know which numbered squares they will be able to place a BINGO bug on until the problem is displayed (see Figure 13.15).

Figure 13.15

Playing Math BINGO.

Referring to Figure 13.15, you will see that sometimes there is more than one instance of a problem's answer on the game board. Since the answer for the problem in this example is 11, the player can tap on any instance of the number 11 to place her bug in that square. This gives the player a little more control over where her bugs are placed.

If a player makes an error, feedback is delivered, with the correct answer displayed at the bottom of the screen (see Figure 13.16).

Figure 13.16

Wrong answers are corrected.

When a row of five BINGO bugs is achieved, the BINGO display will appear, as seen in Figure 13.17.

Scoring is based on the speed of game play. The faster that BINGO is reached, the better the score will be. The app will add two seconds of time to the player's score for each incorrect answer. When players achieve a high score in a particular category of problems, they are given a BINGO bug, which they can play with onscreen by tapping the My BINGO Bugs button in the player score area.

Figure 13.17
BINGO!

Walk Among the Stars

Cost of Solar System: $13.99

Some iPad apps are so cool, they are often instantly identified with the device. As second graders move into the realm of science, they will be able to play more with these kinds of iPad apps and see just what lies out there in the worlds around them.

Two such apps, Solar System and The Elements, let them explore an environment that starts only 50 miles away and stretches billions of light-years into the farthest reaches of the universe.

Check Out the Neighborhood

Space, as you may have gathered, is not far away at all. The Earth's atmosphere is only an average of 50 miles thick (depending on how you measure), so distance-wise it's not that much of a journey. Of course, Earth's gravity well is a bit of an obstacle, requiring *ginormous* rockets to shove fairly small bits of mass away from that well and toward other objects.

And, once you're out in space, 50 miles is about the only time you're going to be dealing with distances that minuscule again. The Moon, which is the nearest object to our planet (we hope), is 238,857 miles away (on average). The other objects in our solar system—planets, moons, comets, dwarf planets, and one mid-sized star—are all ridiculously far away, requiring months, years, or decades for our fastest spacecraft to reach them.

This is why Solar System is a remarkably cool app. It lets anyone explore our home system in remarkable detail without packing a spacesuit.

The Future of Books?

Solar System and The Elements are based on books by the same names. *Solar System* is written by Marcus Chown. (You'll learn more about The Elements in Chapter 15.) Solar System can be explored sequentially, just like a book, with the story leading users through the solar system. But users can also explore the app in any way they want, diving as deep into the information presented as they would like.

Solar System is a visually stunning app, mirroring the book of the same name. Each object described in Solar System has its own section, which can be seen in the animated Home screen shown in Figure 13.18.

Figure 13.18

The worlds around us.

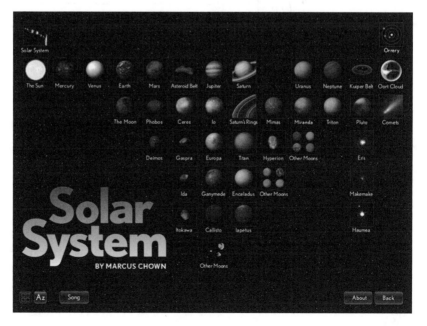

If you want to start at the beginning of the Solar System story, tap the Solar System icon at the top-left corner of the Home screen. This will open the first page of the Solar System section, seen in Figure 13.19.

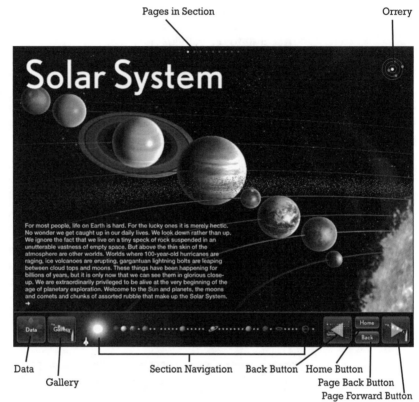

Figure 13.19

The story begins.

There are a lot of navigation tools within Solar System, which should encourage exploration at any user's preference.

✳ **Pages in section.** Each object in the solar system has a collection of pages. This indicator displays which page of the section the reader is in.

✳ **Orrery.** Opens the Orrery tool, a virtual model of the solar system.

✳ **Data.** Opens the data popover menu, which provides relevant data about the object from the app and the Wolfram|Alpha data Web site.

✳ **Gallery.** Displays a gallery of images related to the object displayed.

✳ **Section navigation.** Displays and controls where a user is in the overall book "story" and the position in the solar system. Tap and drag the rocket icon to move to another location in the solar system/story.

✳ **Page back button.** Tap to move one page back in the book story.

✳ **Home button.** Tap to return to the app Home screen.

✳ **Back button.** Tap to return to the most recent section visited.

✳ **Page forward button.** Tap to move one page forward in the book story.

While Solar System can be read as a book, it is by no means a static display of information. Tap any of the highlighted text links to see the referenced object in the solar system (using the Back button to return to where you were, if you desire) or a popover box with more information about the term.

Beyond these Web-like navigation tools, Solar System also enables interactivity with any image displayed in the app. Try it yourself: tap an image on a page. Pinch it, fan it, swipe it. Many of the images have written instructions on how to interact with the image, but some do not. You might be surprised to discover what the app will do with any given image, like the cutaway of Jupiter shown in Figure 13.20.

Figure 13.20

Deep inside the largest planet in our solar system.

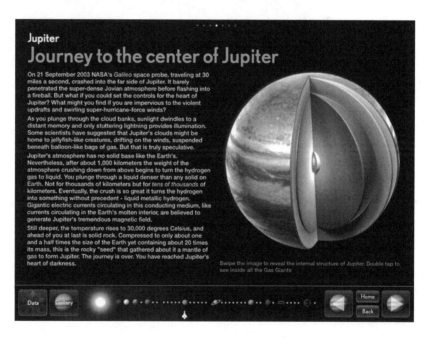

If you tap the Orrery icon at the beginning of each section, you will access the fantastic Orrery tool, centered on the object in question. An Orrery is a model of the solar system. The model in Solar System is virtual, and not quite to scale, but it does feature a time control that enables users to slow down or speed up the passage of time in the model (see Figure 13.21).

Figure 13.21

*The dance of the
planets.*

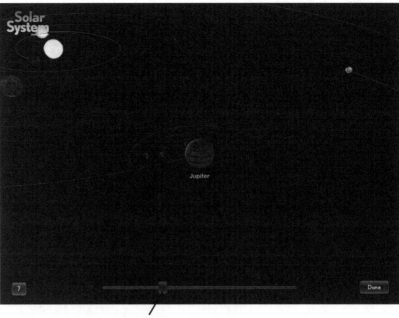

Time Control

To zoom out, pinch the screen; fan the screen to zoom in, or tap another object in the system to center it on the screen. If you slide your finger around the screen, the orientation of the model will shift. Tap Done, and Solar System will return to the last page you left.

Not for Stargazing

The Orrery is a neat model to play with, but it is not accurate for the current position of the planets (nor the size of the objects in the model). So keep that in mind as you explore the model.

Solar System is very much an app for all ages. There is a lot of interesting prose for older children and adults, and more than enough interactivity and visual demonstrations to keep young children fascinated. Second graders may find the vocabulary a little challenging at first, but with parental guidance, this visually stunning app is a great way to make the planets their playground.

The Night Revealed

 Cost of Star Walk: $4.99

At its heart, Star Walk is a very solid astronomy app, to be used by anyone with an interest in the sky. This might not sound like a suitable app for younger children, but in truth, the app is easy enough to use for all ages and can serve as a great launchpad to generate interest in what's beyond the confines of our world. There is a lot of data—over 9,000 sky objects are tracked, with information about each object readily available at the touch of a finger.

There are two ways you can use Star Walk: first, it's a great general astronomy reference tool that lets you explore the sky at your leisure at any time. Pan around the sky, tap individual objects to learn more about them, and move the timeline into the past or future to see how the sky looked as long ago as 1599 or will look all the way in the year 2399.

The second use of the app is a live astronomy tool that you can take outside with you to help locate objects in the night sky using the Star Spotter feature.

When you start Star Walk for the very first time, it will need to establish some base settings for the app, so it generally knows where you are. Typically, it will use the iPad's location settings to figure that out, but you can set this manually if need be.

1. From the main screen, tap the menu control. The menu will appear (see Figure 13.22).

2. Tap the Home Location icon. The Home Location screen will open, as shown in Figure 13.23.

3. If the location is correct, tap the Close icon to return to the main screen. If a new location must be set, navigate to the new home location by one of the three following methods:

   ☀ Pinch, drag, and fan the globe to line up crosshairs on the desired location.

   ☀ Tap the latitude and longitude controls and use the picker controls to enter the coordinates of the location.

   ☀ Tap the Search icon and enter the place name for the location.

4. Tap the Close icon to return to the main screen.

Figure 13.22

The Star Walk menu.

Figure 13.23

Locating home.

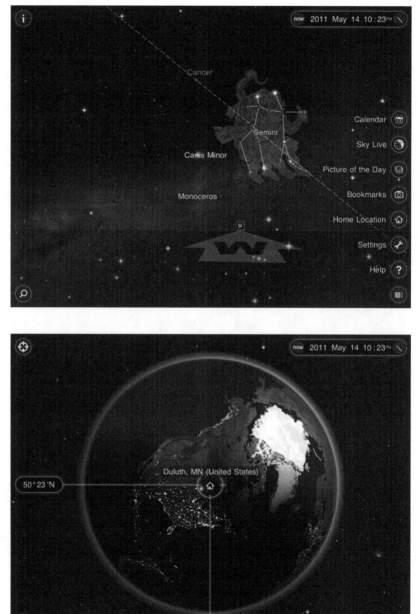

To move around the sky manually, tap and drag the sky around as you want. Pinch to zoom out or fan to zoom in. If you see an object you want to learn more about, tap the object, and then tap the information icon in the upper-left corner of the screen to discover more about the object (see Figure 13.24).

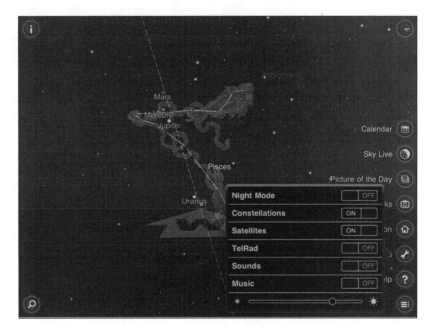

You can also change what objects are displayed on the screen.

1. Tap the menu control. The menu will appear.
2. Tap the Settings icon. The Settings control will open, as shown in Figure 13.25.

3. Tap the control to turn the display of Constellations or Satellite on or off.

4. Tap and drag the Brightness control to adjust the screen for local light pollution.

5. Tap any part of the screen to return to the main screen.

To check out the sky at a different time, tap the clock icon in the upper-right corner of the screen. The time controls will open, as shown in Figure 13.26.

Figure 13.26

Time controls in Star Walk.

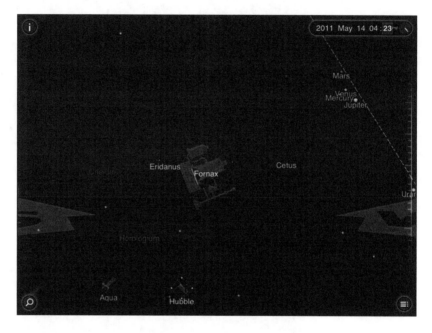

To move the sky to a new point in time, tap the unit of time you want to manipulate, be it year, month, day, hour, or minute. The more you want to move, the higher the unit you should select.

Once the unit is selected, tap and drag the time slider on the right side of the screen. Down moves into the past, and up moves into the future. When you reach the time you want to view, release the control.

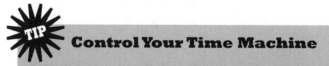

Control Your Time Machine

Flick the time control up or down and Star Walk will keep moving through time indefinitely, creating a nice movie of what's happened or will happen. The faster the flick, the faster the rate of change.

To return to the present time, tap the Now button.

When you want to view the night sky, you can use the sky spotter feature to orient yourself and the app to the sky you're looking at.

In a location with a clear view of the sky, tilt the iPad up. The built-in compass and gyroscope will shift the Star Walk screen to the portion of the sky you are looking at.

 For more complete alignment, tap the align icon to switch on the iPad 2 camera. Orient the device and tap and drag the Star Walk screen until a recognizable object is within the green circle at the center of the screen. Tap the Checkmark button to set the orientation.

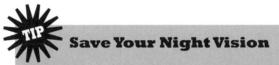

Save Your Night Vision

If you are using Star Walk while observing the sky, make sure the Night mode setting is on. This will set all of the writing and lines in the app to red, which will not affect your night vision.

This is another app that will take some learning for second graders to grow into. At first, they may want to use it as a visual study of sky, using it later as a guide to sky watching.

Conclusion

The universe is definitely opening up for students in the second grade. Math and reading are an integral part of their curriculum, and now science and nature are getting their attention, too.

In Chapter 14, "Apps for Third Grade," we'll look at apps that continue the exploration of the world, as well as history, plus more reading and math practice.

Chapter 14

Apps for
Third Grade

In martial arts, laypeople often believe that the rank black belt represents the pinnacle of achievement within a particular discipline. In actuality, that is not the case: achieving black belt status is regarded as having learned all of the fundamental skills within that martial art. Now the real learning begins.

Third grade, at some levels, is a similar point in the student's academic career. The basics of reading and math have been taught, and now it's time for students to take the skills they have learned and apply them to additional topics and subjects.

In reading, for example, students should know how to read well enough that most sight words are immediately identifiable and any new word can be figured out without much hesitation (although the meaning may need to be defined). With these skills in place, students can start reading anything: prose, poetry, history, science… whatever school and life throw at them.

The same holds true in math: the rules of addition, subtraction, multiplication, and division have been mastered, and now students can start applying what they know to other forms of math, such as geometry, science, and algebra.

There's still a lot to learn, of course. But with reading and math skills in their tool belts, the exchange of knowledge will be a lot broader.

In this chapter, students will continue that exchange by

* Practicing grade-level reading skills with K12 Timed Reading.
* Solving complex math problems with MathBoard.
* Exploring the natural world with GeoWalk HD.
* Learning with Presidents of the United States for iPad.

Achieving Fluency with K12 Timed Reading

 Cost of K12 Timed Reading: $1.99

As phonics is mastered, and words come more easily to students, educators like to focus on reading *fluency*. This is reached when students can read quickly and smoothly, without. pausing. for. every. word. and without readinginamonotonevoicewithoutanyinflectionwhatsoever. This is not as easy as you might remember, but for quite a while children have been focused on reading individual words and not on the rhythm of the sentence in which the words lie. Fluency is when readers get that rhythm and start to absorb not just the meaning of the individual words, but the sentences and longer passages as well.

K12 Timed Reading is an app that has one function: providing grade-level appropriate passages of text that readers can visit and get an idea of how many words per minute they can read. This is done by timing readers as they work through a passage.

K12 Timed Reading is a bit misnamed; it gives the impression that reading levels from kindergarten to 12th grade are examined. In actuality, it's just K–4. This is still useful, to be sure, but parents need to be clear about the app's limitations.

Nor is this an iPad-optimized app—the app is designed for an iPhone interface. Given the simple tasks performed by the user in this app, this is one time when an iPhone-designed app is not a detriment.

Using K12 Timed Reading is simple enough: starting the app for the first time brings up an introductory screen, shown in Figure 14.1.

Tap the purple Settings icon as directed, and the Reading Level screen will open (see Figure 14.2).

Figure 14.1

The K12 Timed Reading introductory screen.

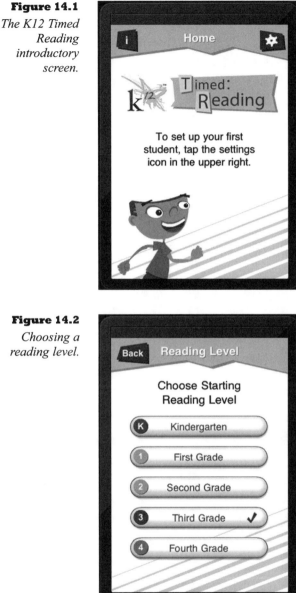

Figure 14.2

Choosing a reading level.

Setting the reading level is straightforward: if the child is in the third grade, then that's the level to tap. The only exception to this, the game's makers recommend, is if a child is in kindergarten and doesn't know how to read yet. For those students, K12 Timed Reading is not recommended. Once they do know how to read, K12 Timed Reading is entirely appropriate.

After the reading level is set, the Add Student screen will automatically appear. Add the student's name and tap Save, as shown in Figure 14.3.

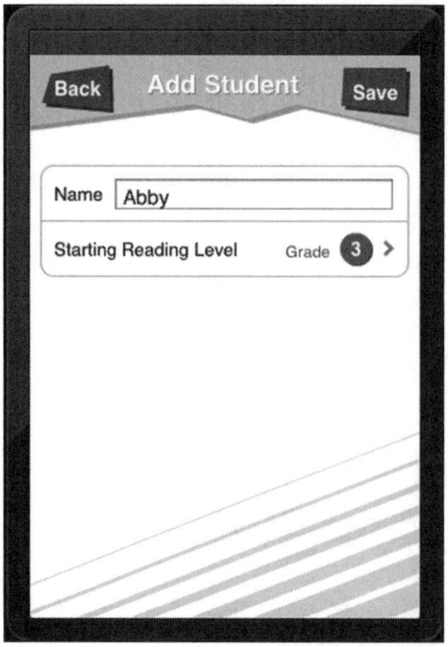

Figure 14.3

Adding a student.

Once the student is added, the Home screen will appear (see Figure 14.4). This will be the screen that will appear every time the app is started from this point forward.

Figure 14.4

The K12 Timed Reading Home screen.

To start a timed reading, tap the student's name. The Activities screen will appear, which gives readers a choice to advance to the next story in the reading level queue or choose from the Reading List (as shown in Figure 14.5).

Figure 14.5

All of K12 Timed Reading's stories are available to read and review.

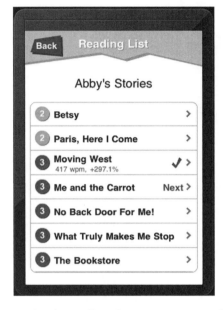

To begin reading the next story, tap the Next Story button. If you would like to read a story from the Reading List, tap the title of the story. After a brief countdown, the story will be presented to the reader (see Figure 14.6).

Figure 14.6

Reading a story.

Tap the Forward button to progress through the story. If you need to stop, tap the Pause button so the app will track reading speed accurately. When the passage is read, tap the Done! button. The Read screen appears, displaying the reader's elapsed time and the number of words read per minute (see Figure 14.7).

Figure 14.7

Seeing the number of words per minute.

Readers can tap Save to record their progress or Don't Save.

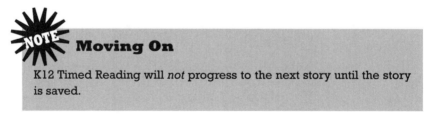

Moving On

K12 Timed Reading will *not* progress to the next story until the story is saved.

Using K12 Timed Reading is a great way to practice and assess reader fluency, and readers are encouraged to read aloud to parents or teachers so they can hear the progress the student is making. You should also find time to ask questions about the story, to make sure that comprehension, a critical part of reading, is also progressing.

Step Up to MathBoard

 Cost of MathBoard: $4.99

MathBoard is a very flexible app that will quiz students on a variety of math problems, all the way up to high-school level math. Because of this customizability, it could be the last math app your student will need.

But because of that flexibility, MathBoard has some drawbacks. Unlike other educational apps, it does not have set grade levels, so parents and teachers will need to figure out manually which settings are appropriate and adjust the game accordingly.

The good news is, once settings have been tuned to a certain level, you can save them as presets in MathBoard, so you can just access them again with one tap.

The interface for MathBoard is actually pretty clever. It has the look and feel of a chalkboard, right down to the virtual pieces of dust that flake down as a student "writes" on the board.

The chalk-like interface continues all the way through the app's configuration settings, which are accessible by tapping any setting in the Settings section of the app. This will open the MathBoard Settings popover box, as shown in Figure 14.8.

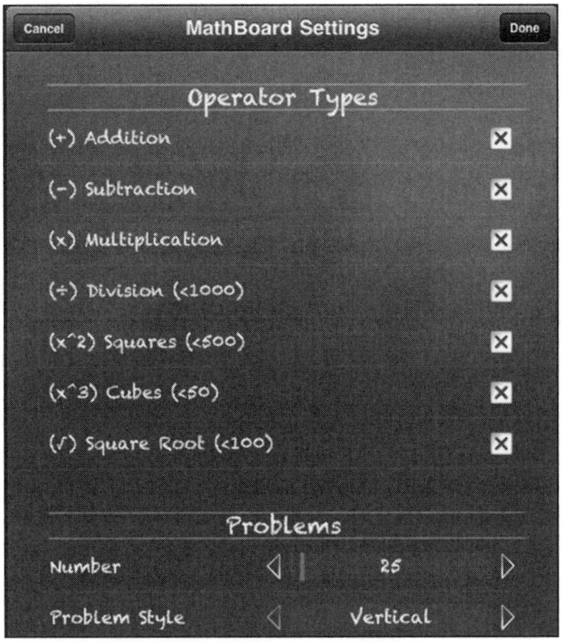

Figure 14.8

Settings in MathBoard.

Setting Up MathBoard

As you will see when you open the Settings popover, there are a lot of possible configurations in MathBoard from which to choose. To illustrate how the important settings work, and to configure the app for a third-grade student, follow these steps:

1. From the Settings box, tap the Squares, Cubes, and Square Root settings. The settings should be deselected.

2. If you want to set the number of problems in any given quiz at an amount different from the default 25 problems, tap the arrows in the Number field to decrease or increase the value. You can set from 1 to 250 questions.

3. Problems in MathBoard are displayed in vertical fashion. To change, tap the arrows in the Problem Style to Horizontal.

4. Answers are given by either typing in a keypad or using pickers for each digit. Select the method your child prefers in the Answer Style field.

5. The Number Range section establishes the difficulty of the problems by setting limits on the possible answers. For third grade, recommended values should be

   * Minimum: 0
   * Maximum: 1000
   * Max Answer: 100

6. The Digit Limit section establishes the difficulty of the problems by setting limits on the digits for answers. For third grade, recommended values should be

   * Min Upper Digits: Off
   * Max Upper Digits: 1
   * Min Lower Digits: Off
   * Max Lower Digits: Off

7. To create a timed quiz, select the Countdown value in the Time section's Style field.

8. When finished with settings, tap the Done button. The MathBoard Settings popover box will close and the settings will be applied.

Saving MathBoard Settings

Once you have the app's settings set to your satisfaction, you can save them as a preset for continued use.

1. Tap the arrow icon next to the title of the Settings section. The Presets action menu will open, as shown in Figure 14.9.

Figure 14.9

Presets for MathBoard.

2. Tap the Add button. The Preset Name message box will open (see Figure 14.10).

Figure 14.10

Name a preset.

3. Type a name and tap Save. The preset will be saved to the app.

To access the preset, tap the Settings icon to open the Presets action menu. The preset will be listed (see Figure 14.11). Tap it to reset your settings to the preset's parameters.

Figure 14.11

Viewing presets.

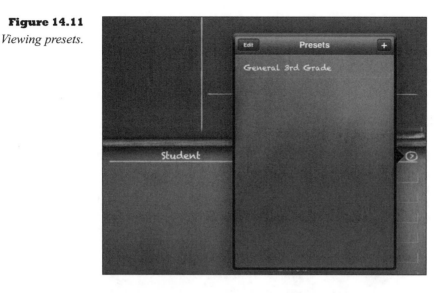

Adding Students to MathBoard

Besides Presets, you can also add students to the app, which will allow you to configure settings for individual students, not just groups of students. After you have settings tailored for a particular student, follow these steps:

1. Tap the arrow icon next to the title of the Student section. The Students action menu will open, as shown in Figure 14.12.

Figure 14.12

Students for MathBoard.

2. Tap the Add button. The Student Name message box will open.

3. Type a name and tap Save. The student will be saved to the app.

To access the student, tap the Student arrow icon to reveal the Students action menu. Tap the student, and the student's name will be listed and settings shifted to that student's capabilities.

Playing MathBoard

To play MathBoard, tap the Play (or Play Again) option on the app's Home screen. This will start a problem set, as seen in Figure 14.13.

Figure 14.13

A MathBoard problem set.

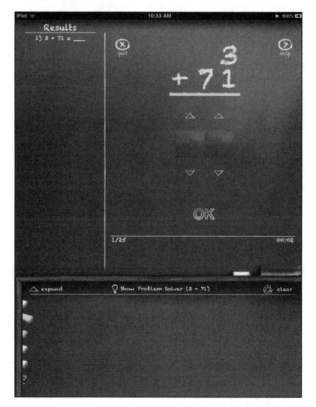

To answer the question using pickers (the method displayed in Figure 14.13), swipe each digit box until the proper answer appears in the boxes. You can also tap the arrow keys to adjust the values of the picker boxes. When finished, tap OK. If the problem is answered correctly, a positive sound will ring, and the next problem will be displayed.

When a challenging problem appears, students can use MathBoard's chalkboard to assist them in solving the problem. Tap the expand option on the lower chalkboard if more space is needed. The board will expand, as shown in Figure 14.14.

Figure 14.14

The chalkboard enables students to work out problems…

Using a stylus or their fingers, students can work out the problem on their own, just as if they were standing at the chalkboard (see Figure 14.15). Tap any of the different colored chalks to get a new color, or the eraser icon to wipe something away and start again.

Once the problem is sufficiently worked, tap the shrink option to return the chalkboard to its normal size so the answer can be entered, as shown in Figure 14.16.

After the quiz is complete, the student's score will be reported to him as a percentage, along with the amount of time it took to answer the questions (see Figure 14.17).

Figure 14.15

...Like this.

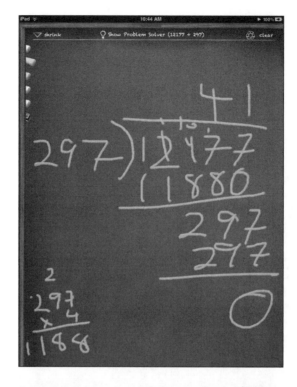

Figure 14.16

A messy problem can yield a clean result.

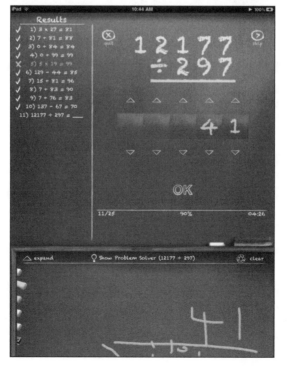

Figure 14.17

The end results.

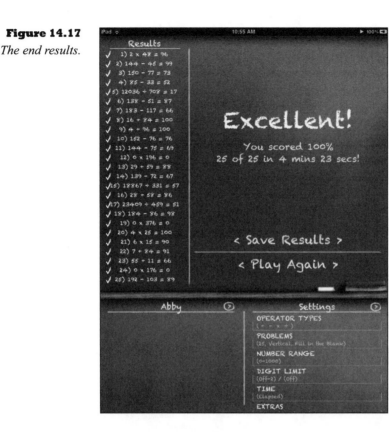

Tap Save Results to keep these results. The Save Results message box will appear. Confirm the date and time and tap Save. The results will be listed in the Student section.

If you want to revisit a quiz (perhaps one that was especially challenging), tap the results of that quiz. The Load Quiz message box will confirm that you want to run that particular quiz again and erase the stored score for that quiz.

Walking the World with GeoWalk HD

 Cost of GeoWalk HD: $2.99

Students have an incredible array of information and knowledge at their fingertips. The Internet represents an unimaginable wealth of information, but at the same time, it can be a daunting place to visit, both in terms of finding information and the dangers that exist on the Web.

GeoWalk HD represents a visual approach to learning that delivers a treasure trove of knowledge, in ways that are clearly organized and safe.

Opening GeoWalk HD will immediately show a globe map of the world, with pictures overlaid across its surface (see Figure 14.18).

Figure 14.18

The world of GeoWalk.

In Earth view, users can swipe the screen to center on another region. Fanning the globe will zoom in, and pinching will zoom out. When a picture is centered in the view, it expands so it can be seen more easily. Tap the picture, and it will expand even further, as seen in Figure 14.19.

To discover more about the object displayed, tap the text icon in the lower-right corner of the picture. The picture will "flip" over to reveal information about the pictured object (see Figure 14.20).

Figure 14.19

Pictures can reveal much about the world.

Figure 14.20

And text will complete the knowledge learned.

Users can share the information learned on Facebook or Twitter, if desired. They can also set the object as a favorite by tapping the star icon on the picture side of the object. This will store the object in the background of the Picture Flow view shown in Figure 14.21.

Favorite Object

Figure 14.21

GeoWalk HD's Picture Flow view.

In Picture Flow view, you can swipe through the pictures to have them displayed randomly. When one strikes your interest, you can view it by tapping, just as in Earth view.

To move between views, tap the appropriate view control at the bottom of the GeoWalk HD screen.

There are four categories of objects displayed in GeoWalk HD: places, animals, plants, and people. To show or hide any of these categories, tap the category's icon at the bottom of the screen.

GeoWalk HD is a fun exploration tool for students to use to view the world and cultures around them. If they feel like they've learned something, they can tap the Quiz icon to start a non-scored quiz (see Figure 14.22). The quiz will continue until the Earth or Picture Flow view is selected.

Figure 14.22

Quiz yourself in GeoWalk HD.

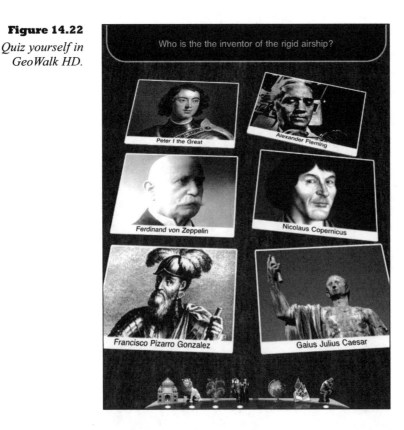

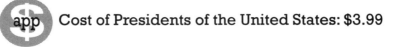

Vote for Presidents of the United States for iPad

$app Cost of Presidents of the United States: $3.99

Quick, how many vice presidents did Franklin D. Roosevelt have during his unprecedented four terms in office? How many presidents didn't even have vice presidents while they served? Those are some of the interesting questions that can be answered in this history app, Presidents of the United States, for iPad.

Presidents, as we'll call this app for short, is a simple app filled chock-full of vital statistics and information about each president of the U.S., from Washington to Obama.

The information is presented in two ways. When the app is first started, the President Reel will be displayed, which is a slideshow that runs through the presidents in chronological order and lists years in office and their vice presidents (see Figure 14.23).

Figure 14.23

*How many FDR
VPs? Three!*

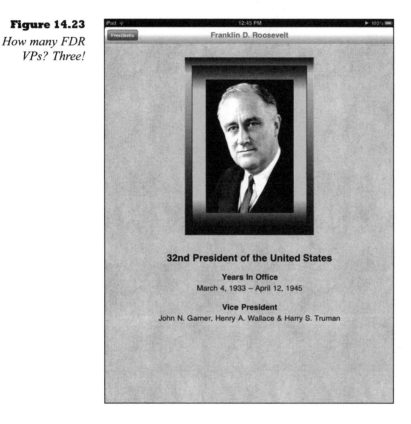

To see an individual president, tap the Presidents button to reveal the Presidents action menu, shown in Figure 14.24.

Tap a president to view that president's information. Vital statistics about the president are listed in the Presidential Info page, shown in Figure 14.25.

Figure 14.24

Choose your president.

Figure 14.25

A governor of Indiana, too.

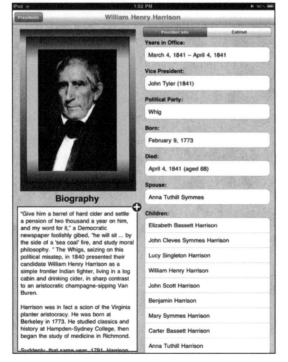

Tap the Cabinet button to view the president's staff. To read the Biography in full page view, tap the plus icon in the Biography section to expand the text out to the full page (see Figure 14.26).

Figure 14.26

One month in office, but still quite a life.

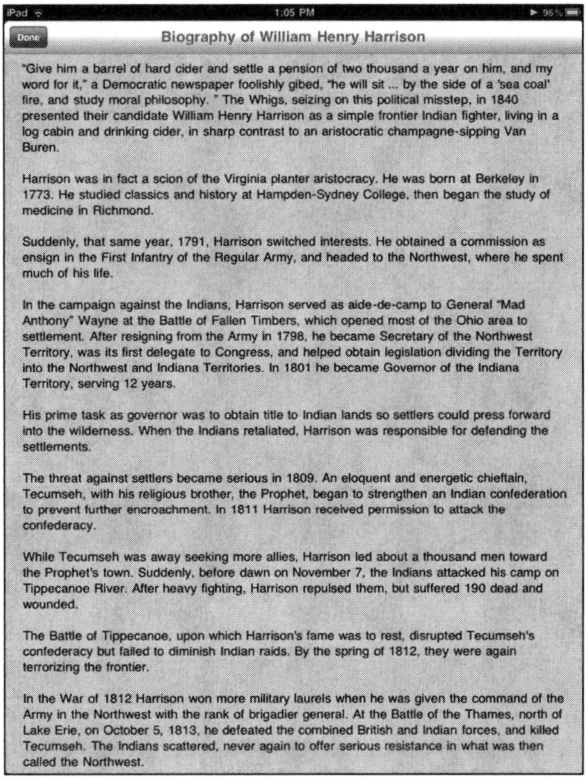

Presidents is not a very interactive app, but it has rich detail that will teach anyone interested in U.S. history about the men who have led the nation and their vice presidents. Except Tyler, Fillmore, Johnson, and Arthur, who didn't have vice presidents.

Conclusion

History and natural science are a big part of early elementary school education, and iPad apps are out there to accommodate anyone interested in these subjects.

In Chapter 15, "Apps for Fourth Grade," the final grade level chapter for this book, we'll look at the best apps for students in that grade, and perhaps beyond.

Chapter 15

Apps for
Fourth Grade

With so many school districts changing, fourth grade can come to mean the end of the elementary school experience, as many middle schools (which are cleverly known as intermediate centers, since "intermediate" sounds fancier than "middle") begin in the fifth grade.

This can be a bit traumatic for parents and students alike, since middle school can represent a not-so-fun time in parents' memories, and the thought of throwing their kid into that sea of raging social storms brought on by the onset of puberty can be, well, scary. Kids may not have such preconceptions, but they are suddenly sensing a change in how they interact with their peers. For boys, girls are no longer so "icky." For girls, boys are still "dumb," but they won't be for long. (Though my wife might challenge that contention.)

Faced with the approach of this new strange environment, fourth graders need to be sure to have all of the basics down as soon as they can. We've covered the reading and math apps in this book pretty thoroughly, but now kids need to learn a new kind of basics: how to learn on their own.

Learning to learn means knowing how to research. In their parents' day, that meant going to the local library and figuring out what you needed for that school report from dusty old encyclopedias written by someone in "Britannia." Today, it means typing a few words in a browser and getting the collective knowledge of millions of people shoved in your face.

It's a common misconception that with so much information at their fingertips, students today don't have to know how to research. In fact, nothing could be further from the truth. The huge influx of so much data is all the more reason that kids need to learn how to turn information into knowledge that they can actually use. What's important to know? Where are the good sources of information? How does this apply to the broader topic they are learning?

Adults, honestly, could use a little brushing up on how to research, too. Just accepting chain-letter emails or what one person writes on the Internet as fact is never a good idea. Research what you hear, if it intrigues you. Who's saying this? What do they know? And who disagrees with them?

With its Safari browser, clearly the iPad can act as a big, wide-open door to the deluge of information that's out there. But there are some great apps for the iPad that have already done a great job of pulling information together into tightly organized packages for students to start their research. In this chapter, we'll look at three such apps, specifically

* iDinoBook, which teaches and quizzes kids on dinosaurs.
* The Elements, a gorgeous interactive app about every element under the sun.
* USA Manual, a vast repository of civics and government information.

Oh, Come On, It's Dinosaurs!

 Cost of iDinoBook: $3.99

It must be a boy thing, but dinosaurs are just…cool.

I say that with tongue firmly in cheek, because I know full well there are lots of brilliant lady paleontologists in the world, but from my own Y-chromosome experiences as a boy and then a father of daughters, I have not met many girls with the kind of raging passion boys seem to exhibit, particularly around this age, for all things dinosaur.

Somehow, the thought of giant lizards with giant teeth running around a primordial forest where dragonflies were the size of eagles has a certain strange appeal to kids at this age. Boys, it seems, get bitten by the dinosaur bug a bit harder.

Regardless of any gender tendencies that may or may not be true, iDinoBook is an iPad app that contains a staggering amount of information about the big lizards from millions of years ago. This is one app that I wish they'd had when I was a kid.

iDinoBook presents its data as a set of file folders, each of which contains information about an individual species of dinosaur. When iDinoBook is started, you can tap one of the three options available on the Main Menu, shown in Figure 15.1.

* **Index.** The first of two organization methods in iDinoBook, the Index screen displays the file folder "drawer," from which you can tap a dinosaur's file to learn more about it.

* **Map.** The second organization method in iDinoBook, the Map screen displays a global map that can explore dinosaur information based on where in the world they lived.

* **Quiz.** This area starts a quiz mode that asks challenging questions about the information in iDinoBook.

Tap Index to explore iDinoBook. You will see the Index screen, shown in Figure 15.2.

There are a lot of elements on the Index screen that users can work with to explore the library of dinosaurs.

Main Extended Search Dinosaur   Dinosaur   Ages Dinosaur Help
Menu   Filter   Filter   List   Images   Lived

Figure 15.2

*The iDinoBook
Index screen.*

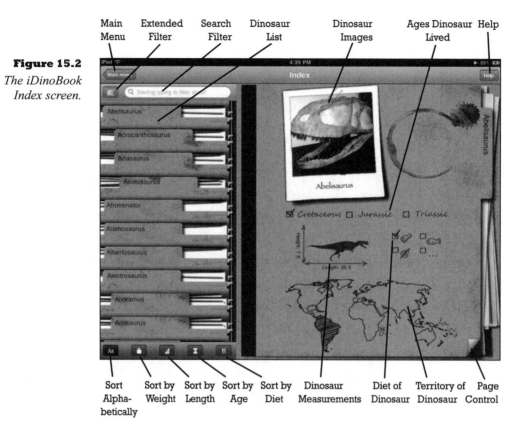

Sort   Sort by   Sort by Sort by Sort by Dinosaur   Diet of   Territory of Page
Alpha-   Weight   Length   Age   Diet   Measurements   Dinosaur   Dinosaur   Control
betically

The filters above the primary list of dinosaurs are useful to narrow the search for a particular dinosaur. Type the name or partial name of the dinosaur, and the list will be filtered to only display dinosaurs with the typed text in their name, as shown in Figure 15.3.

Once a dinosaur of interest is found, tap the file tab for the dinosaur, and the information for that dinosaur will be displayed. You can tell a dinosaur is selected by the off-kilter appearance of the file, as seen in Figure 15.4. To remove a filter from a list, tap the close control in the Search Filter field. Whether a list is filtered or unfiltered, you can sort the list in a number of different ways. By default, iDinoBook sorts dinosaurs alphabetically. Tap the Sort by Weight button, and the list will be sorted by weight, with the heaviest dinosaur on top. Tap the Sort by Weight button again, and the lightest dinosaur will be on top (see Figure 15.5).

Figure 15.3

Tracking a dinosaur.

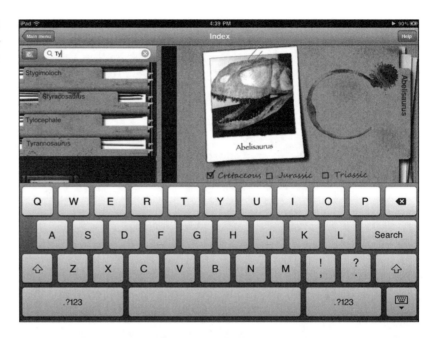

Figure 15.4

Selecting a dinosaur.

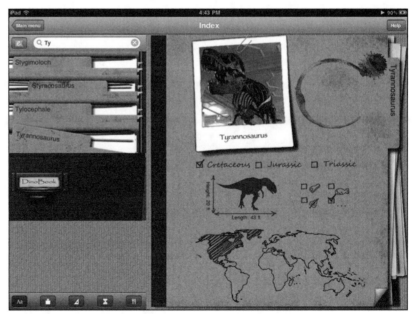

Figure 15.5

*Clearly,
Tyrannosaurus
has weight
issues.*

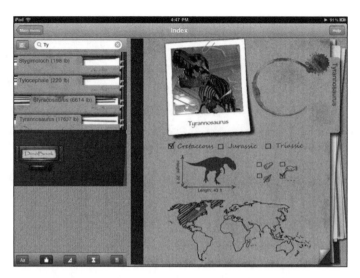

You can also tap the appropriate button to sort the dinosaurs by height, age in which they lived, and the diet they ate.

To view a complete dinosaur record, swipe the selected record from right to left. This will open the record, as seen in Figure 15.6.

Dinosaur   Name   Classification   Main   Font
Images   Definition   Data   Entry   Control

Figure 15.6

*Though with
those teeth, it
can have any
issue it wants.*

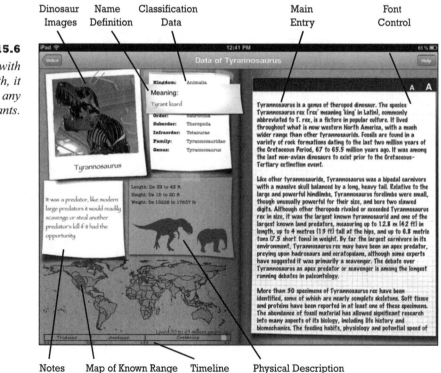

Notes   Map of Known Range   Timeline   Physical Description

You can read the main entry with the font in the default size, but if you want to make the text bigger or smaller, tap the font controls above the entry. iDinoBook overlays the name definition and the classification data sections, but you can toggle back and forth between them with a tap.

To view the images collected for the dinosaur, tap the dinosaur image to open the album for that dinosaur (see Figure 15.7).

Figure 15.7

Picture yourself next to this gal.

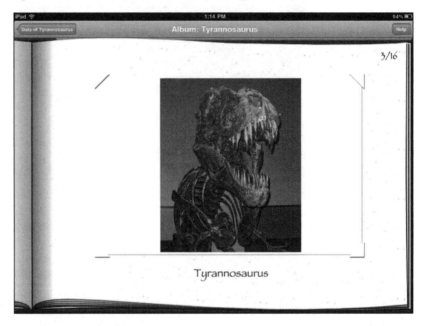

To browse through the album, swipe the pages from right to left to move forward in the album. Swipe from left to right to go to the previous image.

When you are ready to go back to where you came from, tap the back arrow in the upper-left corner of the screen. You can back yourself out all the way to the Main Menu, if you want.

Though the Index is the primary way to find dinosaurs, it's not the only way. Tap the Map option in the Main Menu to visit the Map screen, shown in Figure 15.8.

The Map, for the sake of us humans who have only been around a couple hundred thousand years or so, is conveniently presented with the Earth as it is now, not how it appeared a couple hundred million years in the past, when what would be the United States was somewhere 30 degrees south of the equator.

To find dinosaurs based on their present-day location, tap the location to display the location action menu (see Figure 15.9).

Figure 15.8

Dinosaurs everywhere.

Figure 15.9

Choose a dinosaur by location.

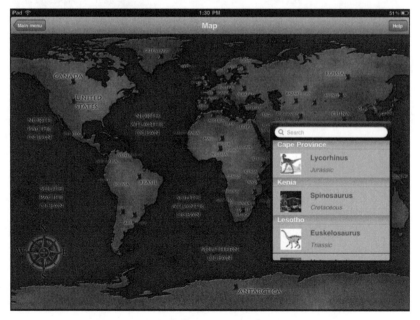

Tap a dinosaur in the location action menu to view its record.

After your children have explored iDinoBook for a while, they may want to test their knowledge with a quiz. Tap Quiz in the Main Menu to open the Game selection screen, shown in Figure 15.10.

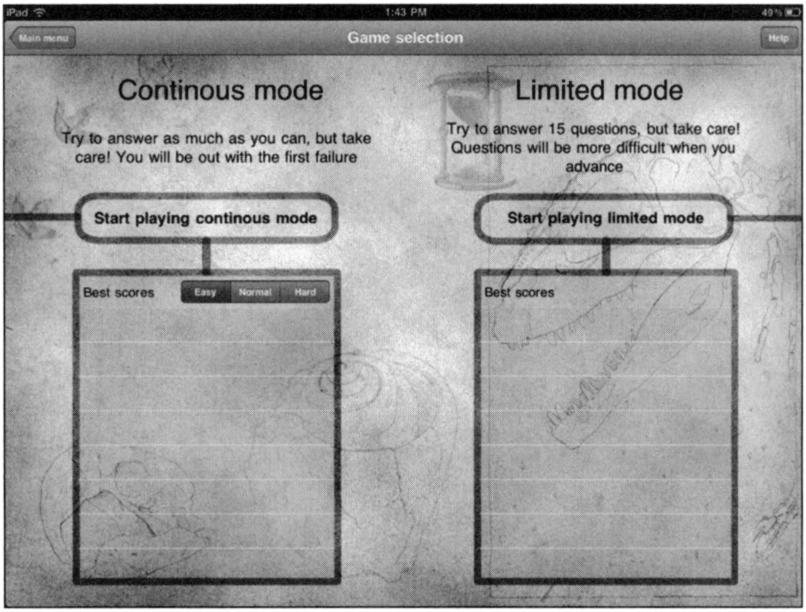

Figure 15.10

Choose your preferred game.

Either quiz mode plays the same way. A question is presented, and you will have a set time in which to answer it (see Figure 15.11). If you're right, you can move on to the next question, but if you miss it, you will be asked to review the card for the related dinosaur.

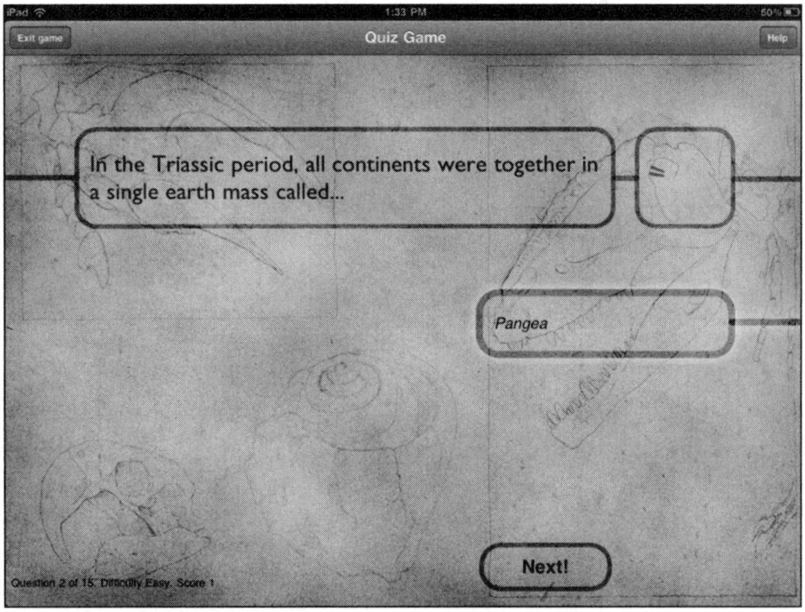

Figure 15.11

Pangea, when the U.S. was closer to the South Pole than the North.

iDinoBook provides a lot of information that any dinosaur enthusiast will gleefully soak up. As your students explore the app, they may note the presence of "Extended" dinosaur records. These records, indicated by a red flagged "e," provide extra interactive tools to learn even more about that dinosaur.

To access these extended features, tap the "e" icon in an Extended record, which will open the Extended screen, shown in Figure 15.12.

Figure 15.12

Explore more with Extended records.

There are a number of fun little extras in the Extended screens. Tap the ruler, for instance, to insert another modern creature, such as an elephant, or a paleontologist, to compare against the size of the dinosaur (see Figure 15.13).

Figure 15.13

Vegetarian, sure, but stay out of its way.

To learn more about the extras in Extended mode, tap the Help icon in the upper-right corner to see what's available.

It's All in the Chemistry

 Cost of The Elements: $13.99

Everything you see around you—everything—was once inside a star. Every element formed in the natural world was formed by the fusion of hydrogen into heavier elements deep inside the furnace of a star that blew up billions of years ago and then reformed into what we see around us.

It's a little more complicated than that, of course, but once upon a time, the entire universe had just one element, hydrogen, but now through fusion, explosions, and other natural calamities has a whole lot more.

Hydrogen and all of those other elements are the topic within the book *The Elements* by Theodore Gray, a lavish reference book that details the properties of all of the elements we know of to date (and some we don't) with pictures of pretty much every element Gray could find.

The Elements is, like Solar System highlighted in Chapter 13, "Apps for Second Grade," a gorgeous app mirroring Gray's book. Each of the 118 elements described in The Elements has its own set of pages, accessed from the animated Home screen shown in Figure 15.14.

Figure 15.14

"Everything you can drop on your foot."

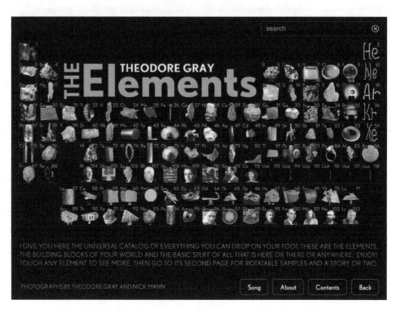

All of the elements in this app are laid out sequentially by their atomic number (the number of protons found in the nucleus of that element, remember?). If you want to start at the beginning, tap the hydrogen icon at the top-left corner of the periodic table on the Home screen. This will open the first page of the hydrogen section, seen in Figure 15.15.

Figure 15.15

The most common element in the universe.

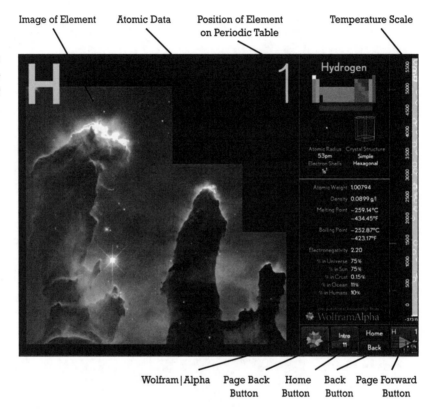

Image of Element   Atomic Data   Position of Element on Periodic Table   Temperature Scale

Wolfram|Alpha   Page Back Button   Home Button   Back Button   Page Forward Button

There are a lot of navigation tools within The Elements, so you and your child can explore to your heart's content.

* **Position of Element.** The periodic table not only lists the elements, but the position of the element on the table also helps illustrate the properties of an element.

* **Atomic Data.** This section details many atomic and chemical properties of an element.

* **Image of Element.** This area displays an animated image of the element.

* **Temperature Scale.** Here is a scale that displays the boiling and melting points of the element, in Celcius.

* **Wolfram|Alpha.** This section opens the Wolfram|Alpha popover, displayed in Figure 15.16. Wolfram|Alpha is a data search engine on the Internet that The Elements taps into for data.

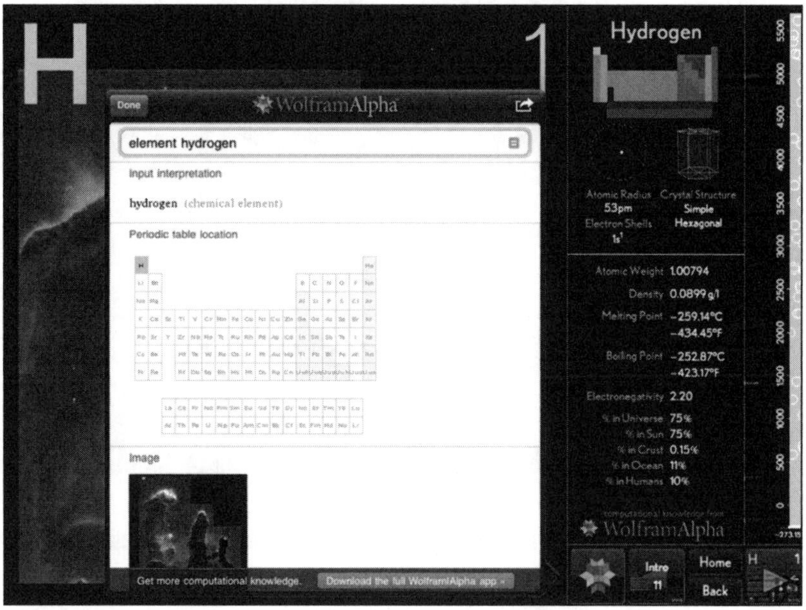

Figure 15.16

The Wolfram|Alpha popover.

* **Page Back Button.** Tap to move one page back in the book story.
* **Home Button.** Tap to return to the app Home screen.
* **Back Button.** Tap to return to the most recent element visited.
* **Page Forward Button.** Tap to move one page forward in the book story.

The Elements can be read as a book, but it is also very interactive. Tap any of the highlighted text links to see the referenced element (using the Back button to return to where you were, if you desire).

Beyond these Web-like navigation tools, The Elements also enables interactivity with every image displayed in the app. Tap or swipe an image on a page, and it will rotate for a 360-degree view or play a small animated movie (see Figure 15.17).

Don't worry if a lot of the raw scientific data is way above your student's (or your) head. Playing with this app is more than enough to intrigue the imagination of most kids, and the casual tone of the prose is very accessible to nonscientific readers.

Figure 15.17

*Lighting
hydrogen-filled
soap bubbles
looks cool.*

Something to Send to Washington

Cost of USA Manual: $4.99

Despite its name, USA Manual is not a how-to guide for government workers to do their jobs.

Darn it.

In the strictest sense, of course, the documents highlighted in USA Manual are the basic instructions for running the United States. Documents from the Declaration of Independence to the Nuclear Test Ban Treaty are contained in the USA Manual app, as well as presidential, state, and Supreme Court information.

For anyone with a need or a desire to read the actual documents that helped shape the direction of this country, USA Manual is a simple little app packed with wonderful civic information.

Navigating USA Manual is simple. When the app is opened, the main screen will appear (see Figure 15.18).

Figure 15.18

The blueprints for the United States.

Store
Additional content available to purchase from the In-App Store ❯

Purchased Items
Additional content appears in this section after purchase from the In-App Store ❯

Declaration of Independence
1776 document text with notes, images, and information about the signers ❯

The Constitution
Article and Amendment texts with notes, images, and information about the signers ❯

List of Presidents
List with images and biographies from 1789 to Present ❯

List of States
State information with list of officials ❯

Supreme Court Justices
List of current Justices with images and biographies ❯

Supreme Court Cases
Selected landmark opinions with additional notes ❯

U.S. Flag
U.S. Flag Code, Image of Flag with measurements ❯

More Documents
Articles of Confederation, Federalist Papers, Anti-Federalist Papers, U.N. Charter, How Our Laws Are Made, Presidential addresses, Treaties, and Acts ❯

Late Developments
Find out about important changes to information (requires internet connection) ❯

To view any section, tap the section to open it. Documents within the section can be read by tapping them in the displayed list, as shown in Figure 15.19.

Figure 15.19

An oldie but a goodie.

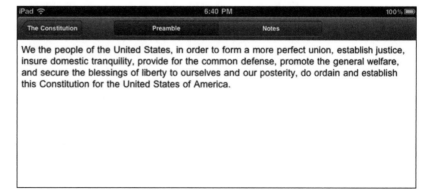

We the people of the United States, in order to form a more perfect union, establish justice, insure domestic tranquility, provide for the common defense, promote the general welfare, and secure the blessings of liberty to ourselves and our posterity, do ordain and establish this Constitution for the United States of America.

If you care to, there are additional documents that can be purchased for viewing in USA Manual. These are listed when tapping the Store option on the main USA Manual screen. You may want to consider such a purchase carefully, since all of these documents are freely available on the Internet or other resources. If you like having them all in one repository on your iPad, however, the option is there for you.

Conclusion

By now, your children are completing their elementary-level education, and the journey to learn what the world has to offer them is just beginning. This is a journey that all children can take, regardless of how they approach the challenges of school.

There are other ways a child can grow their minds, of course, beyond learning in a traditional classroom. Learning through creativity and culture is just as important. The iPad has all the hardware and the software that kids need to start exploring their creativity, which you'll learn in Chapter 16, "Art Class Without Smocks."

Chapter 16

Art Class
Without Smocks

Take out a pencil. Get a piece of paper. Set it in front of you. Wait.

What do you think will happen?

Some of you—the most organized amongst you—may use the opportunity to write down a list. Things to do, groceries to buy, the kids' schedule for next week—that sort of thing. But some of you may use the free time to create something on that sheet of paper that's creative and artistic. It could be a doodle or a sketch or a comic strip—whatever your mind can create and your hand can draw.

The truth is, though we often deny it, there's an artist burgeoning in all of us. There's something in our makeup that encourages us to draw, mold, sculpt, weld, or paint something. We deny it because we think we can't do it well, and while it's true that some people can't, say, draw their way out of a paper bag, they may have a talent for sculpting clay or putting together flower arrangements. Art has nearly infinite forms, and there's going to be something out there for you to create.

iPads are surprisingly good platforms for exploring the visual arts, specifically photography, videography, and drawing. The new iPad 2, in particular, is suitable for the first two disciplines, thanks to its onboard video and still camera. With this feature, you can capture images and edit them directly within the iPad.

The touch surface lends itself well to any drawing app, too. With their fingers or a stylus, your child can create some beautiful artwork on the iPad.

This chapter will focus on apps that work within these three mediums, including three new apps from Apple designed especially for the iPad 2. Specifically, you will explore

* Camera, an app included with the iPad 2 that turns the device into a simple point-and-shoot camera.
* Photo, an app included with the iPad 2 that lets you view and share photos.
* Photo Booth, another included iPad 2 app that generates nifty special effects on the fly.
* iMovie, an Apple app available for purchase that enables users to record and edit movies taken on any iOS device with a camera onboard.
* Glow Draw, a kid-friendly app that lets them get creative without the mess of paint.
* Drawing Pad, a more advanced app for creating art.
* SketchBook Pro, a top-of-the-line drawing app.

Shutterbugging 101

 Cost of Camera: Free

 Cost of Photo: Free

 Cost of Photo Booth: Free

 Cameras used to be things that you would have to lug along with you on family trips, for your parents to grab candid shots of you with ice cream on your nose at the beach, or running away from the bear that entered your campground. Or, more likely, making you stand next to your cousins in an unnatural pose (standing still) to get a picture of everyone for the annual family reunion picture, or taking pictures of you waiting at the top of the stairs to see what gifts Saint Nicholas had delivered overnight.

Cameras used to be formal devices, to be treated reverently. Photos would be taken, but then you would not see them until you had taken the film into the photo-processing center for developing. It would sometimes be days before you saw the final product…only to find that while every cousin in the family looked angelic, you were crossing your eyes at the camera in frustration.

Today, cameras are digital, and you can see what you have taken instantly. They are also pretty much everywhere—it is hard to find a cell phone these days that *doesn't* have a camera onboard. This ubiquity has led to some startling changes in the photo industry. Film-processing centers are gone, replaced by photo-printing services, which basically use giant printers designed to print images on photo paper, or outsource to specialized printing services to get the same images on T-shirts, coffee mugs, and calendars.

What's nice about having a camera on the iPad 2 is that it gives users the opportunity to snap off a quick picture from the same device they are playing or working with. This is called convergence—where fewer devices start performing a multitude of tasks. Like Swiss Army knives.

There are some drawbacks to the cameras on the iPad 2 that should be mentioned up front: there is no flash device on the iPad 2, so any pictures you take will be in natural light. The capabilities of the camera itself are not stunning, either. The reported camera resolution is only 720 pixels, not even a single megapixel. So don't expect high-quality images from the iPad 2 camera.

This is not meant to discourage you from using the iPad for capturing images, but it is important to set realistic expectations for what the camera can do. If you need quick images that are snapped spontaneously, the iPad 2 is more than appropriate for the job.

As you may have noticed throughout the book, the camera's functionality can be embedded within other apps your child may be using. Typically, you can use it to snap a picture of the child that can be used as a personal avatar in the app she is playing.

To take a photo with either of the two cameras on the iPad, tap the Camera app icon to start the camera. The image from the rear-facing camera will appear, as shown in Figure 16.1.

Switch Cameras

Figure 16.1

*The Camera app
in action.*

Last Picture Taken   Take Picture   Still/Video Switch

The Camera app is very simple: point the iPad 2 at the person or thing you want to image; then tap the Camera icon in the bottom center of the screen. A shutter animation and sound effect will indicate the picture has been taken.

If you want to use the front-facing camera and take a picture of the person actually holding the iPad 2, then tap the Switch cameras button to activate that camera. Tap the Take picture button to snap the picture as you normally would (see Figure 16.2).

Pictures taken with the camera are stored in the standard camera roll storage area on the iPad 2. Tap the Last picture taken control in the lower-left corner of the Camera screen to open the Photo app to view that picture and any others you may have taken (see Figure 16.3).

Figure 16.2

The author in action.

Back to Folder   Slideshow   Share   Delete   Done

Figure 16.3

Viewing a photo in Photos.

Image Navigation

You can view photos by swiping back and forth between photos, or tapping the appropriate image along the image navigation bar along the bottom of the screen.

The Camera app is not the only iPad 2 app that grabs images. Photo Booth is a fun little app that's also included with the tablet that simulates some cool effects with which kids will love to play.

Tap the Photo Booth app icon, and you will see a screen like the one shown in Figure 16.4, with nine different views of what the camera is picking up at the moment.

Figure 16.4

The Photo Booth views.

Beyond the Normal view in the center of this screen, there are eight other views presented within Photo Booth. The effects are self-explanatory and visually very interesting. Move the camera around to find the visual effect that's most pleasing to you. When you see something you want to take a photo of, tap the effect window you desire. The window will expand to fill the iPad 2 screen so you can frame the photo, as seen in Figure 16.5.

Figure 16.5

Taking a "thermal" picture.

Last Photos Taken with Photo Booth

Effects Window   Take Picture   Switch Cameras

 Special Effects Only

The Thermal Camera and X-Ray image effects are just that: effects. The Thermal Camera image is just a false-color image based on the amount of light and color of the object being tracked, not an actual infrared camera. The X-Ray effect is basically a negative version of the black-and-white image from the camera. You can't actually see through things.

Once you have the image framed with the desired effect, tap the Take picture icon to snap the shot.

Quiet on the Set!

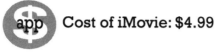 Cost of iMovie: $4.99

 It's not too hard to find video cameras in devices these days. Higher-end phones have video capabilities, and point-and-shoot devices are on the market now for less than $200.

The iPad 2's cameras also have video capabilities, enabling you to capture video quickly and easily. You can record videos using the Camera app, by swiping the Still/Video switch and then tapping the Record button. When the app is recording, a timer will appear in the upper-right corner of the screen to display the current duration of the video shot. To stop recording, tap the flashing Record button.

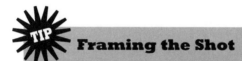

Framing the Shot

You can record a video with the iPad 2 in the vertical position, but it could be difficult to frame the shot properly. If you view the video on another device, chances are that device will be more horizontally oriented, so your iPad 2 should be, too.

To view a video taken with the Camera app, tap the Last Picture/Video Taken button to open the Photos app and navigate to the video, as shown in Figure 16.6.

Tap the video image to start the video playback. To stop the playback, tap the Pause button in the top of the screen.

Using the Camera app to take video will get you straightforward video clips that you can quickly show to others in their raw, unedited form. If you want to create more sophisticated movies with music and effects, you can use the iMovie app from Apple to put together some nice content from your iPad 2.

Back to Folder   Play/Pause Button   Timeline   Share   Delete   Done

Figure 16.6

Viewing a video in Photos.

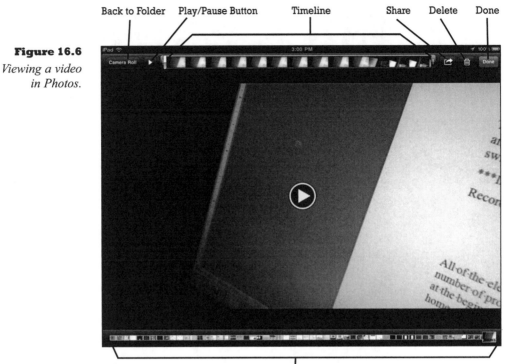

Image Navigation

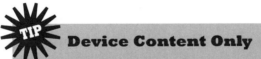

Device Content Only

One of the big limitations of iMovie is its inability to use video recorded from other sources within the app. While you can import still images and music onto the iPad using the usual methods, video recorded on non-iOS cameras can't be used. Only video from iPod Touch and iPhone devices with video camera (or another iPad 2) can be used.

When iMovie is first started, it will display a message box asking to use your current location. Tap OK if this is acceptable, and the iMovie My Projects screen will appear (see Figure 16.7).

Figure 16.7

The iMovie My Projects screen.

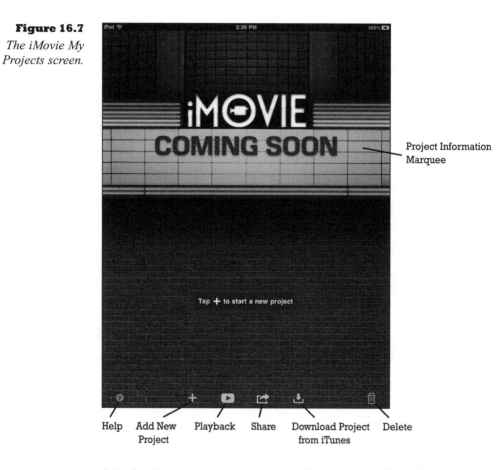

Project Information Marquee

Help   Add New   Playback   Share   Download Project   Delete
       Project   from iTunes

iMovie, like most video-editing applications, handles video content as projects. All of the video, image, and audio clips used in creating a movie are contained within a single project. This is important to keep in mind as you put a video together. In the initial Home screen in Figure 16.7, you are invited to start a new project by tapping the + icon. Tap the New Project icon to open the project editing screen shown in Figure 16.8.

You can use video recorded from the Camera app or record video from within the iMovie app. Tap the Record video button to start recording, as seen in Figure 16.9.

Video   Mode   Playback   Play   Record   Record
Clips   Controls   Monitor   Button   Audio   Video

Figure 16.8

Starting a new project.

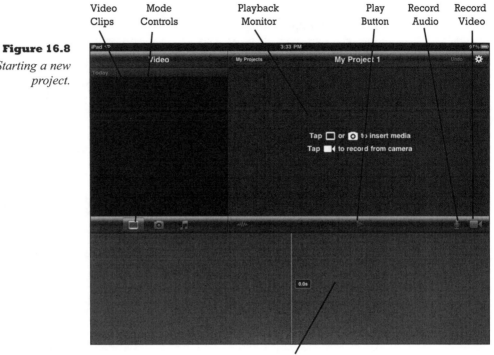

Timeline

Figure 16.9

Recording video from iMovie.

Record/Stop Button

When you are done recording, tap the flashing Record button to stop the video camera and display the clip review screen, as shown in Figure 16.10.

Figure 16.10

Review your clip to make sure it's okay.

Tap the Play button to view the clip again, if need be. If the clip doesn't quite work, tap the Retake button to delete the clip and open the record video screen again. If the clip is acceptable, tap the Use button, which will open the project editing screen once more (see Figure 16.11).

Figure 16.11

The project editing screen with content.

The video clip you have recorded is now in the clips section, and the clip has been selected automatically so it appears in the monitor and time-line sections.

Working in the Cutting Room

The iMovie app is a fairly sophisticated tool that features a lot of editing capabilities. To give you a broader overview of how this interface works, here's how to put together a quick movie with a title screen and some music.

1. Swipe the clip in the timeline so the viewing cursor is at the beginning of the clip.
2. Double-tap the clip in the timeline. The timeline will be selected, and the Clip Settings popover menu will appear (see Figure 16.12).

Figure 16.12

Every clip has its own properties.

3. Tap the Title Style option. The Title Style popover menu will open (see Figure 16.13).

Figure 16.13

Select a title.

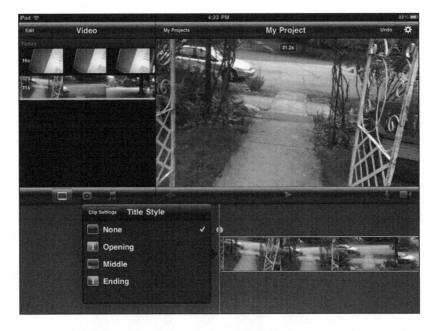

4. Tap Opening. The option will be selected, and placeholder text will appear in the monitor, as seen in Figure 16.14.

Figure 16.14

Enter title text.

5. Tap the Title Text Here placeholder. A keyboard will appear for you to enter a title.

6. Enter a new title and tap Done on the keyboard. The new title will be entered.

7. Tap the Audio mode button. The Audio screen will open, as seen in Figure 16.15.

Figure 16.15

Select your own soundtrack.

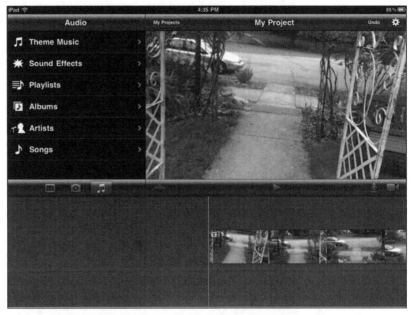

8. Tap the Theme Music option. The Theme Music list will appear.

9. Tap the option that appeals to you. The music will be overlaid on the timeline clip.

10. Tap the Play button to hear the clip. If the music isn't what you want, tap another option to try it instead.

 Use Your Own Tunes

You can also use your own music from the iPad as the audio track for your movie.

11. When your movie is ready, tap the My Projects control. It will now appear in the My Projects window.

12. To change the name of the project, double-tap the name of the project in the project marquee. Use the keyboard to edit the project name (see Figure 16.16).

Figure 16.16

*Display your
project proudly.*

There is a lot more to the iMovie than this; we've only just scratched the surface. The app's Help system, available in the My Projects screen, is very thorough, and should be reviewed by you to help your child really get into editing her own movies.

Drawing for All Ages

The iPad's flat touch-sensitive surface makes for a perfect platform to use fingers or other tools to perform the simple act of drawing. Well, simple for some. Those of us who are not as gifted may find some iPad apps very daunting to try out.

But really, that's the big advantage of using something like the iPad to draw something. If you get something wrong, a couple of taps can undo your mistake and let you try again, without wasting paper, ink…or erasers.

There are three apps that will be highlighted in this section on drawing, each catering to a very specific age or skill level of drawing. Use the descriptions of the apps to determine which app is right for your child.

Glow Draw for Fun

 Cost of Glow Draw: $1.99

Glow Draw is a nifty little app that lets children doodle around on the iPad screen with glowing lines.

Users can use their fingers or a stylus in Glow Draw to create simple drawings. To change the properties of the glowing lines, just tap the draw icon in the lower-left corner of the screen to display the properties toolbar, shown in Figure 16.17.

Figure 16.17

Adjusting the lines in Glow Draw.

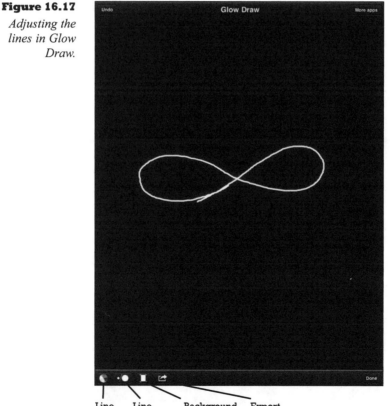

Line Color Line Thickness Background Export

To change the line color, for example, tap the Line color button and select a new color from the options presented. The next time a line is drawn, it will use the new color. Changing the thickness is just as easy; tap the Line thickness button, and then tap and drag the slider control to decrease or increase the thickness of the line.

You can also change the background color in Glow Draw, or even use an image from the iPad's photo collection as a background.

Glow Draw is a very basic drawing tool, but it is something with which even the youngest child can get creative.

Drawing Pad for Intermediate Artists

 Cost of Drawing Pad: $1.99

Drawing Pad offers more tools with which to create artwork, so children can really cut loose on the kind of art they would like to create. Figure 16.18 illustrates some of the tools budding artists can use.

Figure 16.18

The many tools of Drawing Pad.

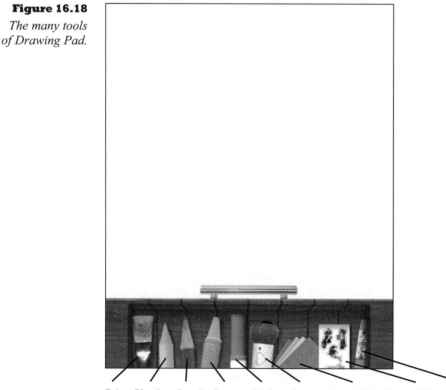

Paint Blender Pencil Crayon Marker Stamp Paper Color/Style Stickers Eraser

To access any tool, tap it. If a tool has different colors available, such as paint, the color options will be displayed in the toolbox (see Figure 16.19).

Figure 16.19

Paint color options.

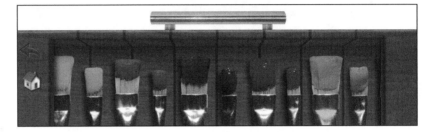

To view all of the color options, swipe the toolbox to the left or right to scroll through the many available colors. When you find the color and size brush you want to use, tap it to select it and then use a finger or stylus to draw what you want on the screen.

Another nice feature of Drawing Pad is the ability to send drawings out of the iPad via other channels. Tap the Share icon in the home toolbox (which looks like a USB cable), and you will see tools to print, email, save, and even share the drawing through Twitter or Facebook. The print function alone will make for instant refrigerator galleries.

For any child with even a passing interest in art, this is a good tool to start with. Toddlers may not enjoy it as much, because of the complexity of the tools, but preschoolers on up will enjoy this app if they like to draw.

Advanced Art with SketchBook Pro

 Cost of SketchBook Pro: $4.99

This app from Autodesk is a fantastic tool for talented artists, and it was named an iPad app of the Week in May 2011.

In some ways, the tools available will not seem as diverse as those offered in Drawing Pad, particularly when you look at Figure 16.20.

Tool Gallery New Information Undo   Brush   Draw   Symmetry   Text   Layer
Bar   Sketch   Redo   Editor   Style   Mode   Transform

Figure 16.20

SketchBook Pro
2 options.

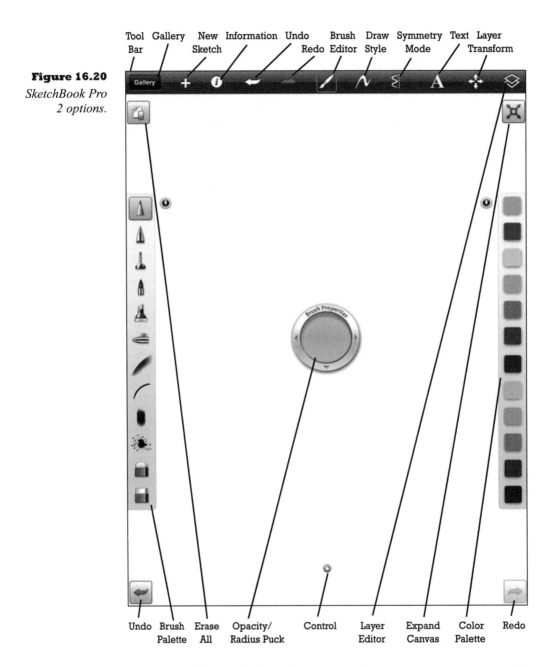

Undo   Brush   Erase   Opacity/   Control   Layer   Expand   Color   Redo
      Palette   All   Radius Puck   Editor   Canvas   Palette

Tap and hold any of the tools or colors in the palettes, and you will
quickly see that the level of control an artist can have in this app is very,
very high (see Figure 16.21).

Figure 16.21

Millions of colors, at your fingertips.

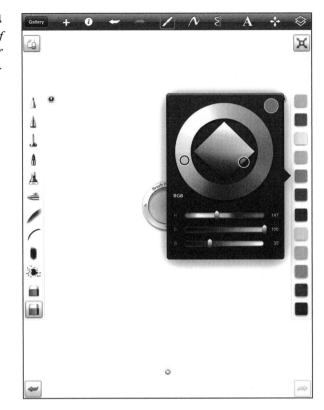

New users to SketchBook Pro are strongly recommended to walk through the introductory Help screens to get a sense of how all of these tools work together. (To visit the Help screens again, tap the Control icon, then the Information icon in the Tool Bar, and finally the Help button.) It is required reading.

You can even add more tools to SketchBook Pro. Tap the Store button in the Information screen, and you will discover additional tools to download to your app, some free of charge.

Artists with experience in using these media on paper will love working with SketchBook Pro. It has a steeper learning curve than other drawing apps, but it makes good use of the iPad's gesturing system to really deliver a sophisticated drawing app.

Conclusion

Art class is not the only way a child can be creative, of course. The stylized rhythmic sounds we like to call music are something else that many kid's brains are wired to respond to.

Music is about creating beauty through sound, and it also gives children the opportunity to stretch their math and literary knowledge. And with the right apps, which we will visit in Chapter 17, "The Musical iPad," your child will be making music in no time.

Chapter 17
The Musical iPad

Let's start at the very beginning. A very good place to start.

Whether it's humming a tune, tapping out fingers, or full-out belting out a song in the shower, most of us enjoy music in some form or another. If we don't like making music, we like listening to music. There is something deeply rich and warm about a good song that immediately brings out emotional responses faster than any other kind of interaction.

When children engage in music, their brains immediately fire up. Studies have cited that the centers for language and reasoning, as well as the ability to form mental pictures of events and objects, get a big boost when kids are exposed to music. Cooperating and discipline are also skills that are enhanced, because music's rhythm and complexity mean that kids have to get with the program and practice to create better music.

And music is so easy to create. Bang a stick on a fence. Tap your feet. Sing. It's all there, a cacophony of sound that with a little effort and practice can be part of a symphony.

When the new iPad 2 was announced, Apple also announced a version of its popular GarageBand app for the iPad platform. This app enables kids of all ages to play with musical tools. Even if they never create a full song, they can use the touch screen to hear and experiment with a variety of instrumental sounds.

GarageBand will be the focus of this chapter, with an overview of the various features of this very rich app. Specifically we will focus on

＊ How to browse the major instrument classes.

＊ Playing with the various instruments manually.

＊ Using the Smart instruments.

Choose Your Instrument

 Cost of GarageBand for iPad: $4.99

When you first start GB, the app will open to the Instruments screen (see Figure 17.1), which enables users to select from an instrument class.

There are two types of instruments available in GB: normal instruments and Smart instruments. Smart instruments will let users play chords, beats, and grooves automatically with just a single touch of the screen.

＊ **Sampler.** Record sounds with the iPad microphone and use the sounds as part of your musical creation.

＊ **Smart Drums.** Establish drum grooves by placing rhythmic tools on a grid to set the beat.

* **Smart Bass.** Build bass lines and grooves with just a few taps.
* **Smart Keyboard.** Create chords and melodies with the Autoplay features.
* **Smart Guitar.** Play chords, grooves, and single notes to rock out.
* **Keyboard.** If a keyboard can do it, so can this virtual version.
* **Drums.** Set the beat manually, without driving parents crazy.
* **Guitar Amp.** Got your own axe? Plug it in and record your own riffs.
* **Audio Recorder.** Get your own voice on track.

Playing Instruments

Let's take a look at one of the manual instruments, the keyboard. Tap the Keyboard option in the Instruments screen to open the Keyboard screen, shown in Figure 17.2.

Figure 17.2

The Grand Piano.

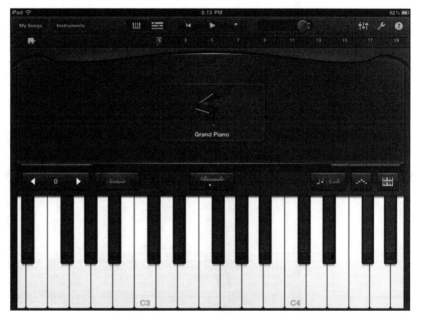

The first keyboard displayed in this class of instruments is the Grand Piano, but that's not the only keyboard instrument available. Tap the Grand Piano button to open the Keyboard popover menu, shown in Figure 17.3.

Figure 17.3

Yes, there's a Heavy Metal Organ.

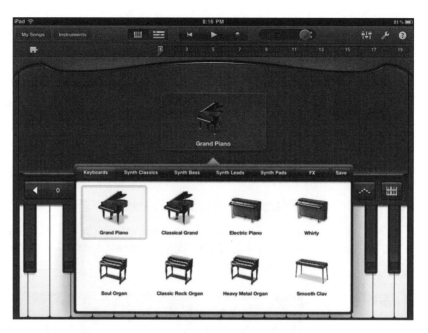

Tap the instrument you want to use. The screen will change to match the look and feel of the instrument selected (see Figure 17.4).

Figure 17.4

Right down to the scratches in the wood.

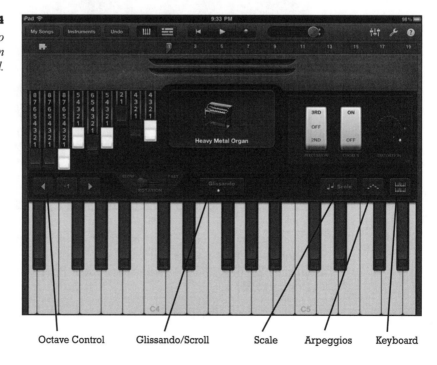

Octave Control   Glissando/Scroll   Scale   Arpeggios   Keyboard

There are variations between the specific keyboard types, but there are some commonalities, such as the octave control, which enables navigation between the octaves on the keyboard.

The Glissando/Scroll slider toggles between these two ways of using the keyboard. Glissando enables players to slide across the keys as with a real keyboard, and Scroll enables players to scroll up and down the entire range of the keyboard.

The Scale button displays the Scale screen, where you can select a scale so the keyboard only plays notes within that scale (see Figure 17.5).

Figure 17.5

Different scales are available.

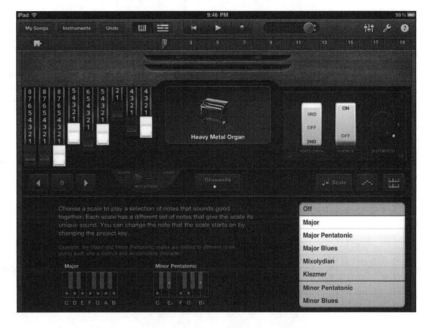

Tap the Arpeggiator button to display the Arpeggiator action menu. Slide the Run control to On to play arpeggios, which are fast sequences of notes, for the key or keys played (see Figure 17.6). Players can choose the speed, how many notes are in a sequence, and what order they are played in.

You can also change the layout of the keyboard by tapping the Keyboard button, which shows the Keyboard action menu shown in Figure 17.7. Set the width of your keyboard so it shows more or fewer keys, or display a second keyboard over the first so you can play both at once.

Figure 17.6

Get those notes flying.

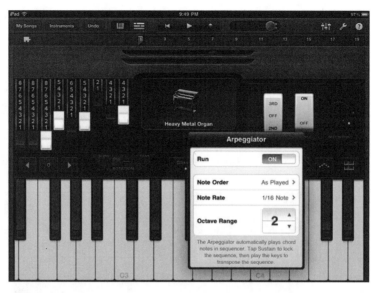

Sizing the Instruments Up

If a younger child is playing with GB, set the instruments to be as wide or large as possible to help little fingers find their way.

Figure 17.7

Set your keyboard size.

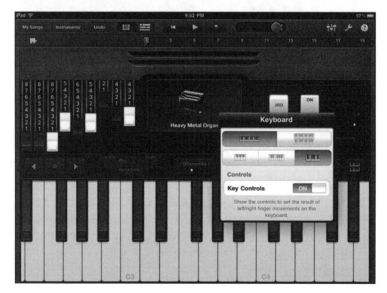

Compare this keyboard with the Smart Keyboard options, shown in Figure 17.8.

Figure 17.8

The Smart version of the organ.

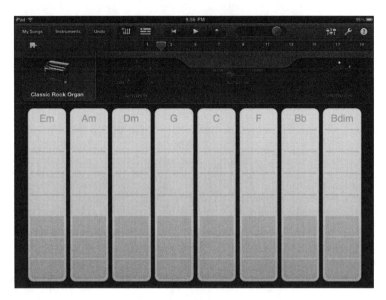

When you first open a Smart Keyboard, you'll see a series of towers with chord names on top. Tap or swipe the chord towers to hear the notes and chords.

Tap the Autoplay knob, and the towers will be split in two, as seen in Figure 17.9. Tap either of these parts and Autoplay will perform a pattern of notes based on the selected chords. The other Autoplay settings will offer different patterns.

What's really exceptional about all of the instruments in GB is the way dynamics are played. Tap the screen softly, and the instrument will play softer sounds. Tap the screen with more force and the sounds are louder. This is evident in the keyboards and in the drum sets like the one shown in Figure 17.10.

Figure 17.9

Using Autoplay.

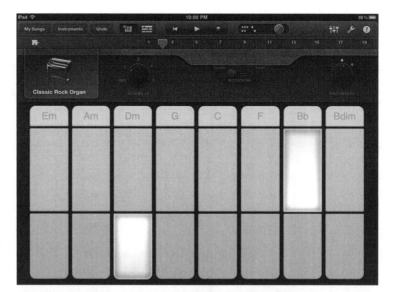

Figure 17.10

Bang those drums.

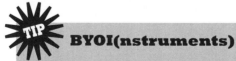

BYOI(nstruments)

Not only can you create music with GarageBand's instruments, but you can also bring your own instruments to the jam session. Plug your electric guitar or keyboard into the iPad with a headphone or USB adapter, and the app can record your instrument for inclusion in any song you want to create.

Getting Smart

Though we have already looked at the Smart Keyboard in the previous section, let's examine the Smart Guitar to get a better idea of the "smart" capabilities of GB.

Unlike the keyboard or drums, the Smart Guitar doesn't have a non-smart version. This means the Guitar is always going to be a little automated, though you can still play notes on individual strings.

Figure 17.11 shows an acoustic Smart Guitar in action. Swipe your finger across the strings in the chord towers and the notes will sound for those strings based on that chord.

Figure 17.11

Chords can be played as a whole or in part.

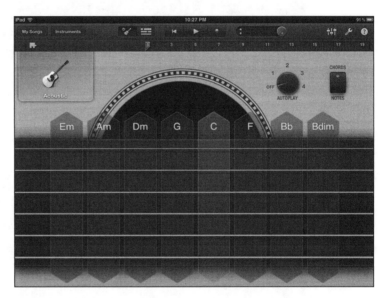

Swipe down to play all of the notes in a chord or just play individual strings or part of the strings from that chord. You can also tap the top of the chord tower to play all strings simultaneously.

As you do with the Smart Keyboard, tap Autoplay to have GarageBand play melodies automatically. Autoplay will remove the strings for the guitar, so you can only interact at the chord level (see Figure 17.12).

Figure 17.12

Autoplay in Smart Guitar.

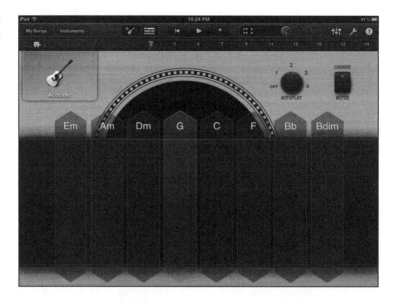

For individual note playing, tap the switch from Chords to Notes. In this mode, you'll see a more traditional guitar layout where you can play individual notes and even bend notes (see Figure 17.13).

Figure 17.13

Note playing in Smart Guitar.

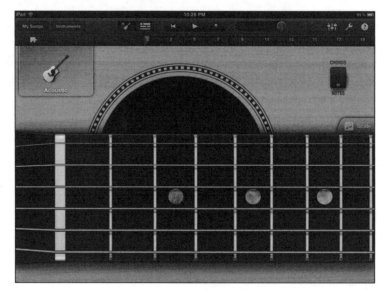

Conclusion

There are a lot of great instruments to play in GarageBand, and even children who have never played an instrument will find it interesting to tap, pluck, and otherwise play with instruments that will never break and never wear out. Along the way, maybe they can start working on their own songs as they explore their own musical talents.

In Chapter 18, "Homework: Documenting with Pages," you will learn how to start creating written documents for schoolwork and other projects, using the first of three great tools found in the iWork suite of apps: Pages.

Appendix
Apps for
Learning
Challenges

Every loving parent of every child wants her child to flourish, to reach out and meet the challenges that life gives that person head on.

Sometimes, though, children have extra challenges, beyond what most kids have to face. The challenges can be physical, mental, emotional, or environmental, and can range from minor to life-changing obstacles.

To be with children that face such challenges is at once heart-wrenching and mind-boggling. It usually doesn't take long to really see the spirit of the children come barreling out, smacking you on the brain, and challenging your own preconceptions about what's "normal."

The iPad makes for a very good platform for children with disabilities. With the right apps, learning is possible for every child. A lot of this comes from the very simple form factor of the iPad, too. There's no mouse or keyboard to use, just a touchscreen. This means that apps can be created to accept input without these traditional input devices and *without special hardware*. The onboard camera and microphone can also be used for input, which is a big plus.

The portability of the iPad tablet is also a big advantage, because unlike a desktop computer, or even a laptop, iPads can be taken almost anywhere. A child can be comfortable and work with the iPad alone or in a group. This is a kind of flexibility computers can't always offer.

Because there is a huge range of challenges for children, this book cannot address in detail all of the apps available that are designed to work with kids who need them. There would be, frankly, enough to fill a whole book in and of itself. The approach of this appendix will be to list apps that have been highly recommended in the area of communication.

These apps not only enable children to learn, but also facilitate communication between disabled children and others. This is done through alternate ways of getting ideas and concepts across. A child with reduced motor skills, for instance, can speak to the iPad and create written documents. A child with autism can use the iPad to reach out beyond the walls that surround her and speak to her loved ones.

It seems like such a little thing, but we are social creatures, and communication is the basis of how we live with each other. And how we love.

Dragon Dictation

 Cost of Dragon Dictation: Free

Dragon Dictation is an app that enables users to speak to the iPad and have their spoken words translated to written form.

This application is stunningly good, because it uses a connection to the Internet to tap into an online text-recognition database in real time. That means you don't have to load such a massive database onto the iPad, though it does mean you will need to have an active Internet connection to run the app.

Dragon Dictation has an easy interface, too. Tap the single big red Record button to start a new recording and tap the screen again to stop it. Once the recording is done, the text appears on the screen for editing or sending to someone via email, Twitter, and Facebook. The text can also be cut and pasted into other iPad apps.

iCommunicate

 Cost of iCommunicate: $49.99

Parents of autistic children and those with behavioral problems that can degrade traditional forms of communication can use iCommunicate to create pictures, flashcards, storyboards, routines, and visual schedules.

Parents can also record custom audio in any language, and there is a text-to-speech converter in the app, too.

The idea behind the app is to create pictures of known objects and then enable the child to string them together to form the concept he wants to communicate. This is done in a storyboard format, which can be configured to allow for various degrees of coordination.

iConverse

 Cost of iConverse: $9.99

iConverse is another app for those with communication challenges, which uses Augmentative Alternative Communication (AAC) to get ideas across. It is similar to the iCommunicate app, except that it uses standard AAC iconography and concepts to build concepts.

iConverse is not optimized for the iPad, but it still gives children with language issues an easy way to communicate.

Look2Learn

 Cost of Look2Learn: $14.99

Look2Learn is another AAC software app. It has more flexibility than iConverse, in that users, parents, and teachers can record their own voice within the program. Also, picture sizes can be adjusted up or down to compensate for children with visual or motor function challenges.

Pictures can be added to Look2Learn, and they can also be removed, which is useful if fewer choices are needed.

Proloquo2Go

 Cost of Proloquo2Go: $189.99

Another AAC app, but this one could be the last one you and your child will need. Like other AAC apps listed in this appendix, Proloquo2Go has text-to-speech and customizability.

It also brings 8,000 symbols and conjugations to the user, which is a significantly high number. But it also brings a high price tag. At $189.99, it is by far the most expensive app in this book.

Is the cost worth it? The designers seem to think so; they point out that dedicated AAC devices can cost a lot more. Parents should take a look at this app and do the legwork to make sure it's right for their child before purchasing it.

Index